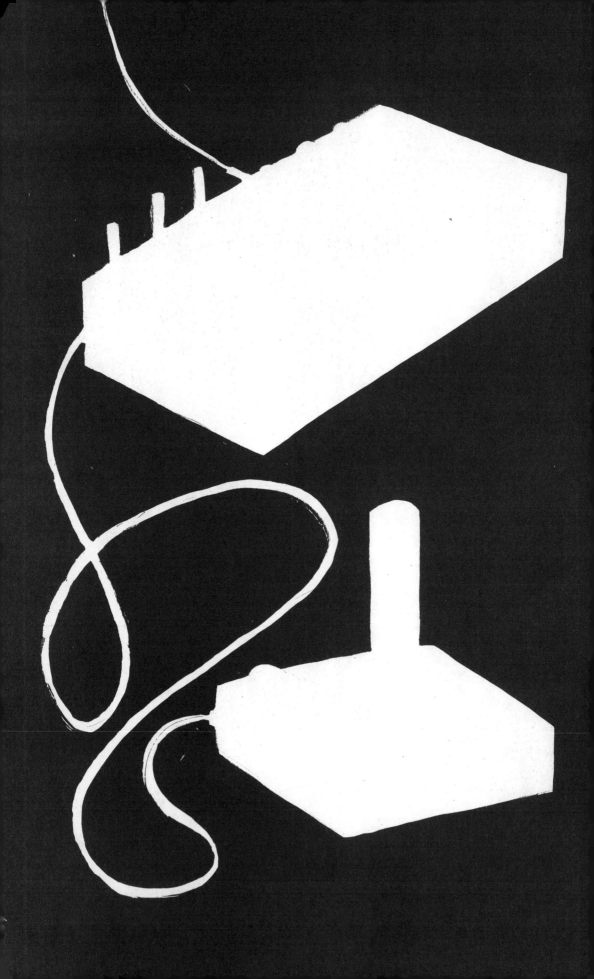

POWER UP ™

BY DOUG TENNAPEL

POWER UP

Doug TenNapel - *Writer/Artist*
Jennifer Barker - *Letterer*
Allen Hui - *Book Designer*

www.tennapel.com

IMAGE COMICS, INC.
www.imagecomics.com

Robert Kirkman - *chief operating officer*
Erik Larsen - *chief financial officer*
Todd McFarlane - *president*
Marc Silvestri - *chief executive officer*
Jim Valentino - *vice-president*

ericstephenson - *publisher*
Joe Keatinge - *pr & marketing coordinator*
Branwyn Bigglestone - *accounts manager*
Tyler Shainline - *administrative assistant*
Traci Hui - *traffic manager*
Allen Hui - *production manager*
Drew Gill - *production artist*
Jonathan Chan - *production artist*
Monica Howard - *production artist*

International Rights Representative: **Christine Jensen** *(christine@gfloystudio.com)*

ISBN: 978-1-60706-093-2
First Printing

PRINTED IN CANADA

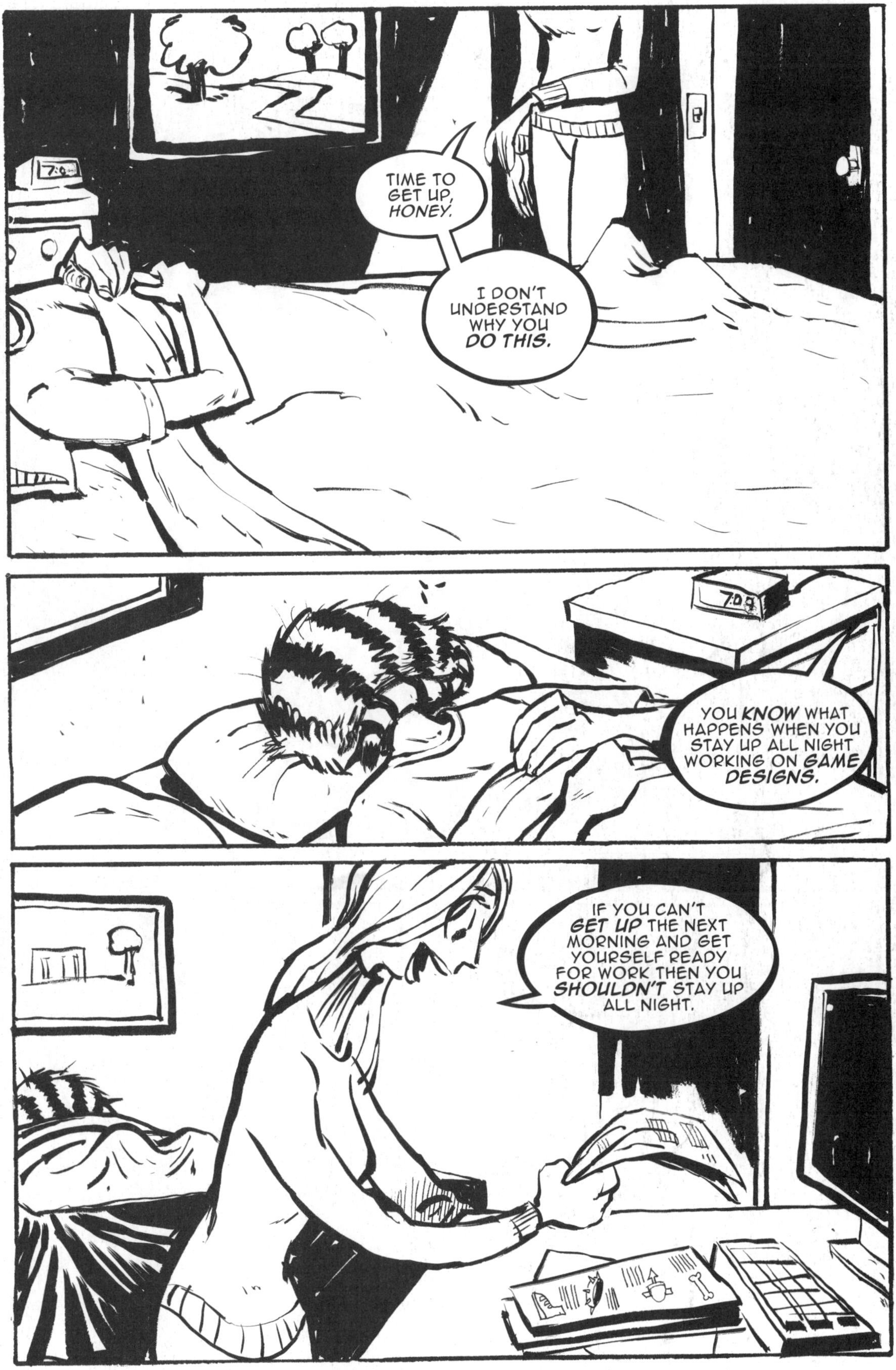
TIME TO GET UP, HONEY.
I DON'T UNDERSTAND WHY YOU DO THIS.
YOU KNOW WHAT HAPPENS WHEN YOU STAY UP ALL NIGHT WORKING ON GAME DESIGNS.
IF YOU CAN'T GET UP THE NEXT MORNING AND GET YOURSELF READY FOR WORK THEN YOU SHOULDN'T STAY UP ALL NIGHT.

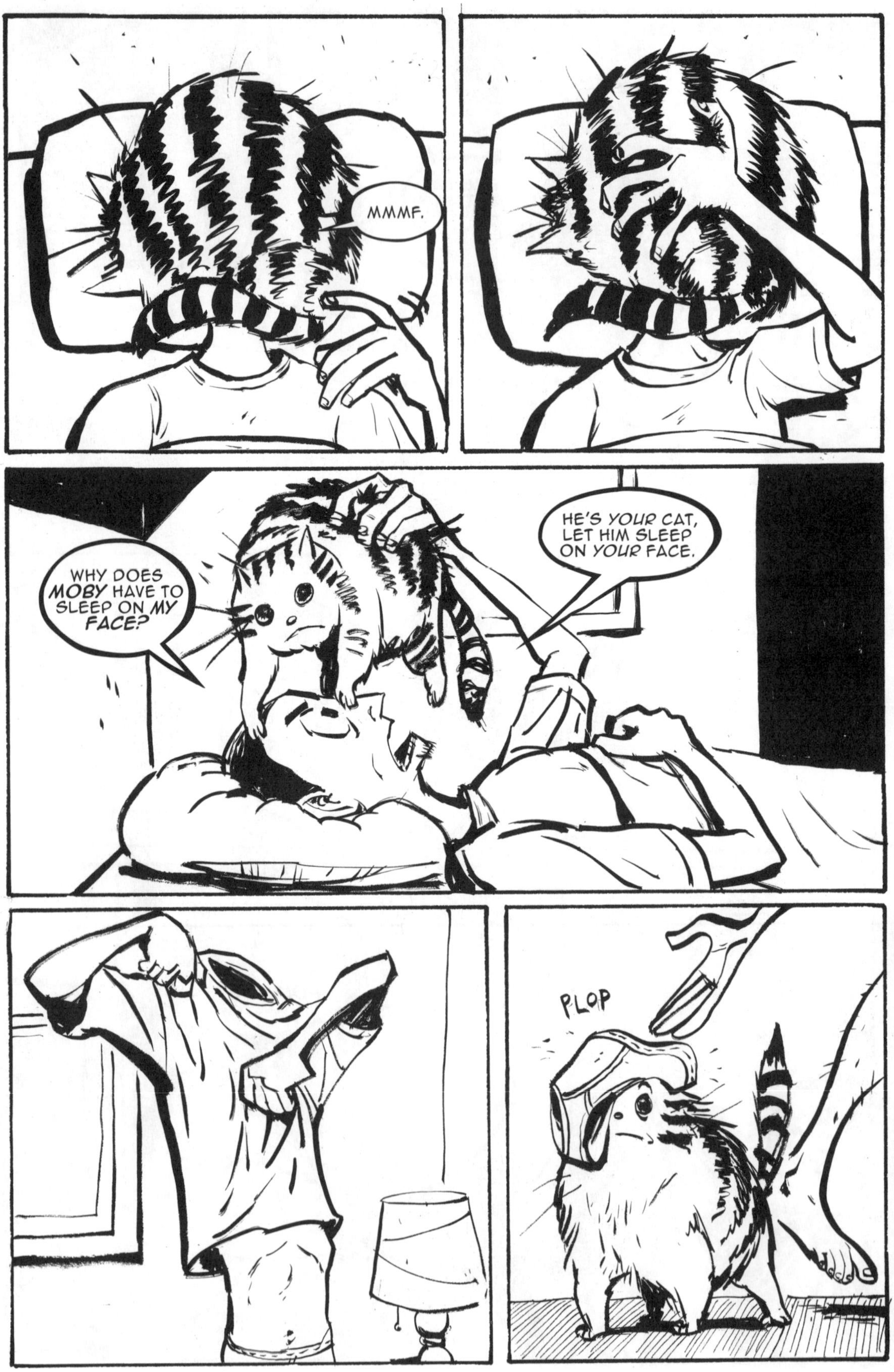
MMMF.
WHY DOES MOBY HAVE TO SLEEP ON MY FACE?
HE'S YOUR CAT, LET HIM SLEEP ON YOUR FACE.
PLOP

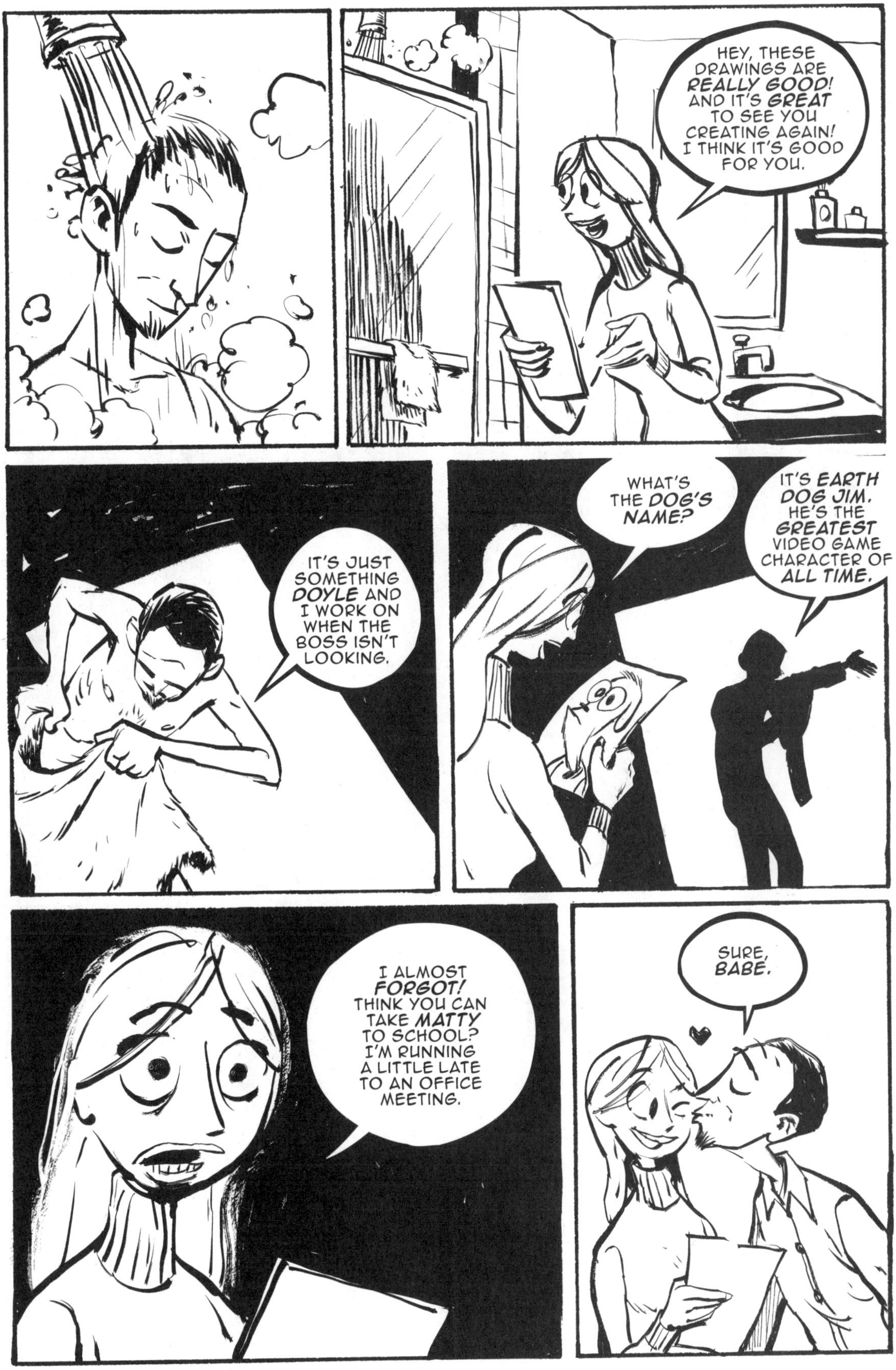
HEY, THESE DRAWINGS ARE REALLY GOOD! AND IT'S GREAT TO SEE YOU CREATING AGAIN! I THINK IT'S GOOD FOR YOU.
IT'S JUST SOMETHING DOYLE AND I WORK ON WHEN THE BOSS ISN'T LOOKING.
WHAT'S THE DOG'S NAME?
IT'S EARTH DOG JIM. HE'S THE GREATEST VIDEO GAME CHARACTER OF ALL TIME.
I ALMOST FORGOT! THINK YOU CAN TAKE MATTY TO SCHOOL? I'M RUNNING A LITTLE LATE TO AN OFFICE MEETING.
SURE, BABE.

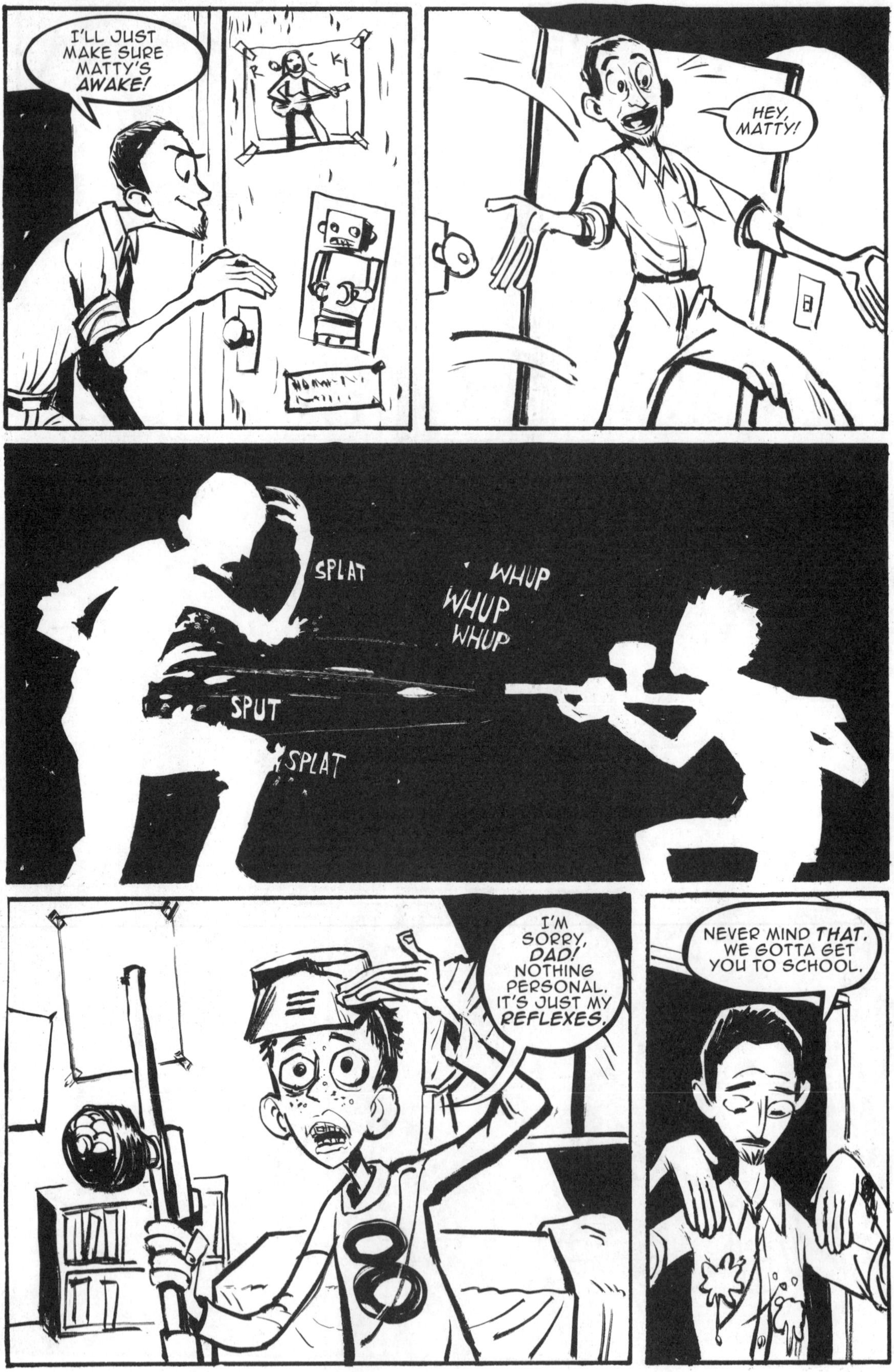
ROCKY
I'LL JUST MAKE SURE MATTY'S AWAKE!
HEY, MATTY!
SPLAT
WHUP
WHUP
WHUP
SPUT
SPLAT
I'M SORRY, DAD! NOTHING PERSONAL. IT'S JUST MY REFLEXES.
NEVER MIND THAT. WE GOTTA GET YOU TO SCHOOL.

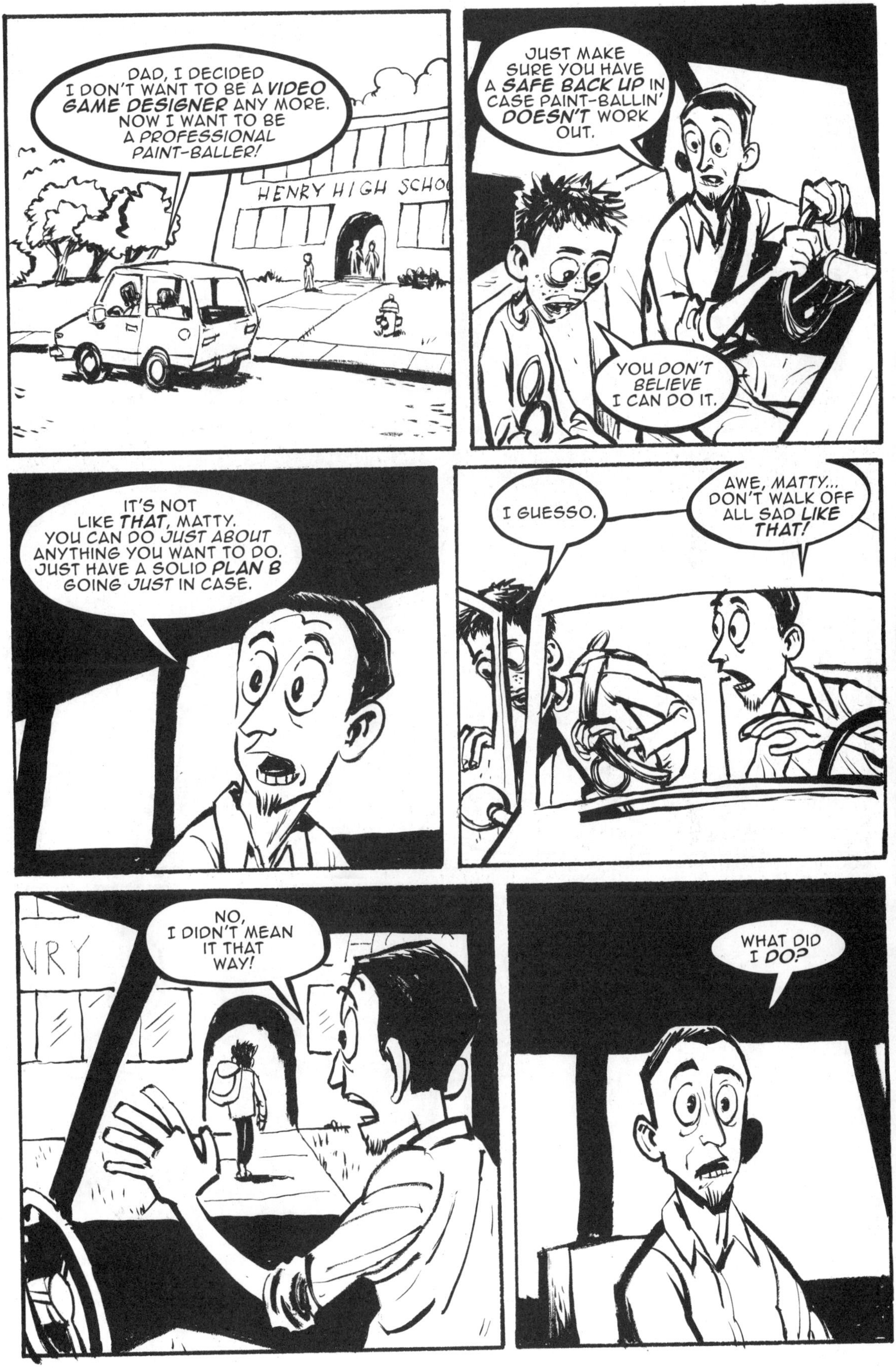
DAD, I DECIDED I DON'T WANT TO BE A VIDEO GAME DESIGNER ANY MORE. NOW I WANT TO BE A PROFESSIONAL PAINT-BALLER!
HENRY HIGH SCHO
JUST MAKE SURE YOU HAVE A SAFE BACK UP IN CASE PAINT-BALLIN' DOESN'T WORK OUT.
YOU DON'T BELIEVE I CAN DO IT.
IT'S NOT LIKE THAT, MATTY. YOU CAN DO JUST ABOUT ANYTHING YOU WANT TO DO. JUST HAVE A SOLID PLAN B GOING JUST IN CASE.
I GUESSO.
AWE, MATTY... DON'T WALK OFF ALL SAD LIKE THAT!
NO, I DIDN'T MEAN IT THAT WAY!
WHAT DID I DO?

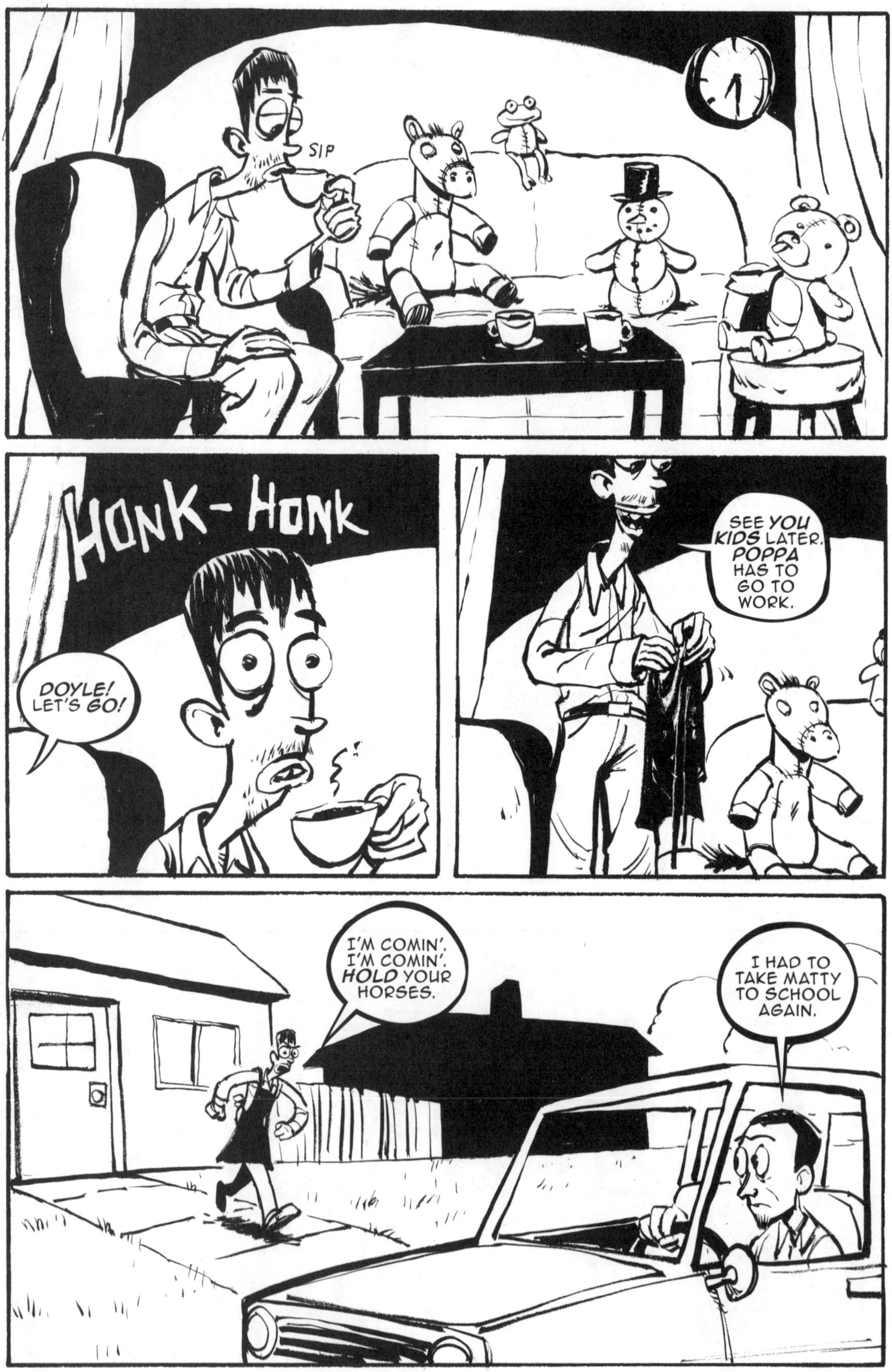
SIP
HONK-HONK
DOYLE! LET'S GO!
SEE YOU KIDS LATER. POPPA HAS TO GO TO WORK.
I'M COMIN'. I'M COMIN'. HOLD YOUR HORSES.
I HAD TO TAKE MATTY TO SCHOOL AGAIN.

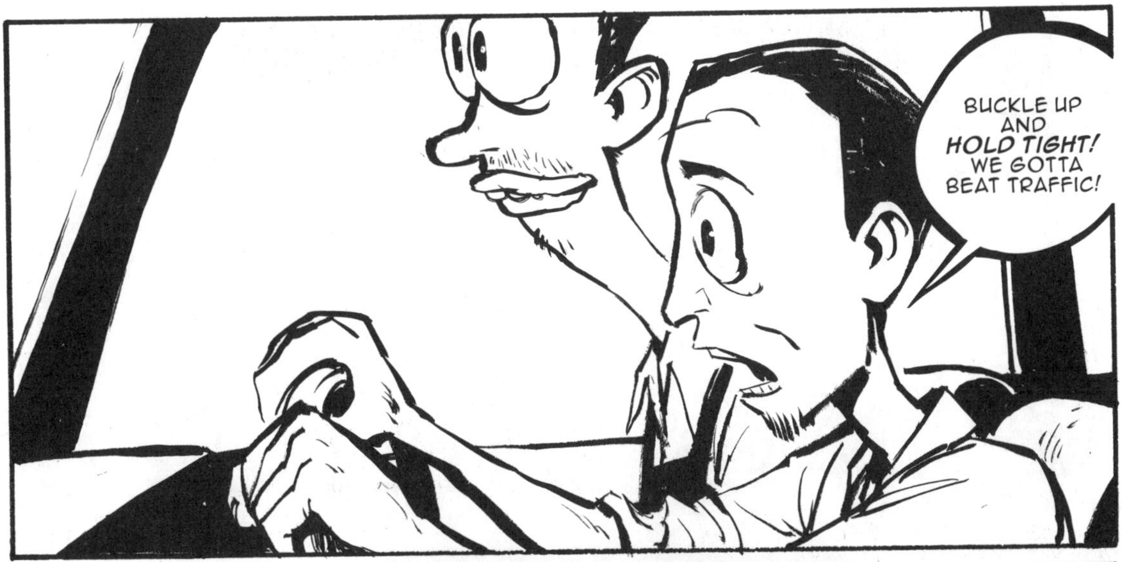
BUCKLE UP AND HOLD TIGHT! WE GOTTA BEAT TRAFFIC!

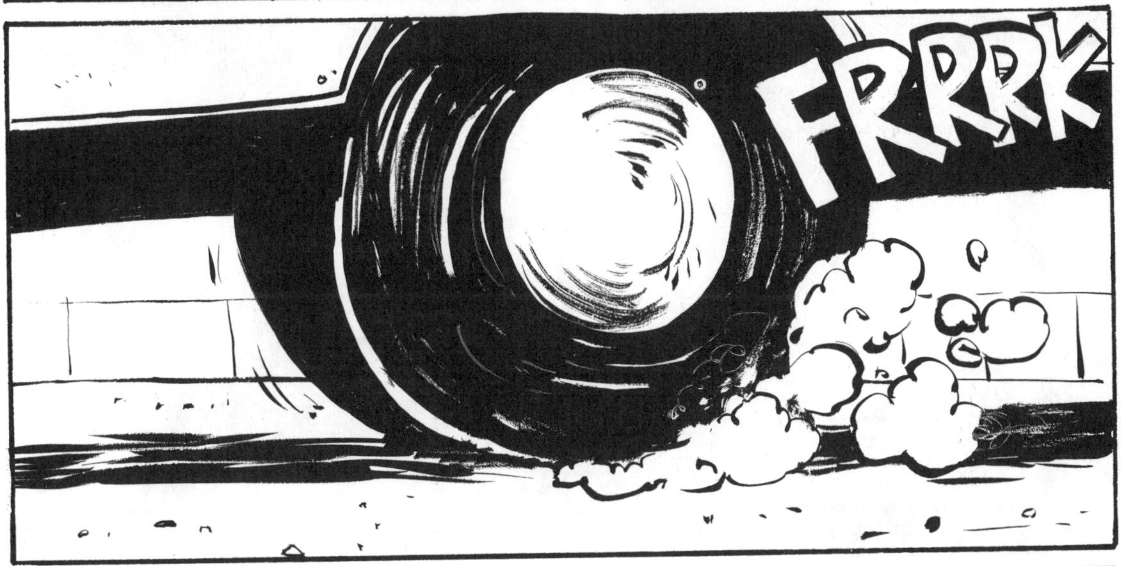
FRRRK

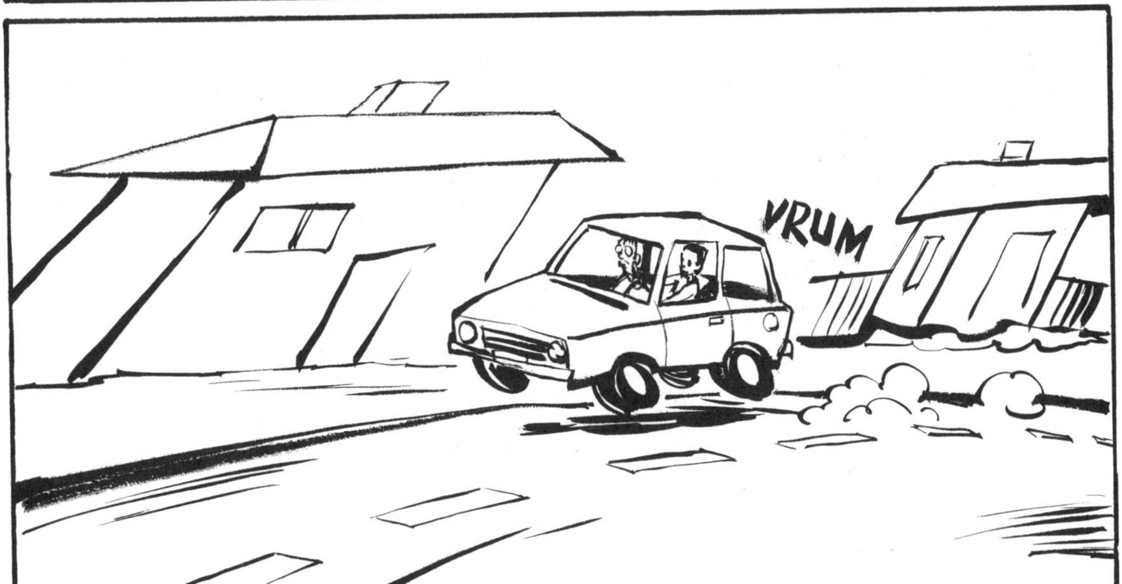
VRUM

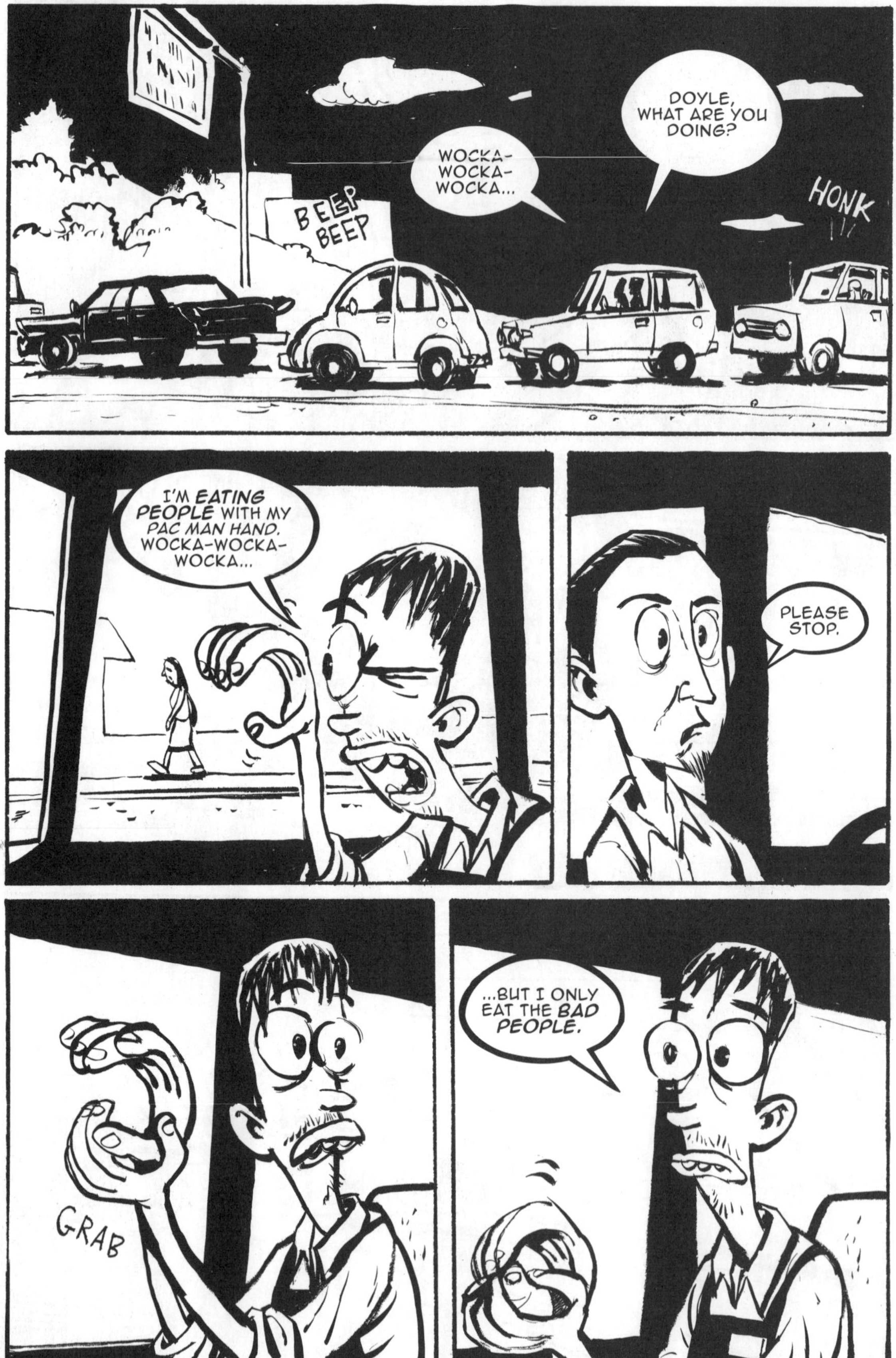
BEEP BEEP
WOCKA-WOCKA-WOCKA...
DOYLE, WHAT ARE YOU DOING?
HONK
I'M EATING PEOPLE WITH MY PAC MAN HAND. WOCKA-WOCKA-WOCKA...
PLEASE STOP.
GRAB
...BUT I ONLY EAT THE BAD PEOPLE.

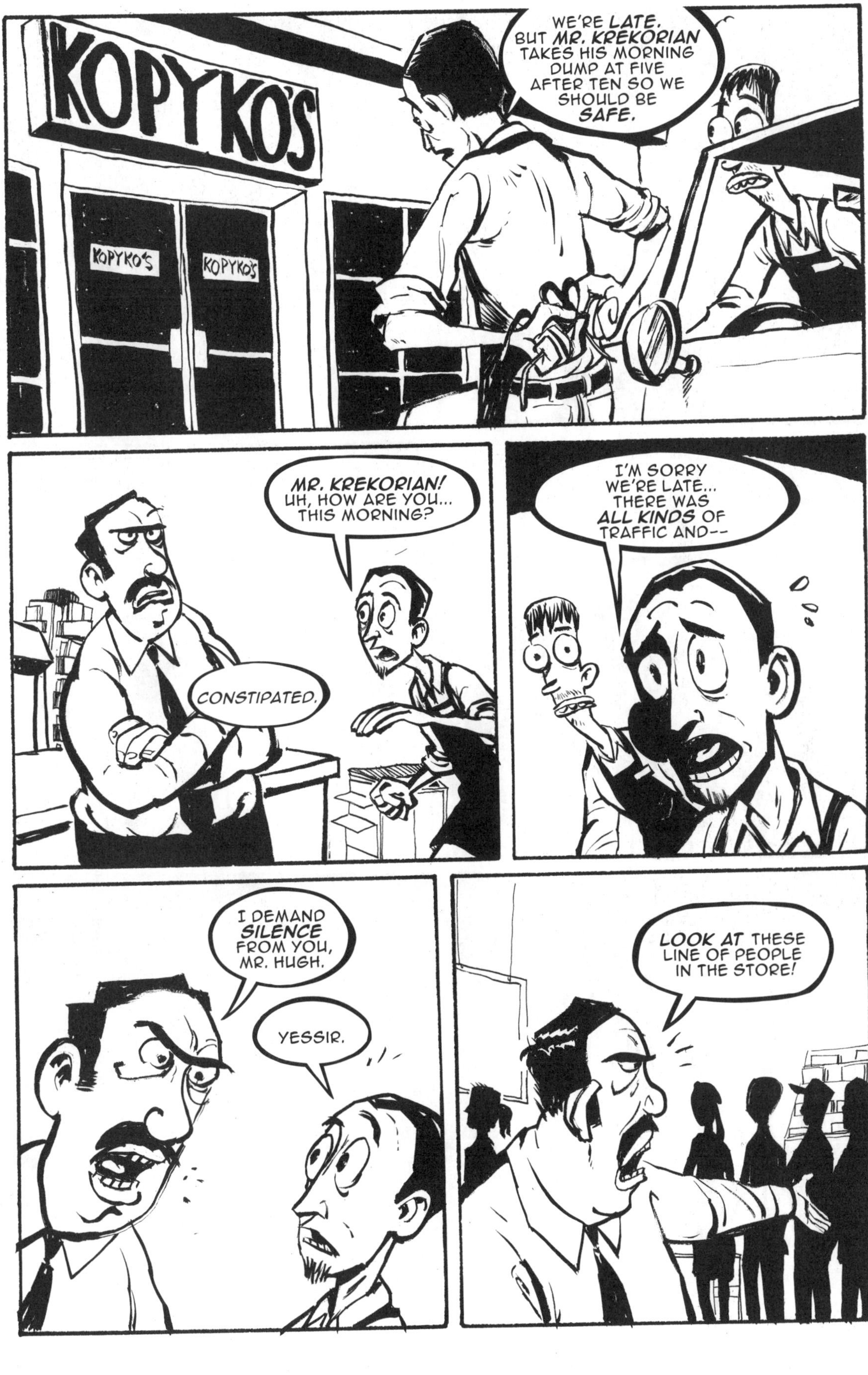
KOPYKO'S
KOPYKO'S
KOPYKO'S
WE'RE LATE. BUT MR. KREKORIAN TAKES HIS MORNING DUMP AT FIVE AFTER TEN SO WE SHOULD BE SAFE.
MR. KREKORIAN! UH, HOW ARE YOU... THIS MORNING?
CONSTIPATED.
I'M SORRY WE'RE LATE... THERE WAS ALL KINDS OF TRAFFIC AND--
I DEMAND SILENCE FROM YOU, MR. HUGH.
YESSIR.
LOOK AT THESE LINE OF PEOPLE IN THE STORE!

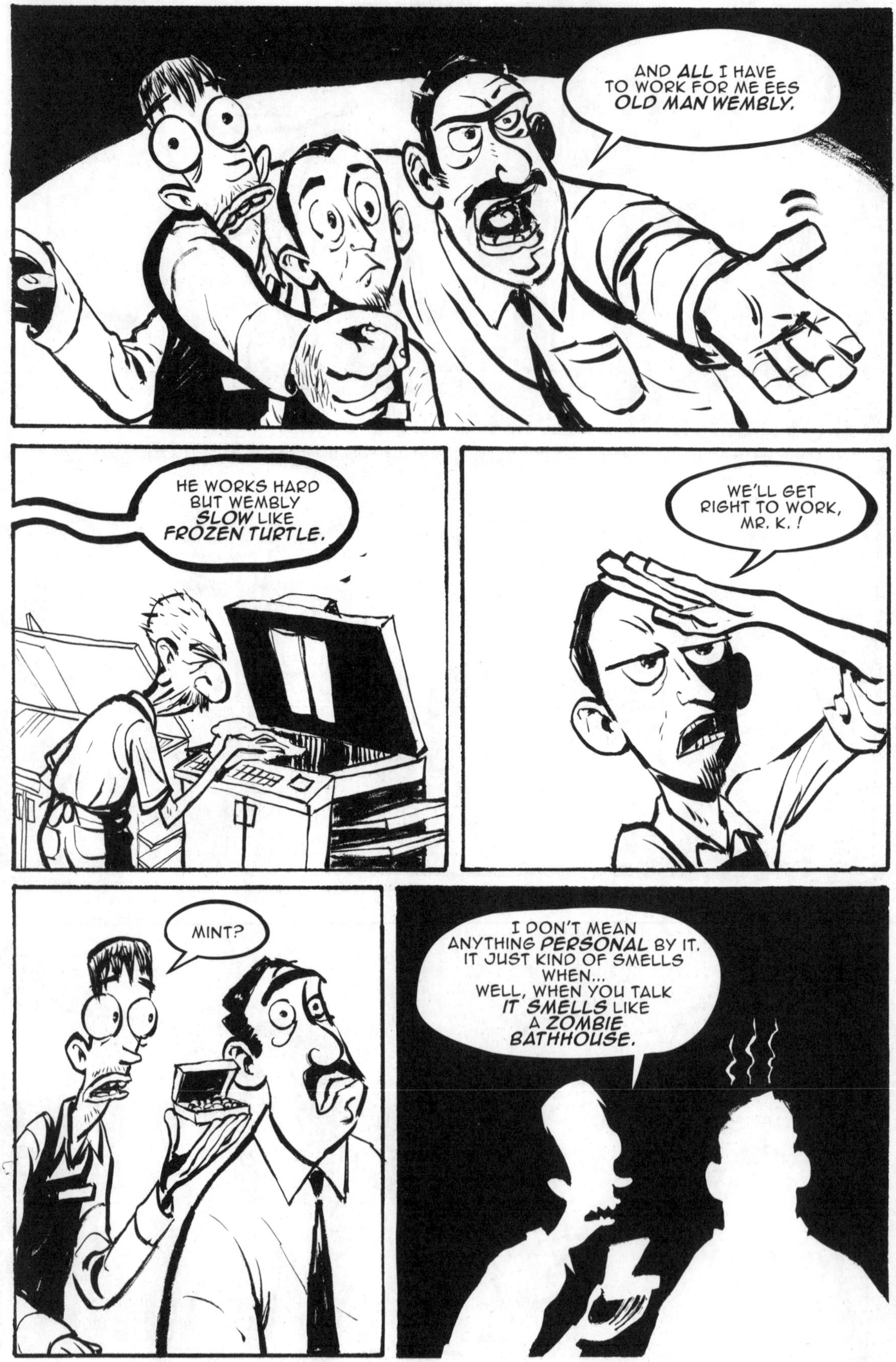
AND ALL I HAVE TO WORK FOR ME EES OLD MAN WEMBLY.
HE WORKS HARD BUT WEMBLY SLOW LIKE FROZEN TURTLE.
WE'LL GET RIGHT TO WORK, MR. K. !
MINT?
I DON'T MEAN ANYTHING PERSONAL BY IT. IT JUST KIND OF SMELLS WHEN... WELL, WHEN YOU TALK IT SMELLS LIKE A ZOMBIE BATHHOUSE.

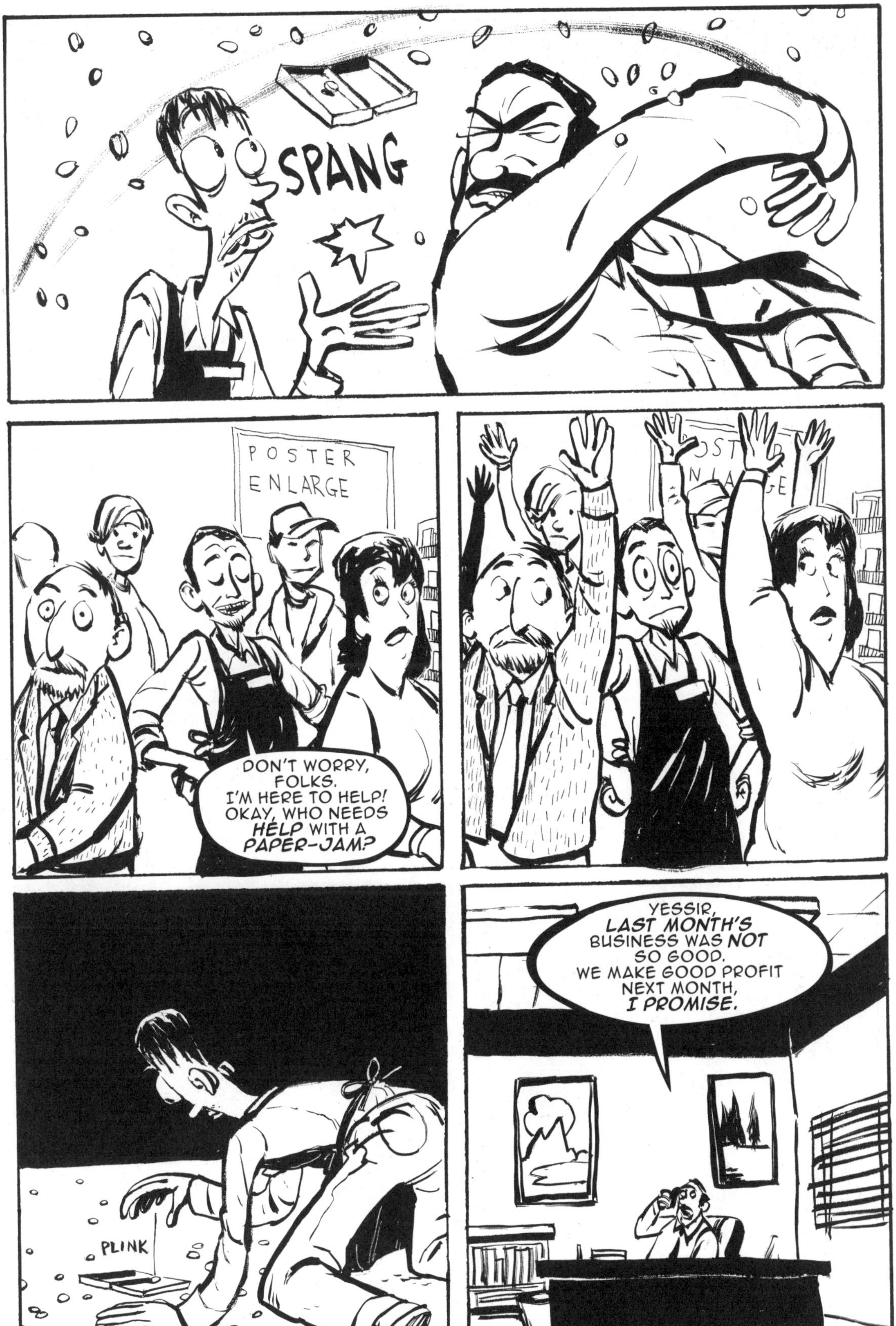
SPANG
POSTER ENLARGE
DON'T WORRY, FOLKS. I'M HERE TO HELP! OKAY, WHO NEEDS *HELP* WITH A *PAPER-JAM?*
PLINK
YESSIR, *LAST MONTH'S* BUSINESS WAS *NOT* SO GOOD. WE MAKE GOOD PROFIT NEXT MONTH, *I PROMISE.*

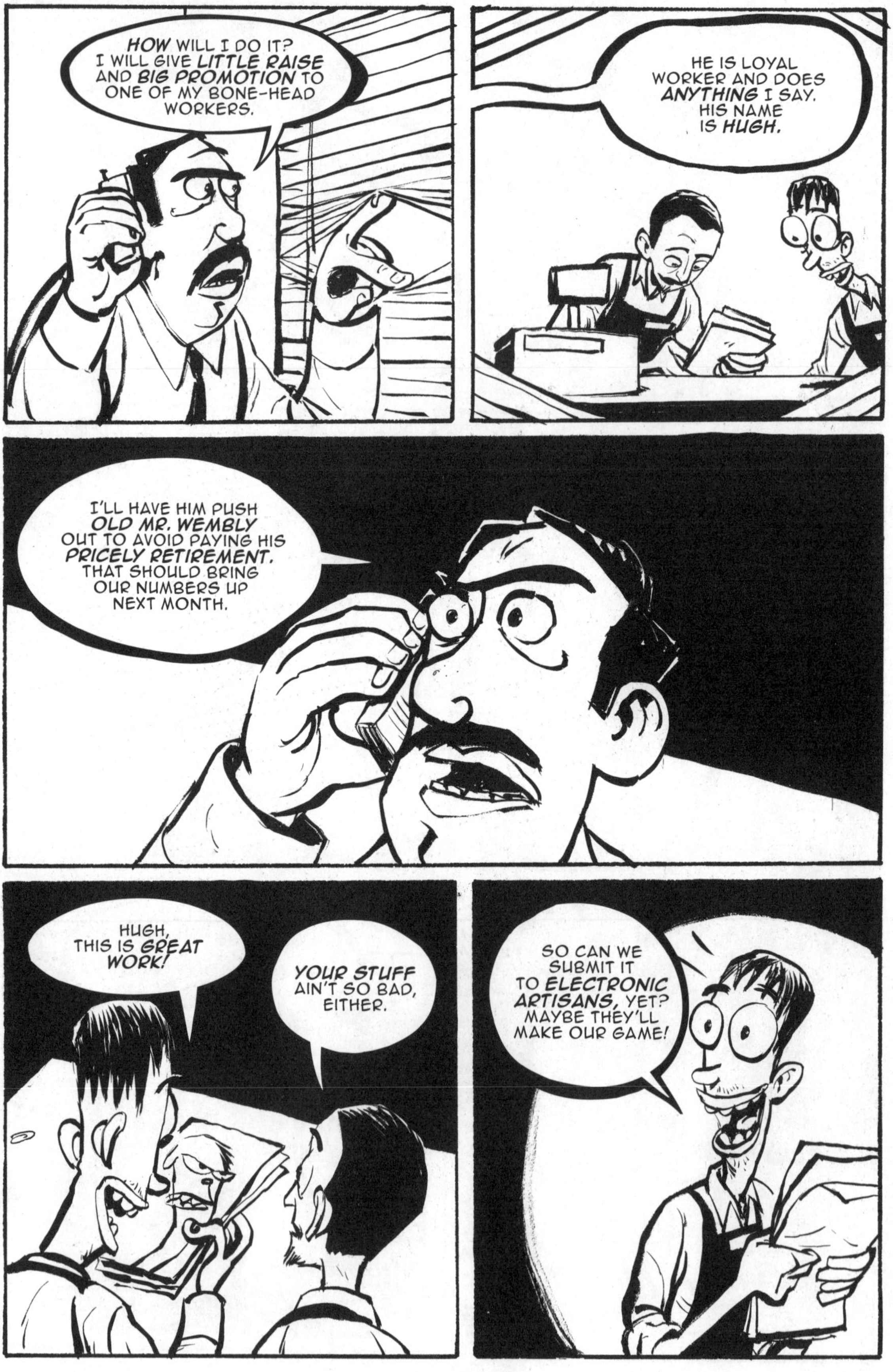
HOW WILL I DO IT? I WILL GIVE LITTLE RAISE AND BIG PROMOTION TO ONE OF MY BONE-HEAD WORKERS.
HE IS LOYAL WORKER AND DOES ANYTHING I SAY. HIS NAME IS HUGH.
I'LL HAVE HIM PUSH OLD MR. WEMBLY OUT TO AVOID PAYING HIS PRICELY RETIREMENT. THAT SHOULD BRING OUR NUMBERS UP NEXT MONTH.
HUGH, THIS IS GREAT WORK!
YOUR STUFF AIN'T SO BAD, EITHER.
SO CAN WE SUBMIT IT TO ELECTRONIC ARTISANS, YET? MAYBE THEY'LL MAKE OUR GAME!

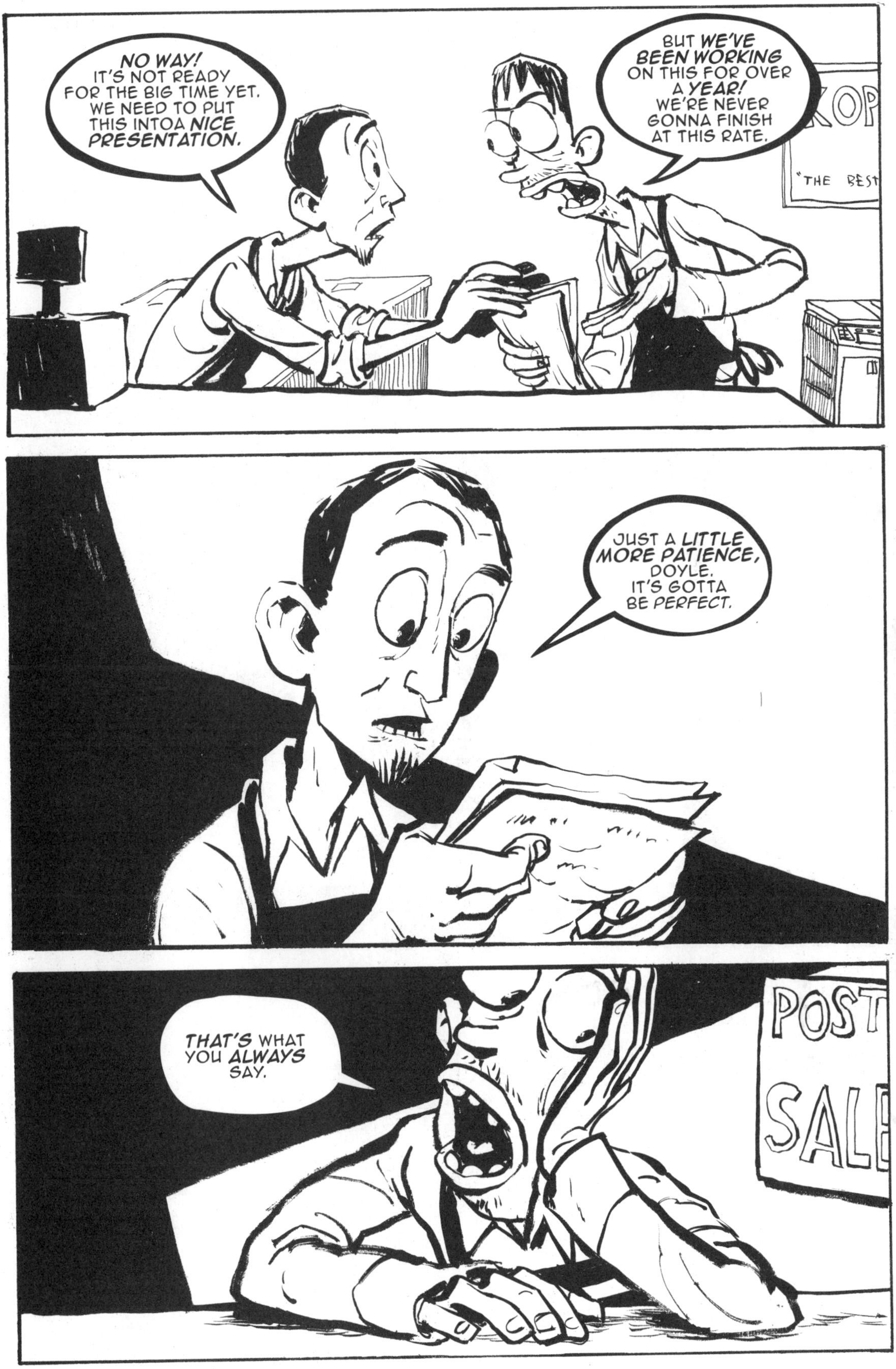
NO WAY! IT'S NOT READY FOR THE BIG TIME YET. WE NEED TO PUT THIS INTOA NICE PRESENTATION.
BUT WE'VE BEEN WORKING ON THIS FOR OVER A YEAR! WE'RE NEVER GONNA FINISH AT THIS RATE.
"THE BEST
JUST A LITTLE MORE PATIENCE, DOYLE. IT'S GOTTA BE PERFECT.
THAT'S WHAT YOU ALWAYS SAY.
POST
SALE

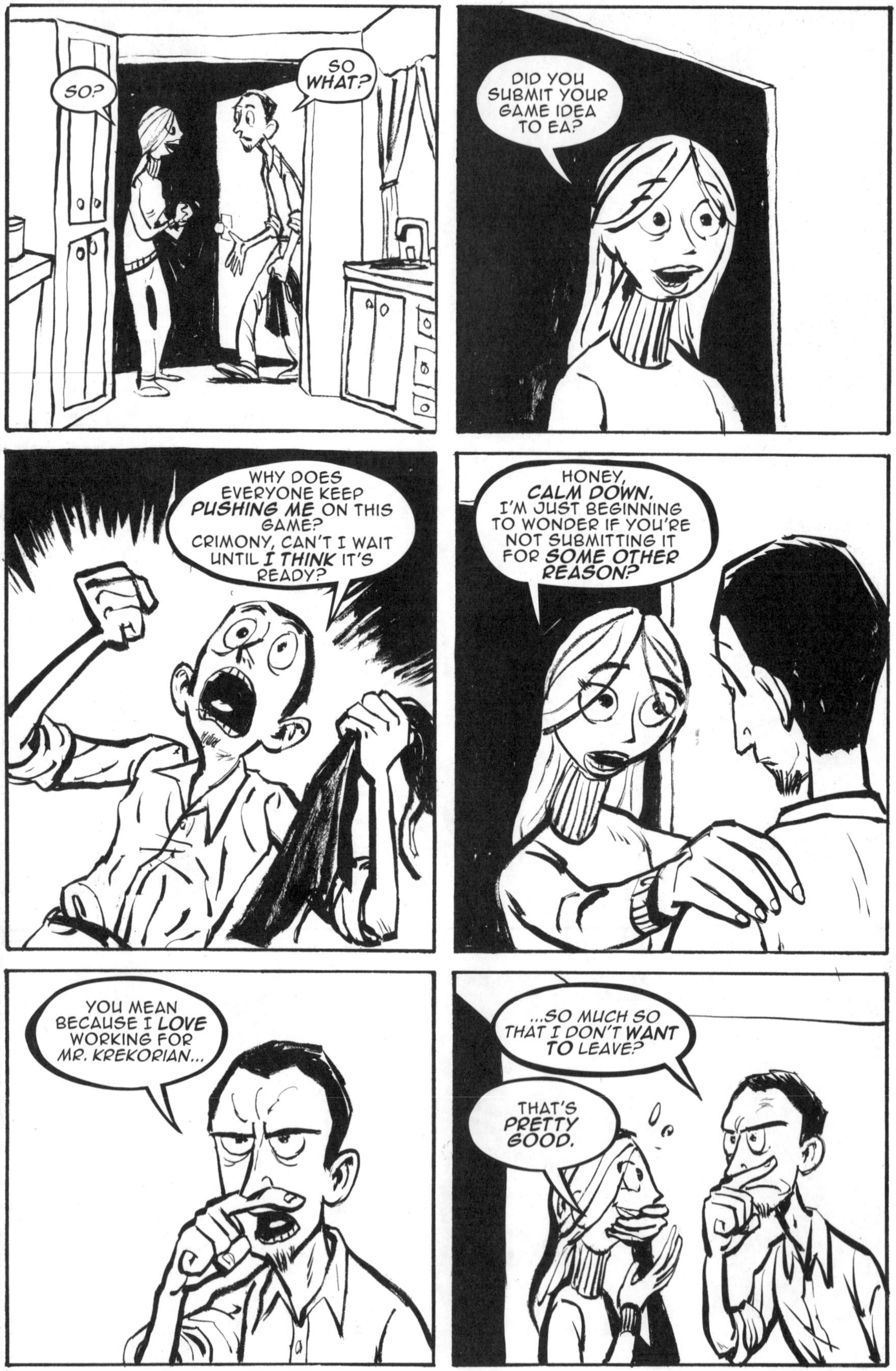
SO?
SO WHAT?
DID YOU SUBMIT YOUR GAME IDEA TO EA?
WHY DOES EVERYONE KEEP PUSHING ME ON THIS GAME? CRIMONY, CAN'T I WAIT UNTIL I THINK IT'S READY?
HONEY, CALM DOWN. I'M JUST BEGINNING TO WONDER IF YOU'RE NOT SUBMITTING IT FOR SOME OTHER REASON?
YOU MEAN BECAUSE I LOVE WORKING FOR MR. KREKORIAN...
...SO MUCH SO THAT I DON'T WANT TO LEAVE?
THAT'S PRETTY GOOD.

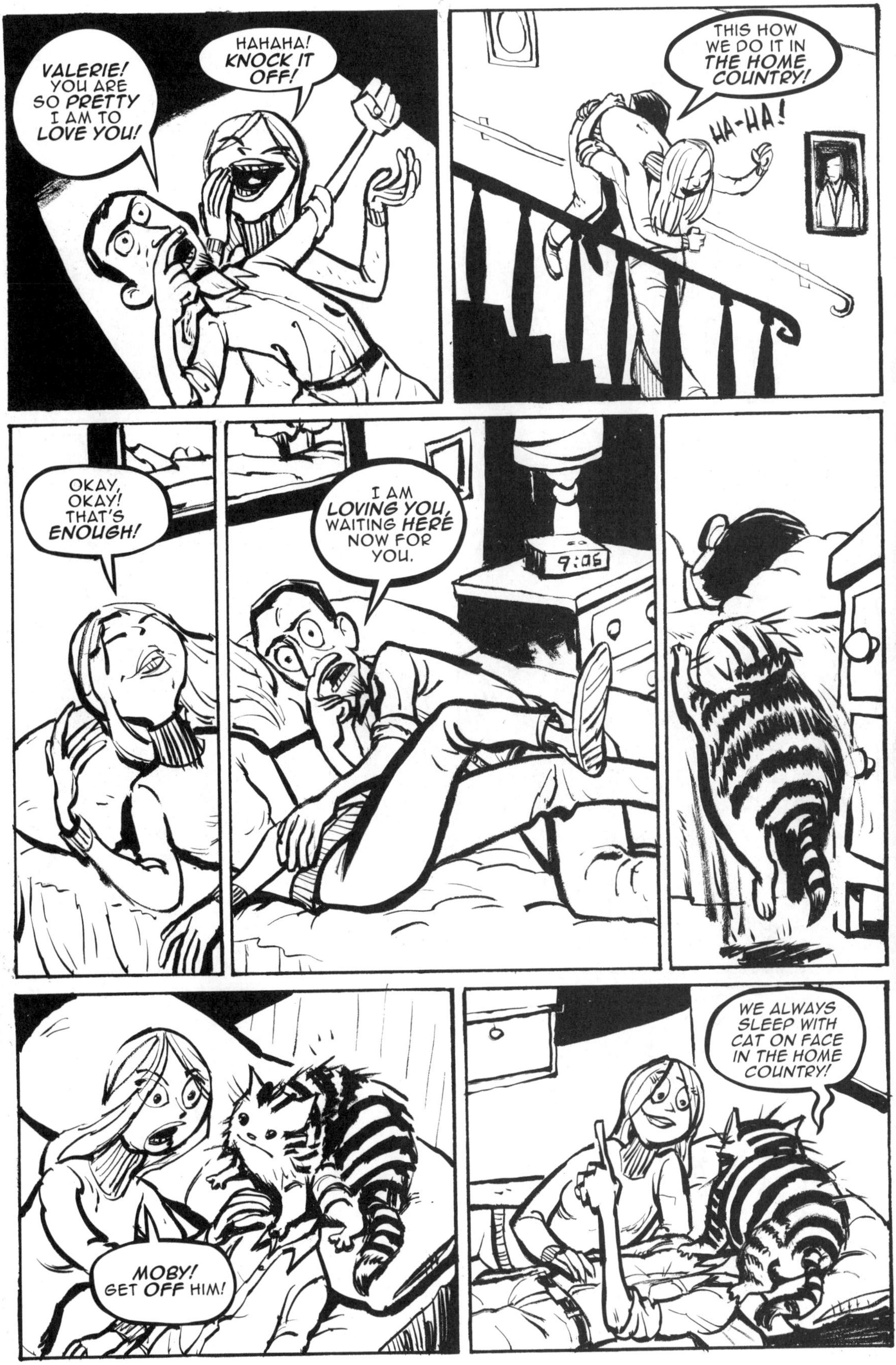

VALERIE! YOU ARE SO PRETTY I AM TO LOVE YOU!
HAHAHA! KNOCK IT OFF!
THIS HOW WE DO IT IN THE HOME COUNTRY!
HA-HA!
OKAY, OKAY! THAT'S ENOUGH!
I AM LOVING YOU, WAITING HERE NOW FOR YOU.
9:06
MOBY! GET OFF HIM!
WE ALWAYS SLEEP WITH CAT ON FACE IN THE HOME COUNTRY!

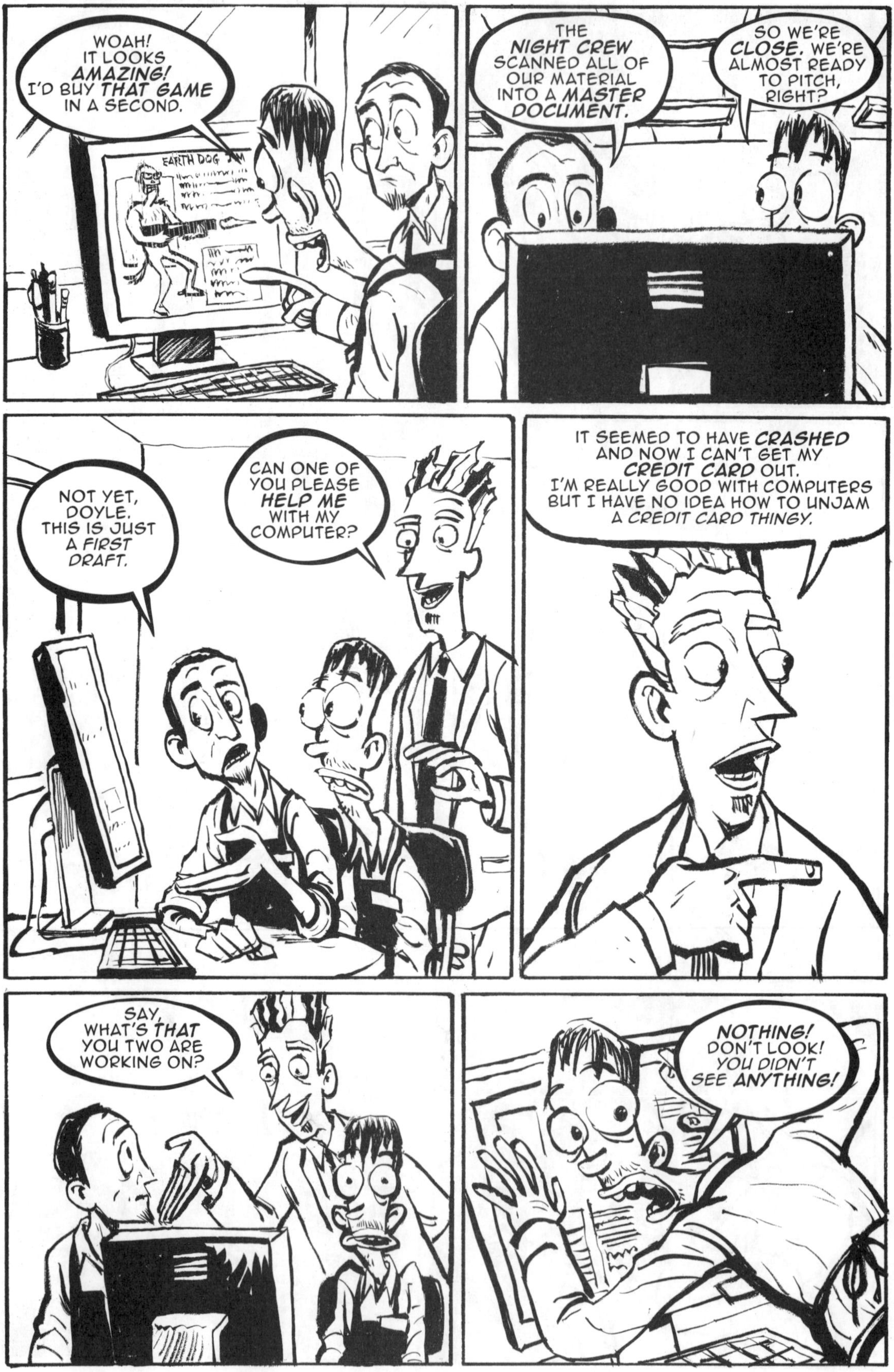
WOAH! IT LOOKS AMAZING! I'D BUY THAT GAME IN A SECOND.
EARTH DOG JIM
THE NIGHT CREW SCANNED ALL OF OUR MATERIAL INTO A MASTER DOCUMENT.
SO WE'RE CLOSE. WE'RE ALMOST READY TO PITCH, RIGHT?
NOT YET, DOYLE. THIS IS JUST A FIRST DRAFT.
CAN ONE OF YOU PLEASE HELP ME WITH MY COMPUTER?
IT SEEMED TO HAVE CRASHED AND NOW I CAN'T GET MY CREDIT CARD OUT. I'M REALLY GOOD WITH COMPUTERS BUT I HAVE NO IDEA HOW TO UNJAM A CREDIT CARD THINGY.
SAY, WHAT'S THAT YOU TWO ARE WORKING ON?
NOTHING! DON'T LOOK! YOU DIDN'T SEE ANYTHING!

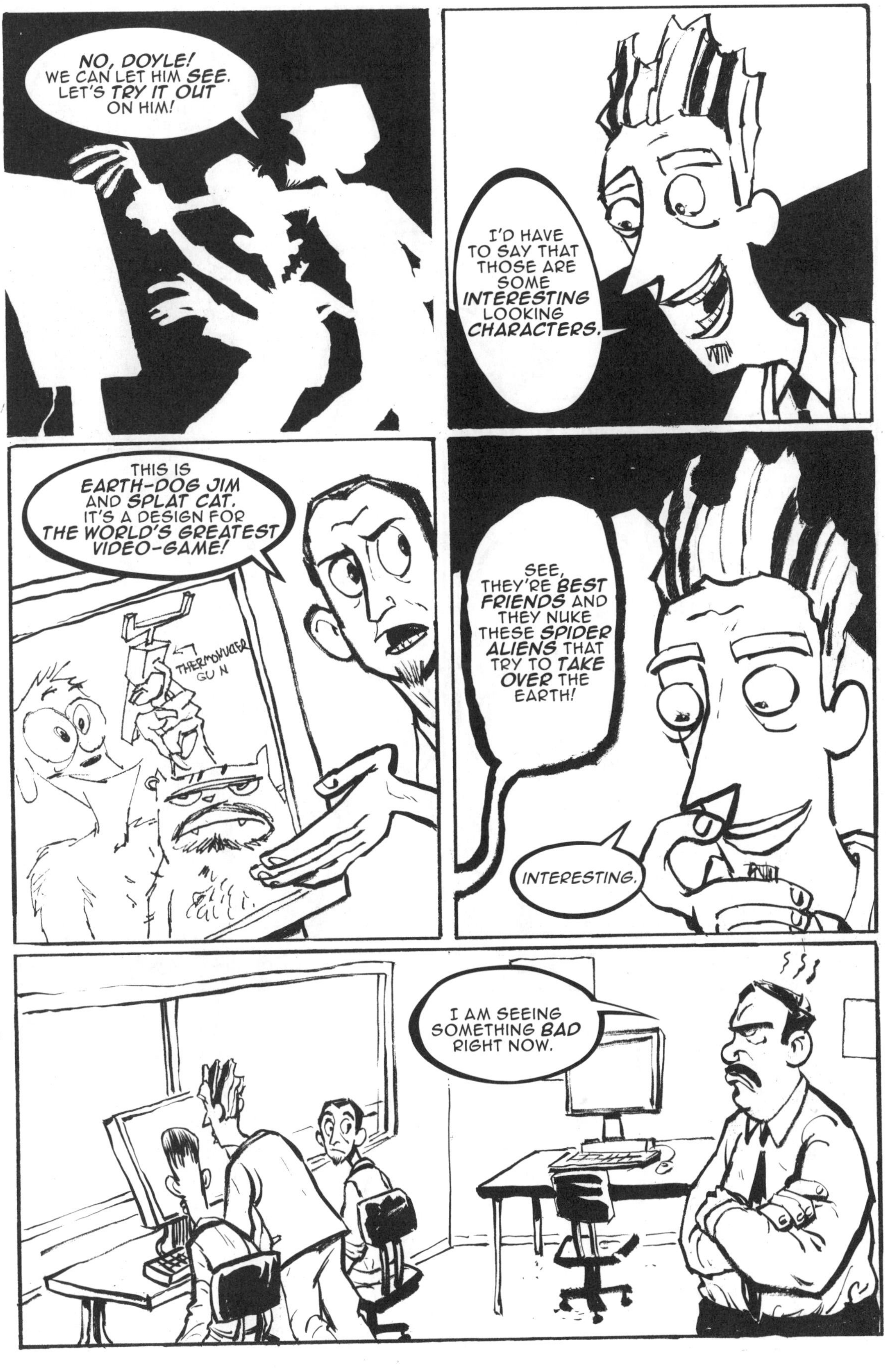
NO, DOYLE! WE CAN LET HIM SEE. LET'S TRY IT OUT ON HIM!
I'D HAVE TO SAY THAT THOSE ARE SOME INTERESTING LOOKING CHARACTERS.
THIS IS EARTH-DOG JIM AND SPLAT CAT. IT'S A DESIGN FOR THE WORLD'S GREATEST VIDEO-GAME!
THERMONUCLEAR GUN
SEE, THEY'RE BEST FRIENDS AND THEY NUKE THESE SPIDER ALIENS THAT TRY TO TAKE OVER THE EARTH!
INTERESTING.
I AM SEEING SOMETHING BAD RIGHT NOW.

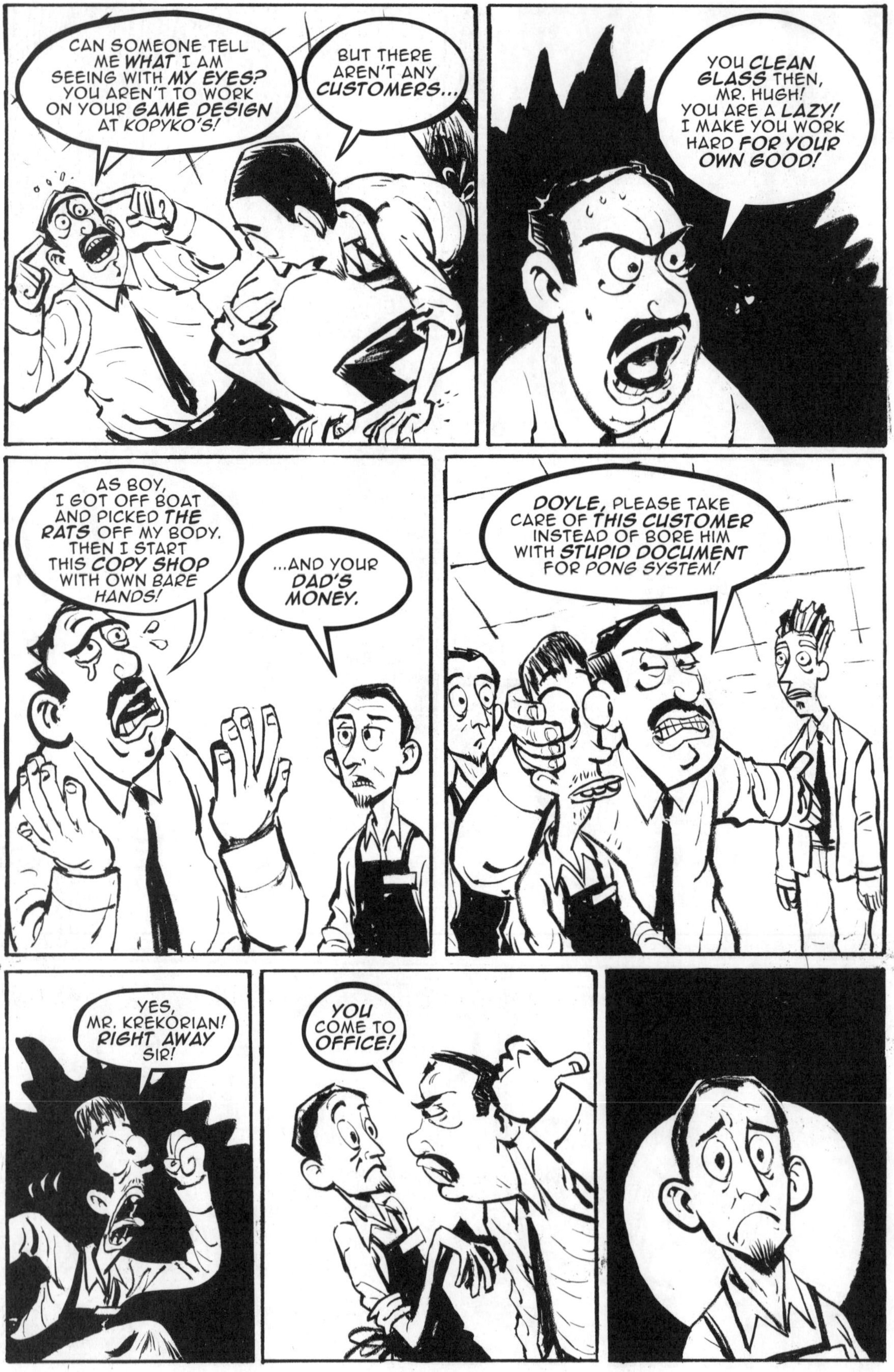
CAN SOMEONE TELL ME WHAT I AM SEEING WITH MY EYES? YOU AREN'T TO WORK ON YOUR GAME DESIGN AT KOPYKO'S!
BUT THERE AREN'T ANY CUSTOMERS...
YOU CLEAN GLASS THEN, MR. HUGH! YOU ARE A LAZY! I MAKE YOU WORK HARD FOR YOUR OWN GOOD!
AS BOY, I GOT OFF BOAT AND PICKED THE RATS OFF MY BODY. THEN I START THIS COPY SHOP WITH OWN BARE HANDS!
...AND YOUR DAD'S MONEY.
DOYLE, PLEASE TAKE CARE OF THIS CUSTOMER INSTEAD OF BORE HIM WITH STUPID DOCUMENT FOR PONG SYSTEM!
YES, MR. KREKORIAN! RIGHT AWAY SIR!
YOU COME TO OFFICE!

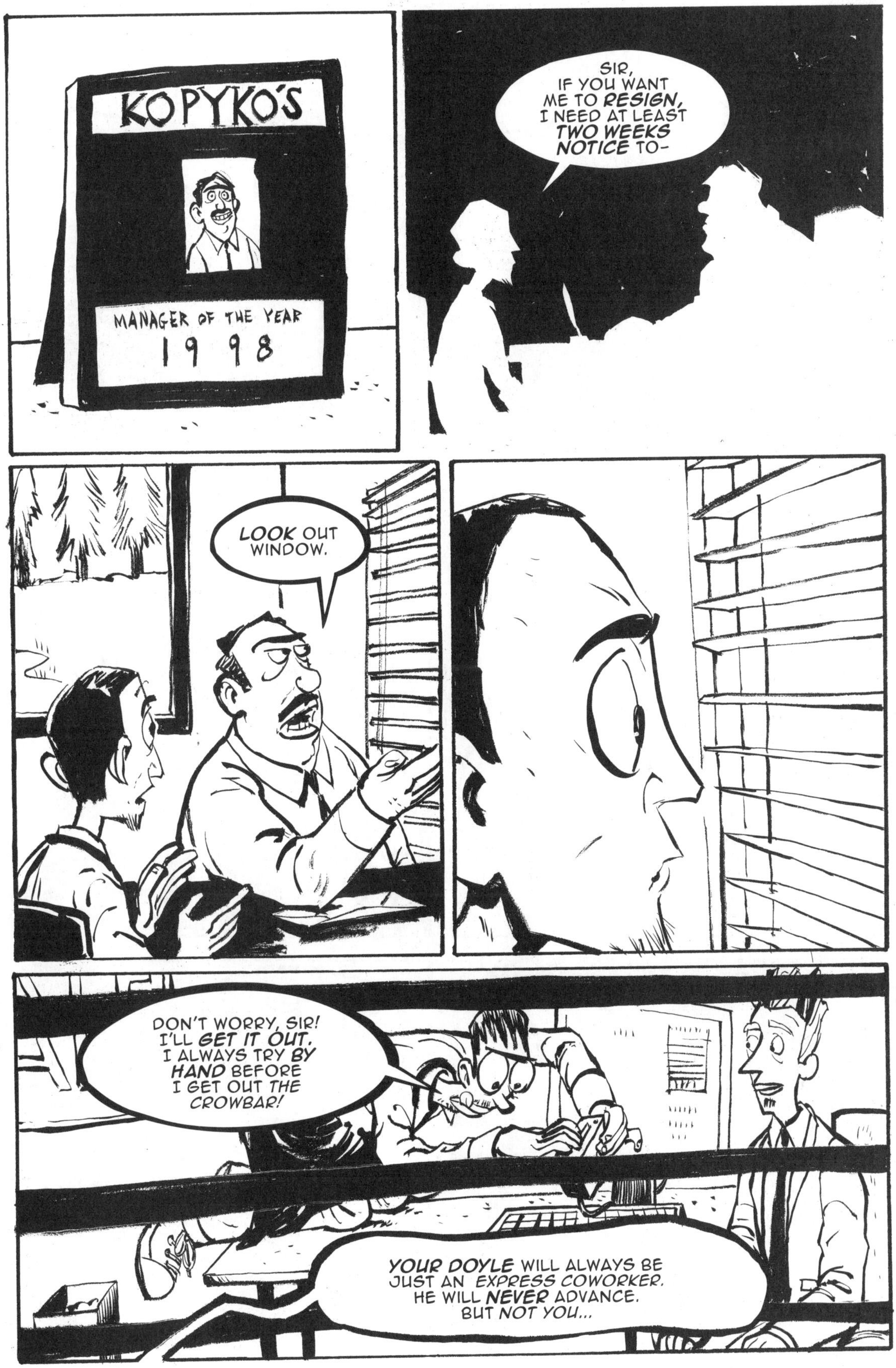
KOPYKO'S
MANAGER OF THE YEAR
1998
SIR, IF YOU WANT ME TO RESIGN, I NEED AT LEAST TWO WEEKS NOTICE TO-
LOOK OUT WINDOW.
DON'T WORRY, SIR! I'LL GET IT OUT. I ALWAYS TRY BY HAND BEFORE I GET OUT THE CROWBAR!
YOUR DOYLE WILL ALWAYS BE JUST AN EXPRESS COWORKER. HE WILL NEVER ADVANCE. BUT NOT YOU...

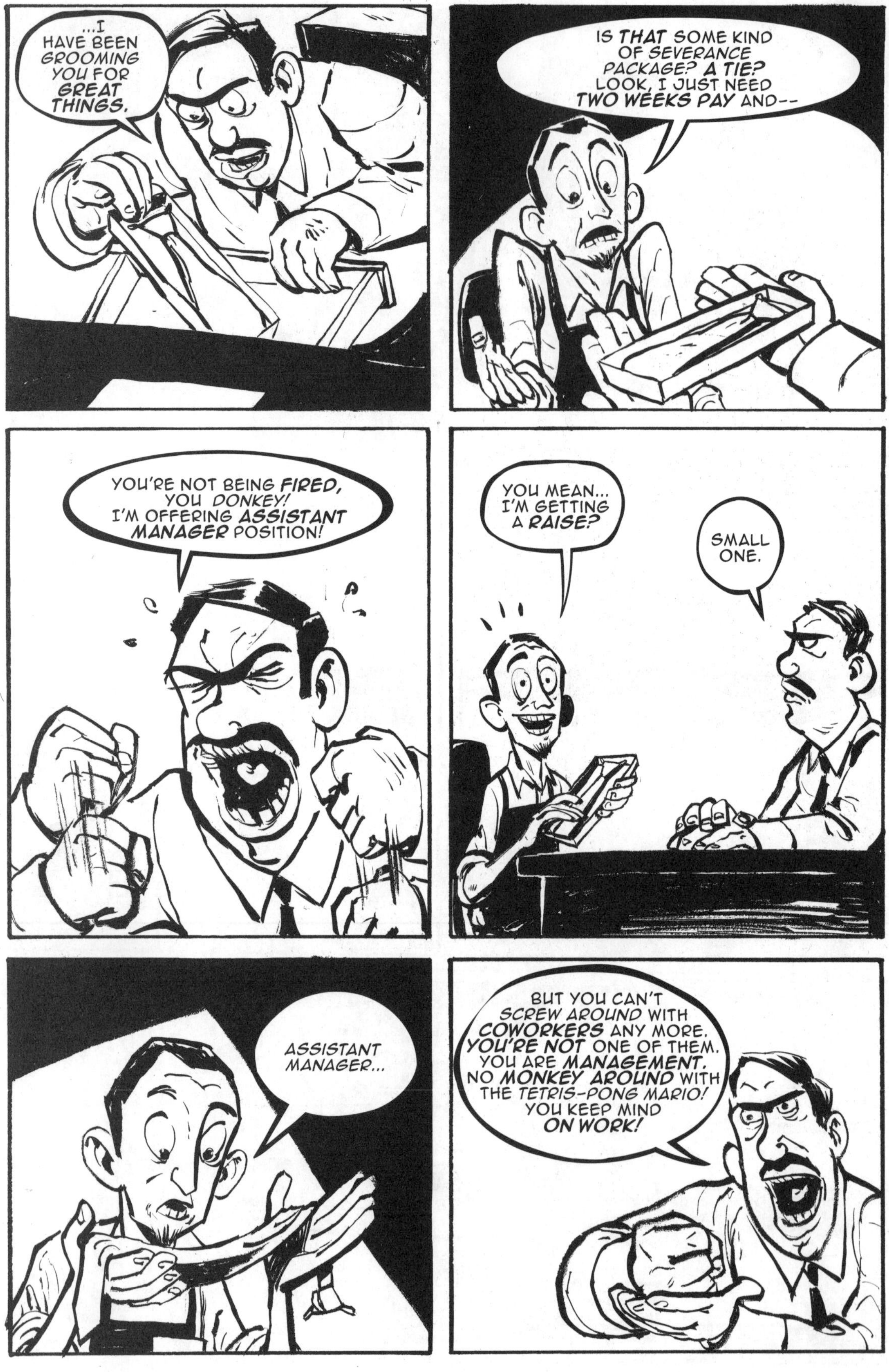

...I HAVE BEEN GROOMING YOU FOR GREAT THINGS.
IS THAT SOME KIND OF SEVERANCE PACKAGE? A TIE? LOOK, I JUST NEED TWO WEEKS PAY AND--
YOU'RE NOT BEING FIRED, YOU DONKEY! I'M OFFERING ASSISTANT MANAGER POSITION!
YOU MEAN... I'M GETTING A RAISE?
SMALL ONE.
ASSISTANT MANAGER...
BUT YOU CAN'T SCREW AROUND WITH COWORKERS ANY MORE. YOU'RE NOT ONE OF THEM. YOU ARE MANAGEMENT. NO MONKEY AROUND WITH THE TETRIS-PONG MARIO! YOU KEEP MIND ON WORK!

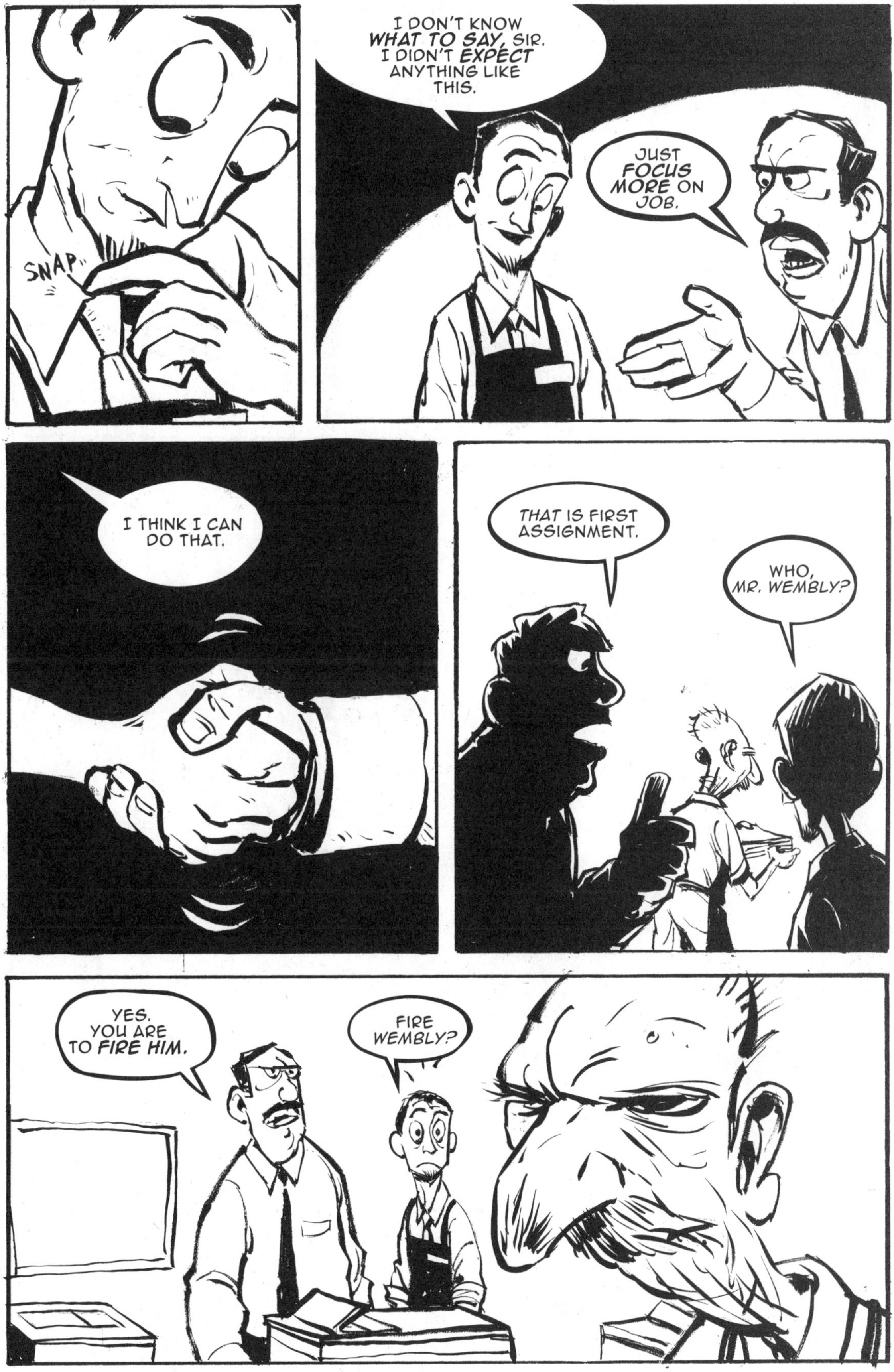
SNAP
I DON'T KNOW WHAT TO SAY, SIR. I DIDN'T EXPECT ANYTHING LIKE THIS.
JUST FOCUS MORE ON JOB.
I THINK I CAN DO THAT.
THAT IS FIRST ASSIGNMENT.
WHO, MR. WEMBLY?
YES. YOU ARE TO FIRE HIM.
FIRE WEMBLY?

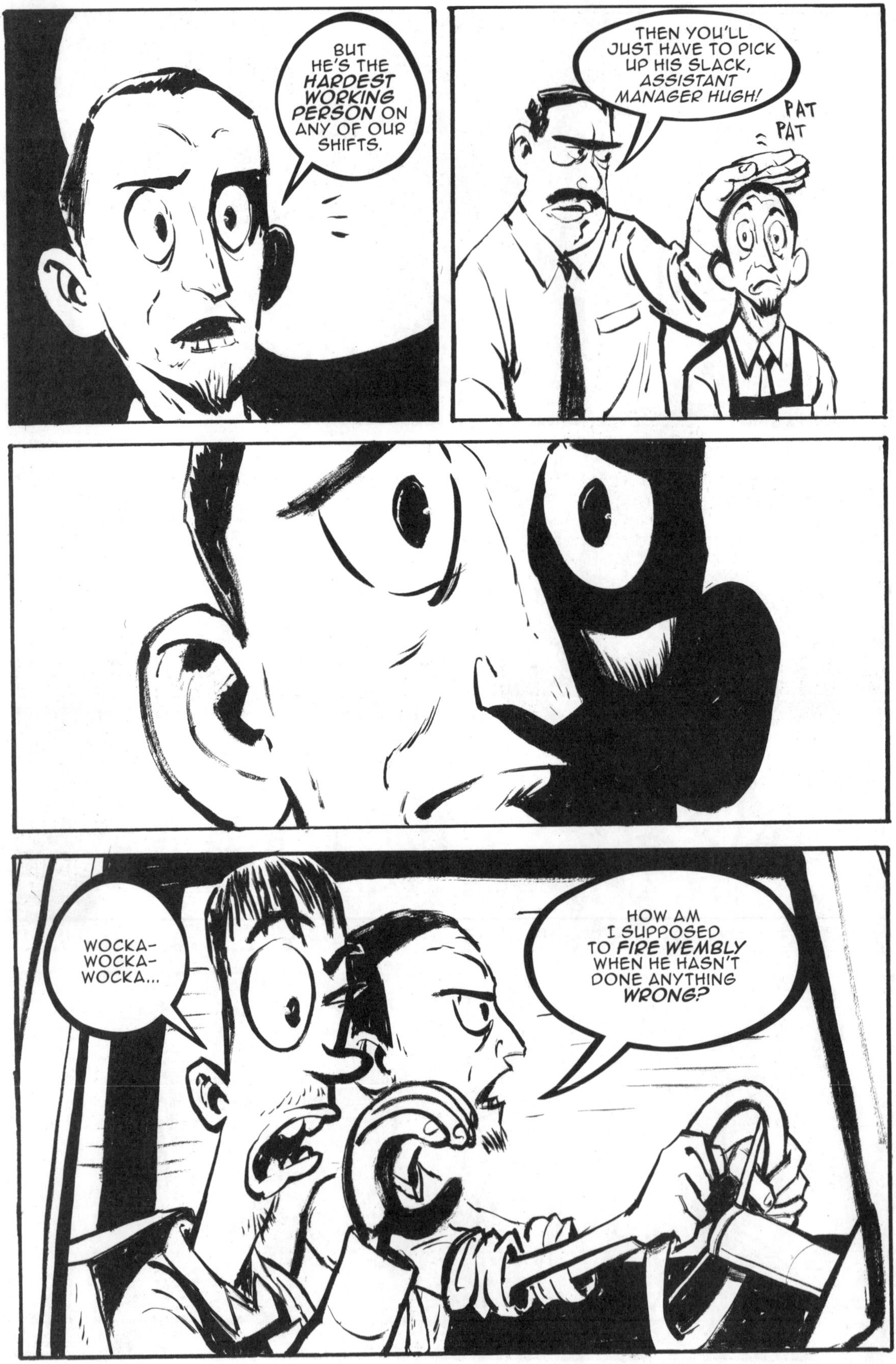
BUT HE'S THE HARDEST WORKING PERSON ON ANY OF OUR SHIFTS.
THEN YOU'LL JUST HAVE TO PICK UP HIS SLACK, ASSISTANT MANAGER HUGH!
PAT PAT
WOCKA-WOCKA-WOCKA...
HOW AM I SUPPOSED TO FIRE WEMBLY WHEN HE HASN'T DONE ANYTHING WRONG?

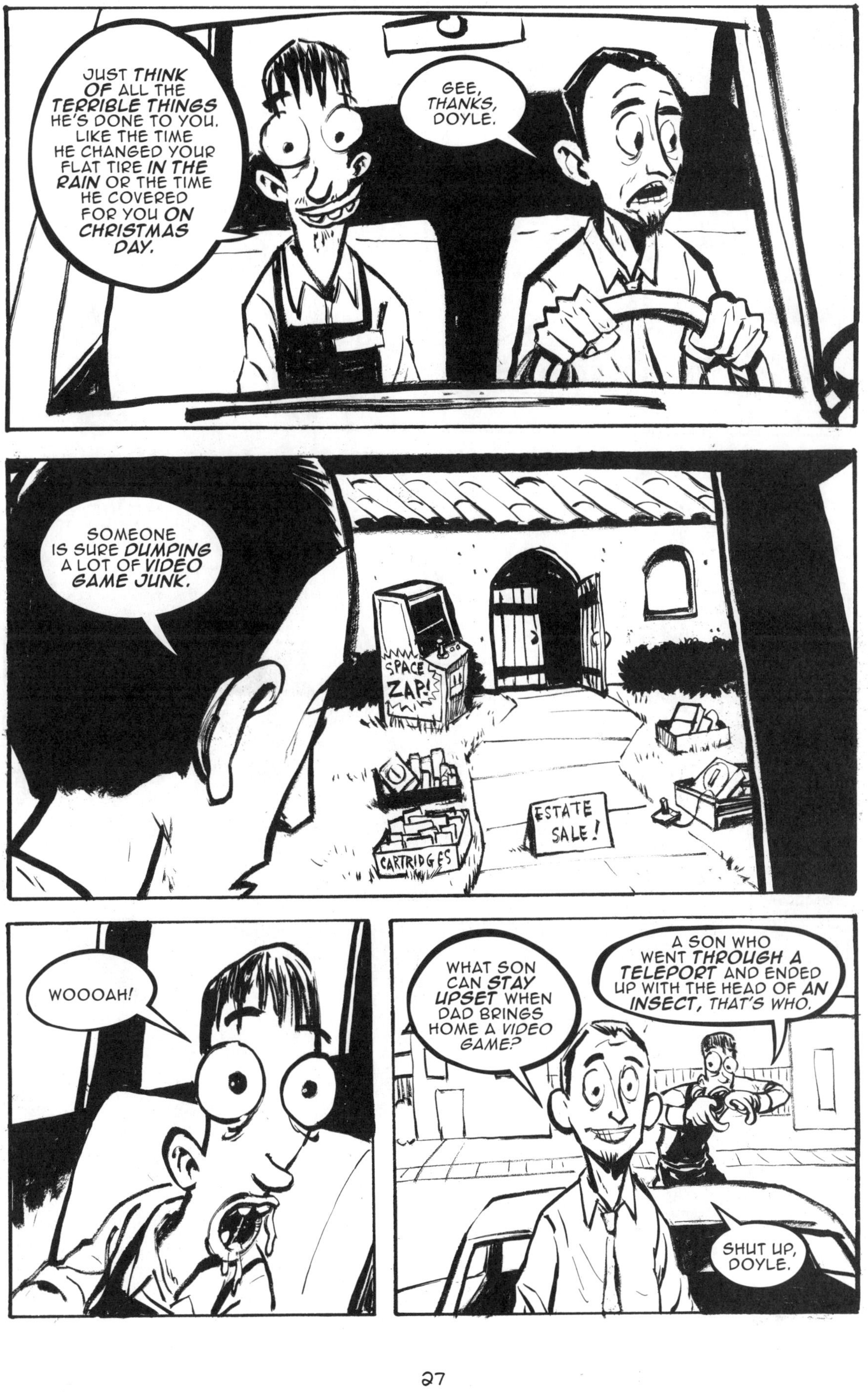
JUST THINK OF ALL THE TERRIBLE THINGS HE'S DONE TO YOU. LIKE THE TIME HE CHANGED YOUR FLAT TIRE IN THE RAIN OR THE TIME HE COVERED FOR YOU ON CHRISTMAS DAY.
GEE, THANKS, DOYLE.
SOMEONE IS SURE DUMPING A LOT OF VIDEO GAME JUNK.
SPACE ZAP!
CARTRIDGES
ESTATE SALE!
WOOOAH!
WHAT SON CAN STAY UPSET WHEN DAD BRINGS HOME A VIDEO GAME?
A SON WHO WENT THROUGH A TELEPORT AND ENDED UP WITH THE HEAD OF AN INSECT, THAT'S WHO.
SHUT UP, DOYLE.

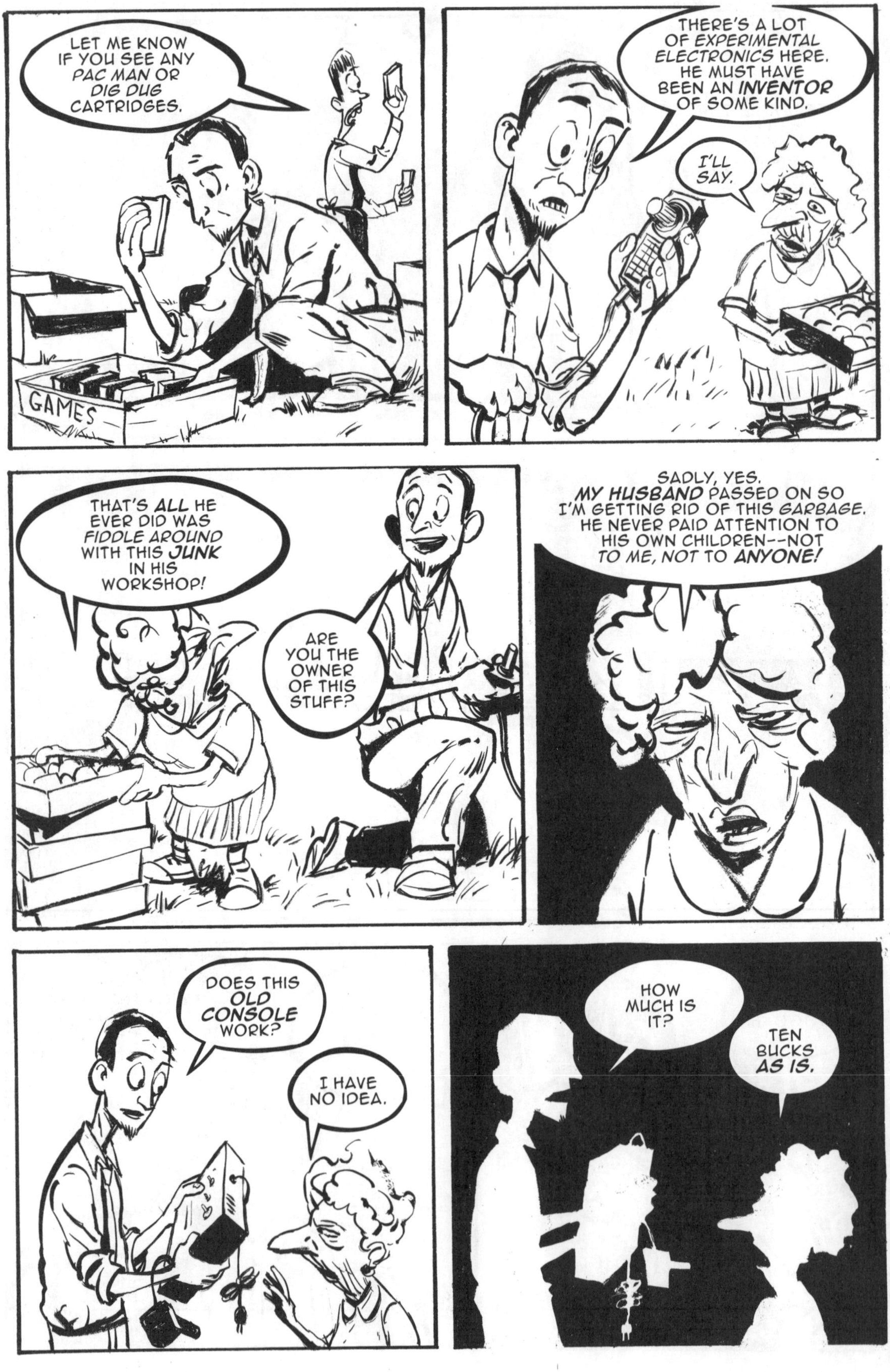
LET ME KNOW IF YOU SEE ANY PAC MAN OR DIG DUG CARTRIDGES.
GAMES
THERE'S A LOT OF EXPERIMENTAL ELECTRONICS HERE. HE MUST HAVE BEEN AN INVENTOR OF SOME KIND.
I'LL SAY.
THAT'S ALL HE EVER DID WAS FIDDLE AROUND WITH THIS JUNK IN HIS WORKSHOP!
ARE YOU THE OWNER OF THIS STUFF?
SADLY, YES. MY HUSBAND PASSED ON SO I'M GETTING RID OF THIS GARBAGE. HE NEVER PAID ATTENTION TO HIS OWN CHILDREN--NOT TO ME, NOT TO ANYONE!
DOES THIS OLD CONSOLE WORK?
I HAVE NO IDEA.
HOW MUCH IS IT?
TEN BUCKS AS IS.

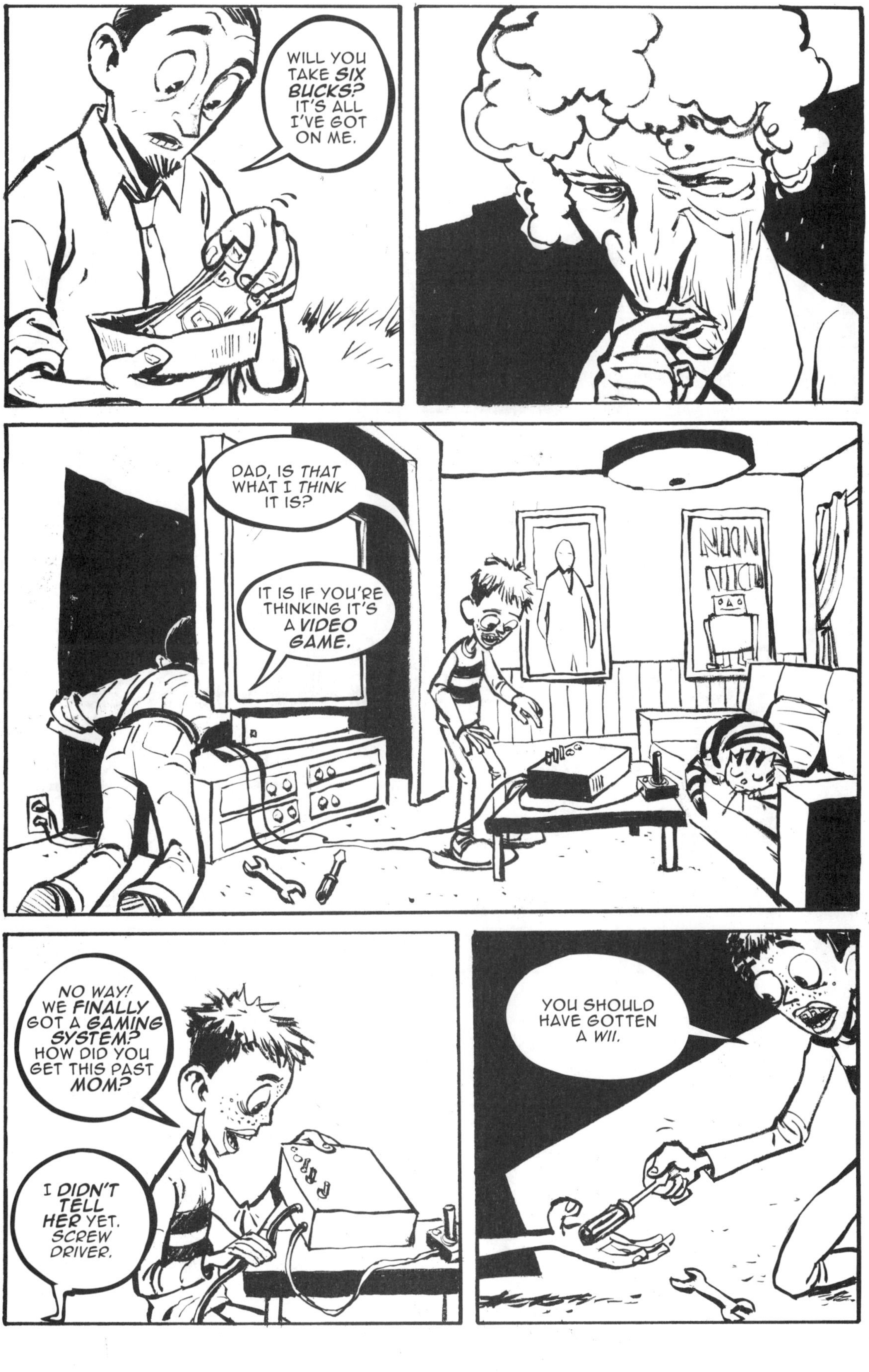

WILL YOU TAKE SIX BUCKS? IT'S ALL I'VE GOT ON ME.
DAD, IS THAT WHAT I THINK IT IS?
IT IS IF YOU'RE THINKING IT'S A VIDEO GAME.
NO WAY! WE FINALLY GOT A GAMING SYSTEM? HOW DID YOU GET THIS PAST MOM?
I DIDN'T TELL HER YET. SCREW DRIVER.
YOU SHOULD HAVE GOTTEN A WII.

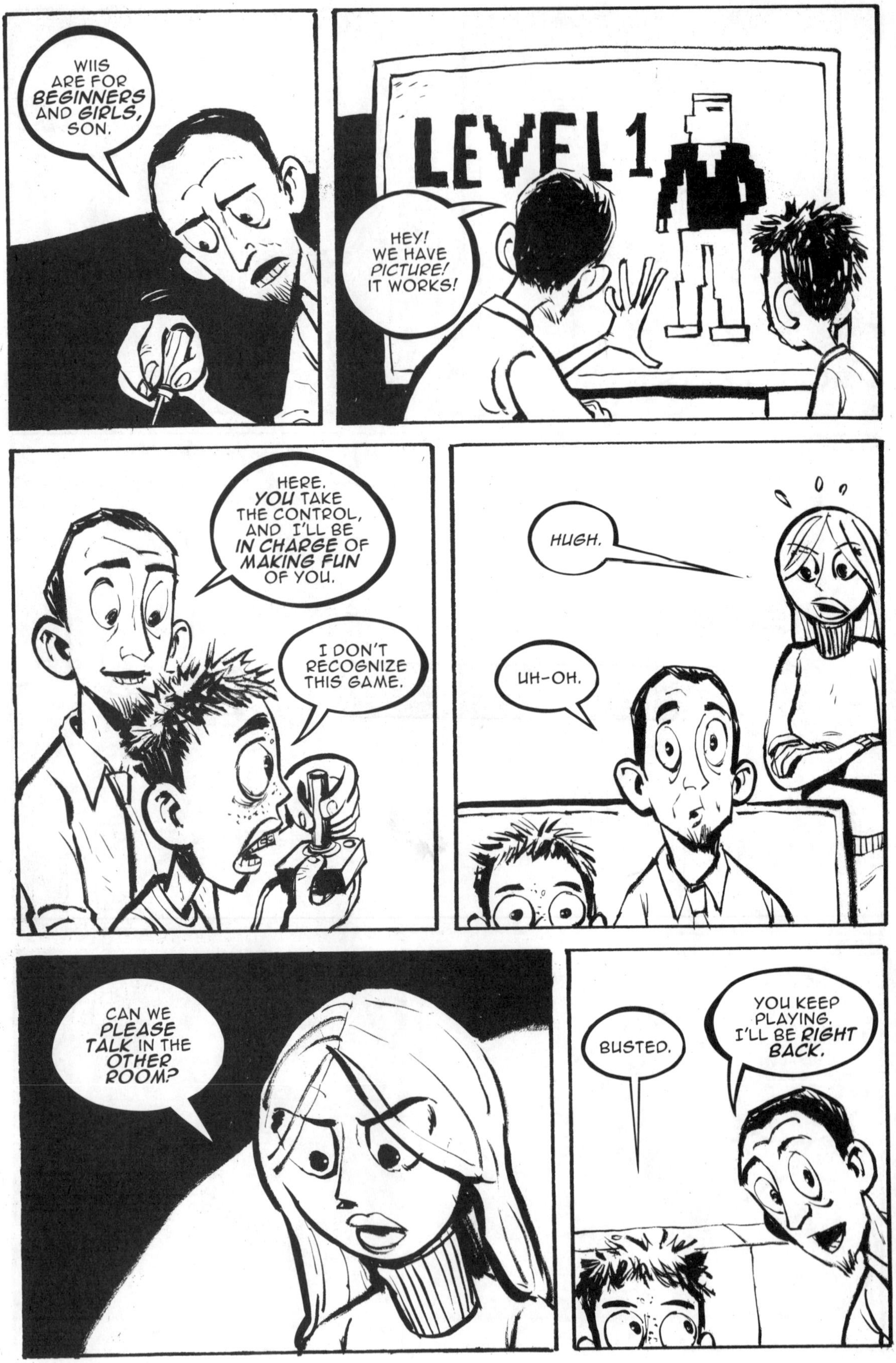
WIIS ARE FOR BEGINNERS AND GIRLS, SON.
LEVEL 1
HEY! WE HAVE PICTURE! IT WORKS!
HERE. YOU TAKE THE CONTROL, AND I'LL BE IN CHARGE OF MAKING FUN OF YOU.
I DON'T RECOGNIZE THIS GAME.
HUGH.
UH-OH.
CAN WE PLEASE TALK IN THE OTHER ROOM?
BUSTED.
YOU KEEP PLAYING. I'LL BE RIGHT BACK.

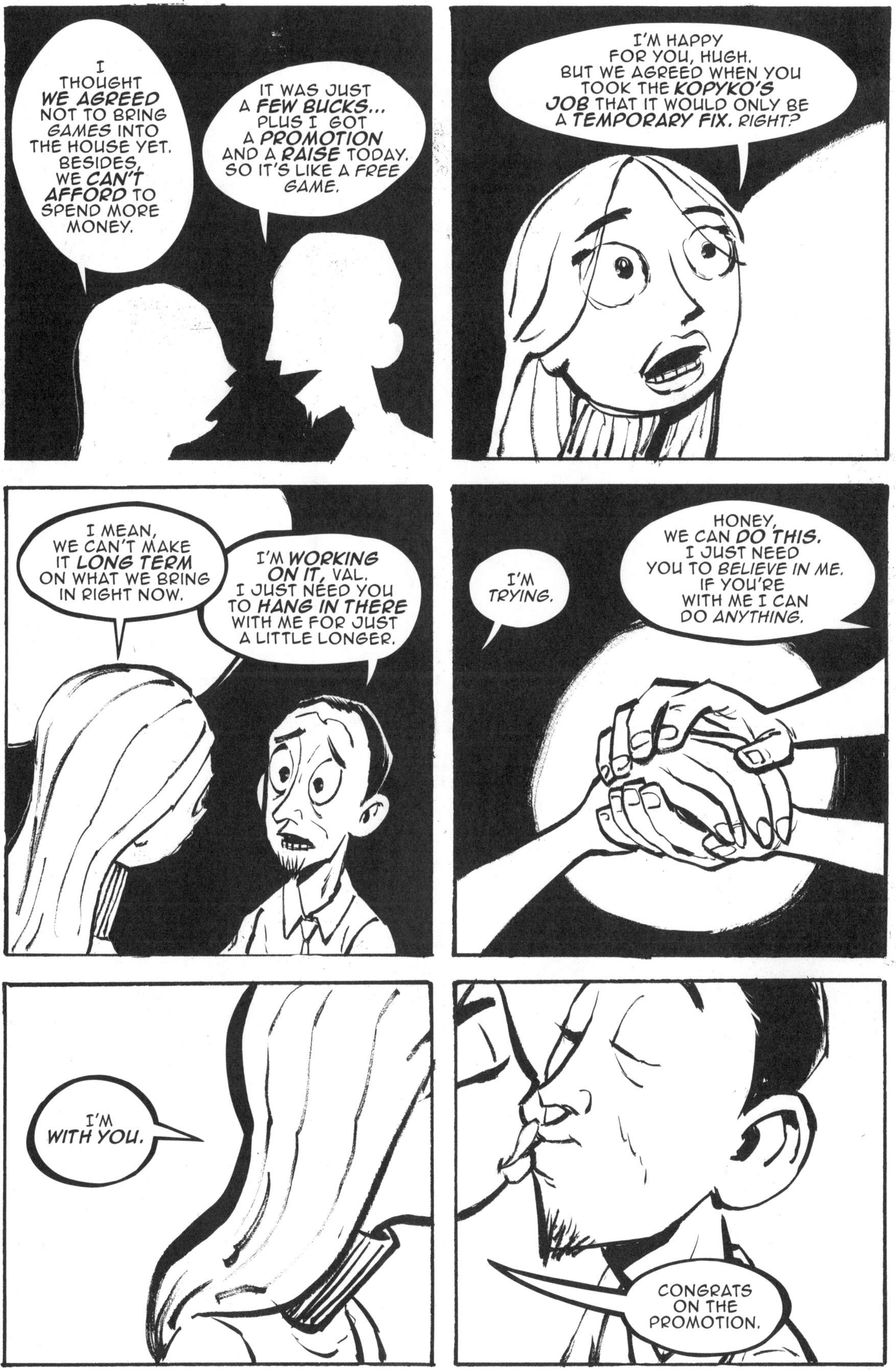
I THOUGHT WE AGREED NOT TO BRING GAMES INTO THE HOUSE YET. BESIDES, WE CAN'T AFFORD TO SPEND MORE MONEY.
IT WAS JUST A FEW BUCKS... PLUS I GOT A PROMOTION AND A RAISE TODAY. SO IT'S LIKE A FREE GAME.
I'M HAPPY FOR YOU, HUGH. BUT WE AGREED WHEN YOU TOOK THE KOPYKO'S JOB THAT IT WOULD ONLY BE A TEMPORARY FIX. RIGHT?
I MEAN, WE CAN'T MAKE IT LONG TERM ON WHAT WE BRING IN RIGHT NOW.
I'M WORKING ON IT, VAL. I JUST NEED YOU TO HANG IN THERE WITH ME FOR JUST A LITTLE LONGER.
I'M TRYING.
HONEY, WE CAN DO THIS. I JUST NEED YOU TO BELIEVE IN ME. IF YOU'RE WITH ME I CAN DO ANYTHING.
I'M WITH YOU.
CONGRATS ON THE PROMOTION.

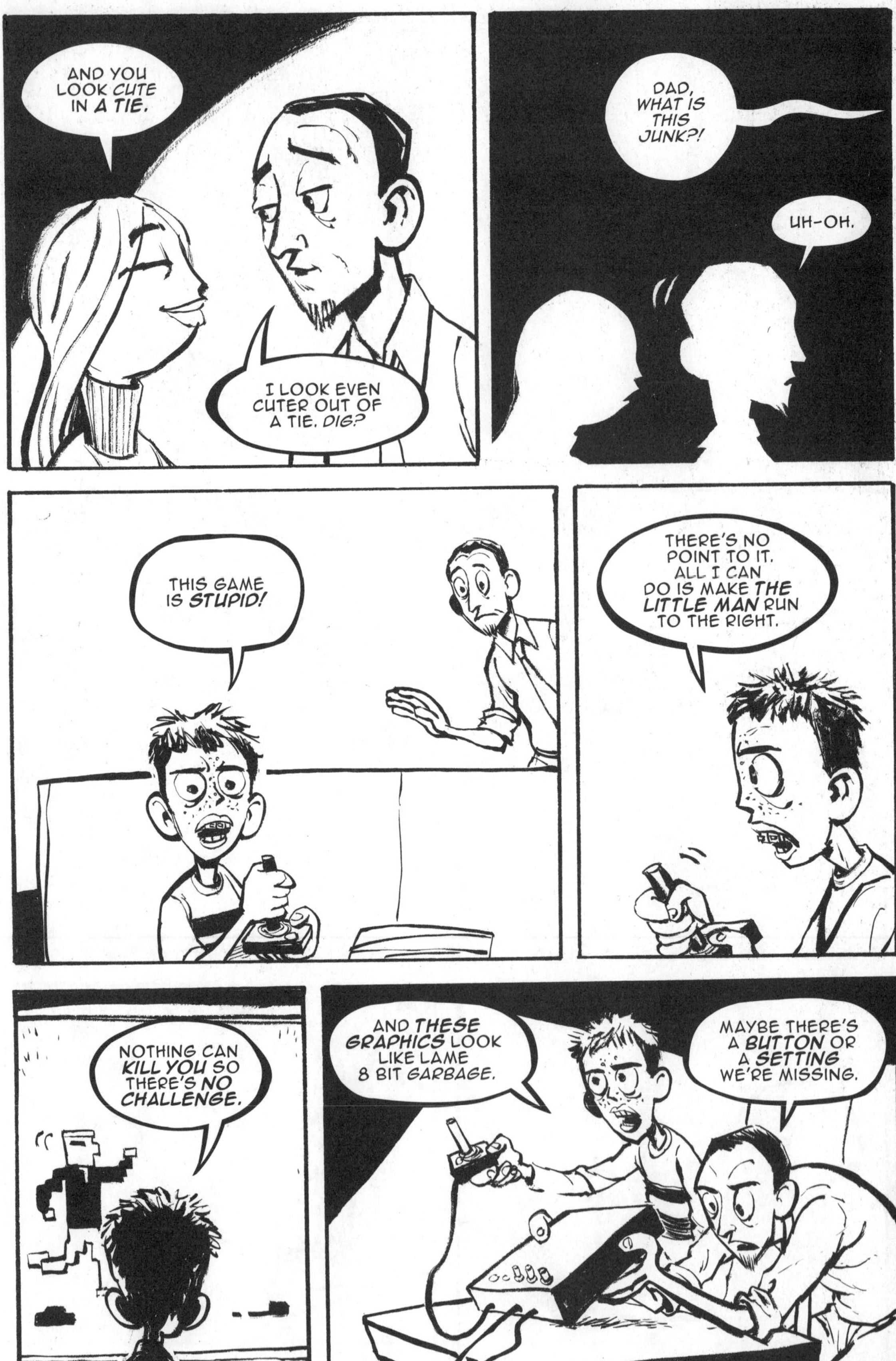
AND YOU LOOK CUTE IN A TIE.
I LOOK EVEN CUTER OUT OF A TIE. DIG?
DAD, WHAT IS THIS JUNK?!
UH-OH.
THIS GAME IS STUPID!
THERE'S NO POINT TO IT. ALL I CAN DO IS MAKE THE LITTLE MAN RUN TO THE RIGHT.
NOTHING CAN KILL YOU SO THERE'S NO CHALLENGE.
AND THESE GRAPHICS LOOK LIKE LAME 8 BIT GARBAGE.
MAYBE THERE'S A BUTTON OR A SETTING WE'RE MISSING.

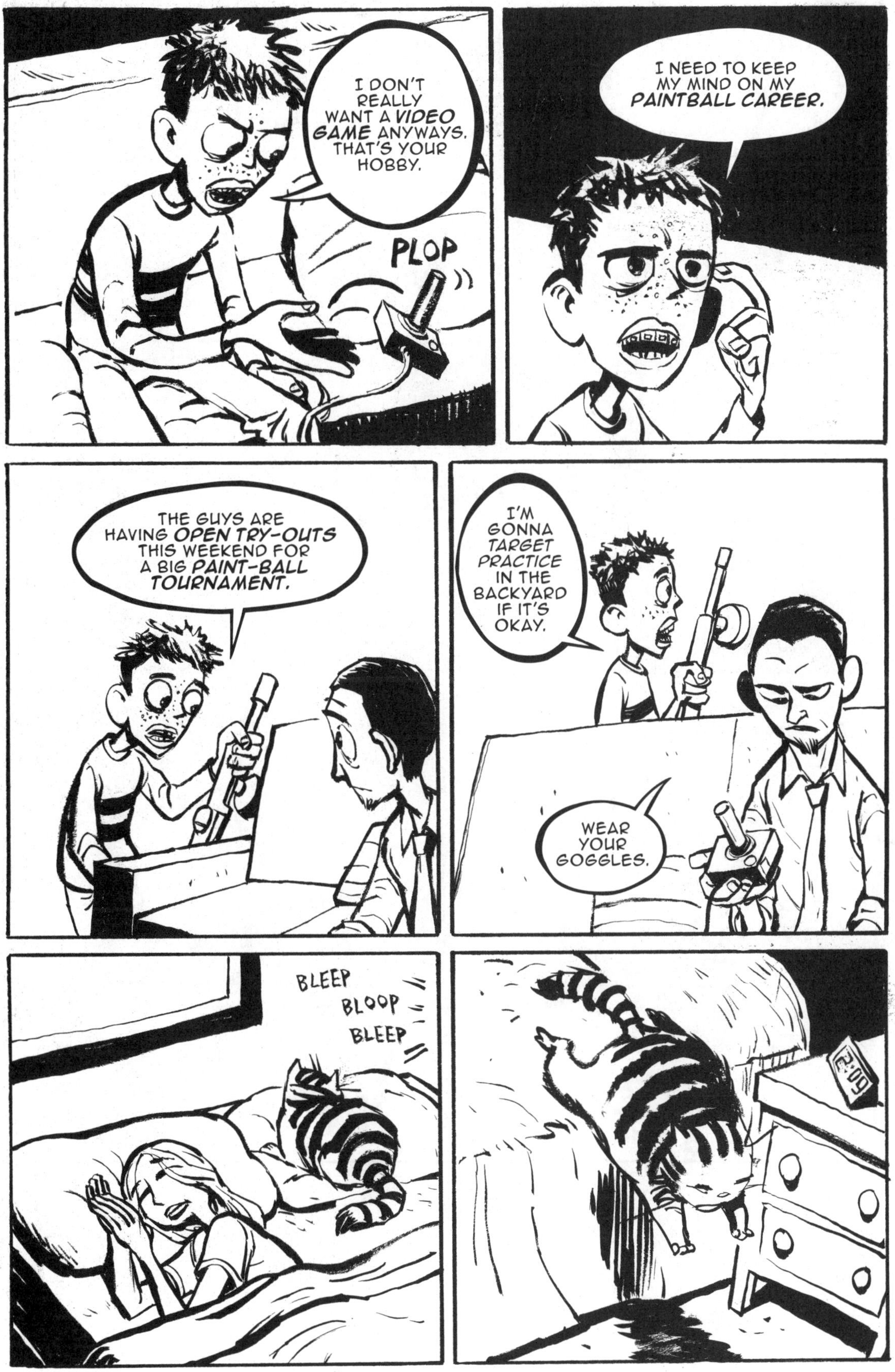
I DON'T REALLY WANT A VIDEO GAME ANYWAYS. THAT'S YOUR HOBBY.
PLOP
I NEED TO KEEP MY MIND ON MY PAINTBALL CAREER.
THE GUYS ARE HAVING OPEN TRY-OUTS THIS WEEKEND FOR A BIG PAINT-BALL TOURNAMENT.
I'M GONNA TARGET PRACTICE IN THE BACKYARD IF IT'S OKAY.
WEAR YOUR GOGGLES.
BLEEP
BLOOP
BLEEP
2:09

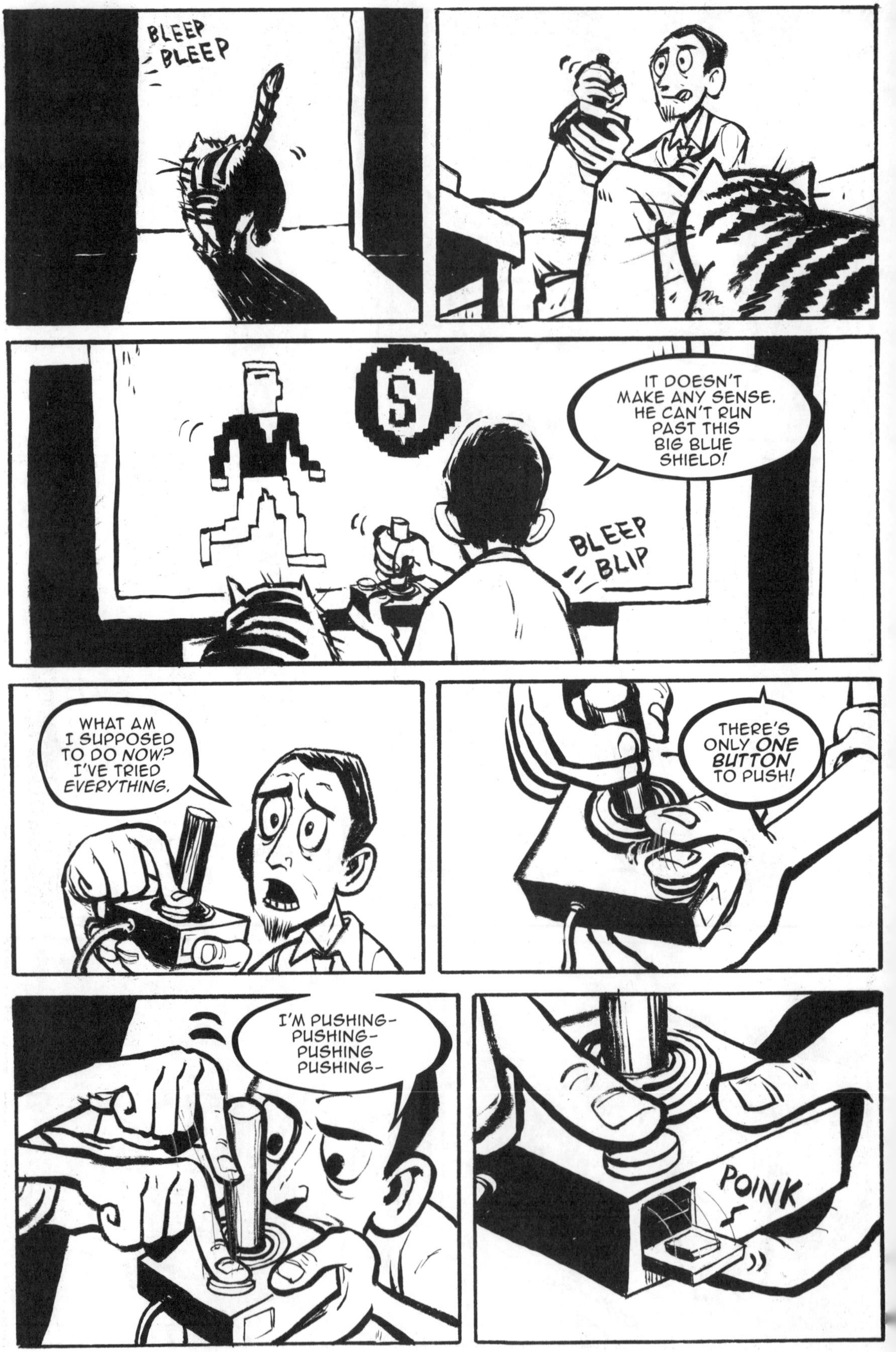
BLEEP
BLEEP
IT DOESN'T MAKE ANY SENSE. HE CAN'T RUN PAST THIS BIG BLUE SHIELD!
BLEEP
BLIP
WHAT AM I SUPPOSED TO DO *NOW?* I'VE TRIED *EVERYTHING.*
THERE'S ONLY ***ONE BUTTON*** TO PUSH!
I'M PUSHING-
PUSHING-
PUSHING
PUSHING-
POINK

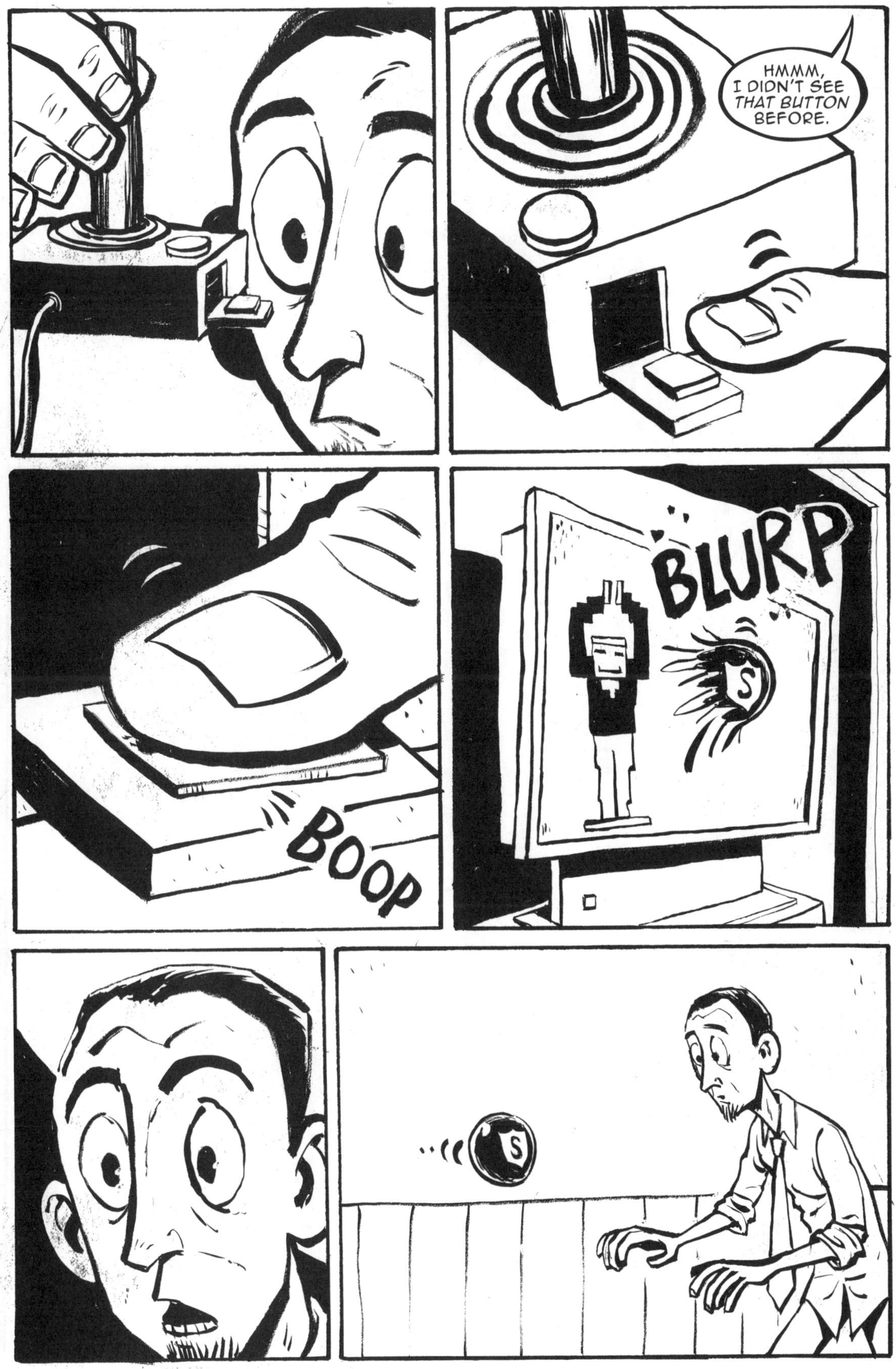
HMMM, I DIDN'T SEE THAT BUTTON BEFORE.
BOOP
BLURP
S
S

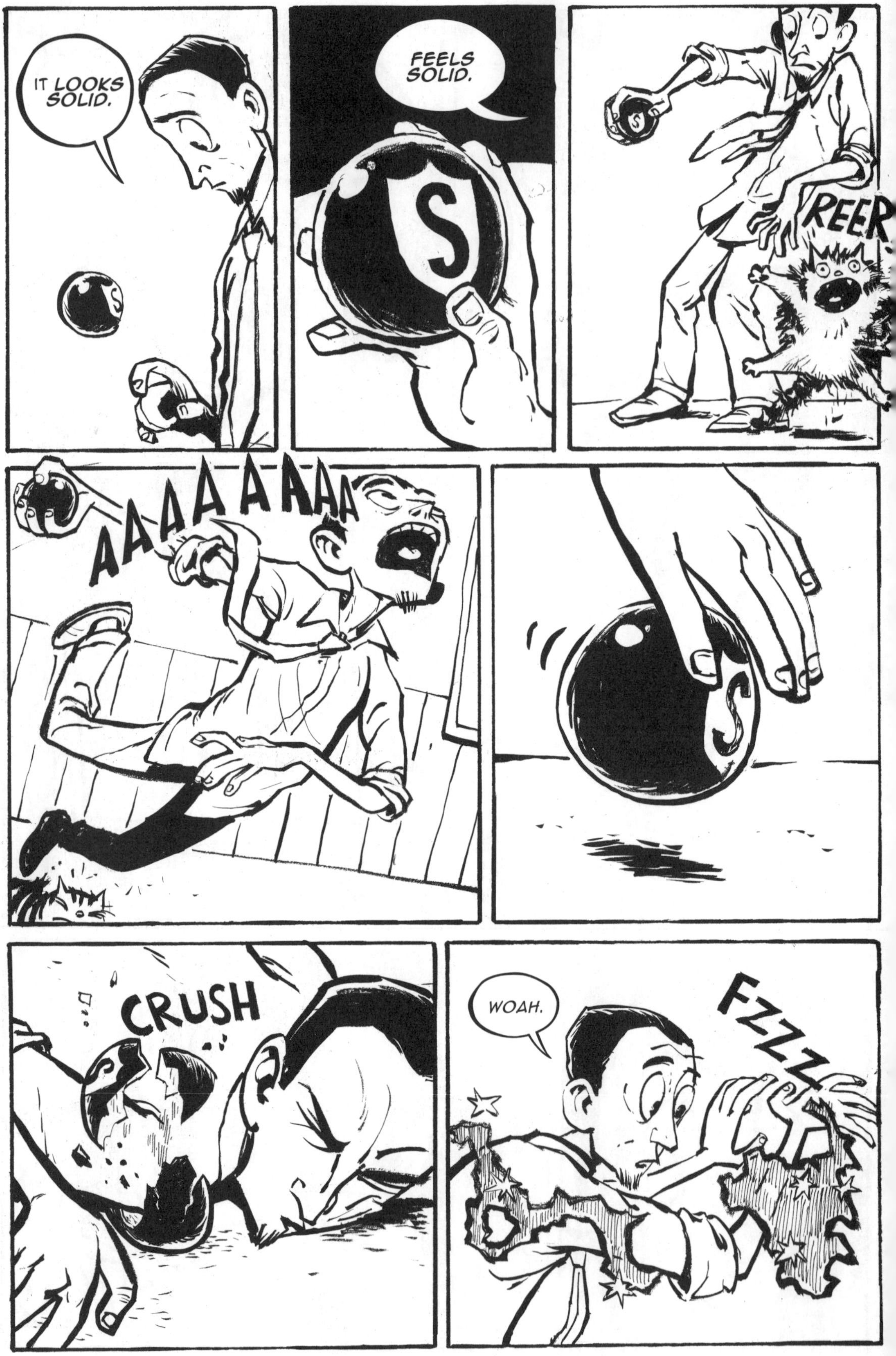
IT LOOKS SOLID.
FEELS SOLID.
S
S
REER
AAAAAAAA
S
CRUSH
WOAH.
FZZZ

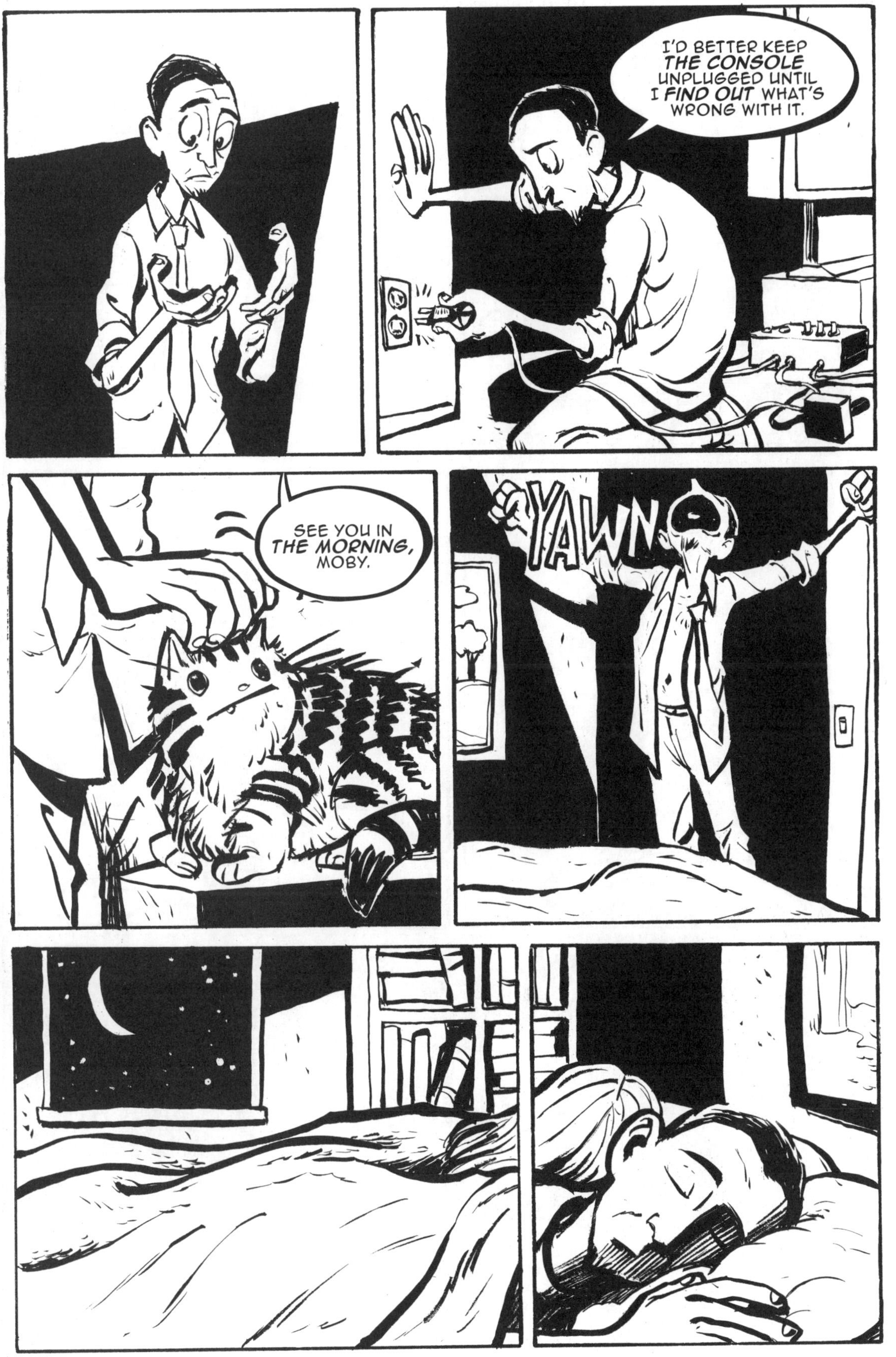
I'D BETTER KEEP THE CONSOLE UNPLUGGED UNTIL I FIND OUT WHAT'S WRONG WITH IT.
SEE YOU IN THE MORNING, MOBY.
YAWN

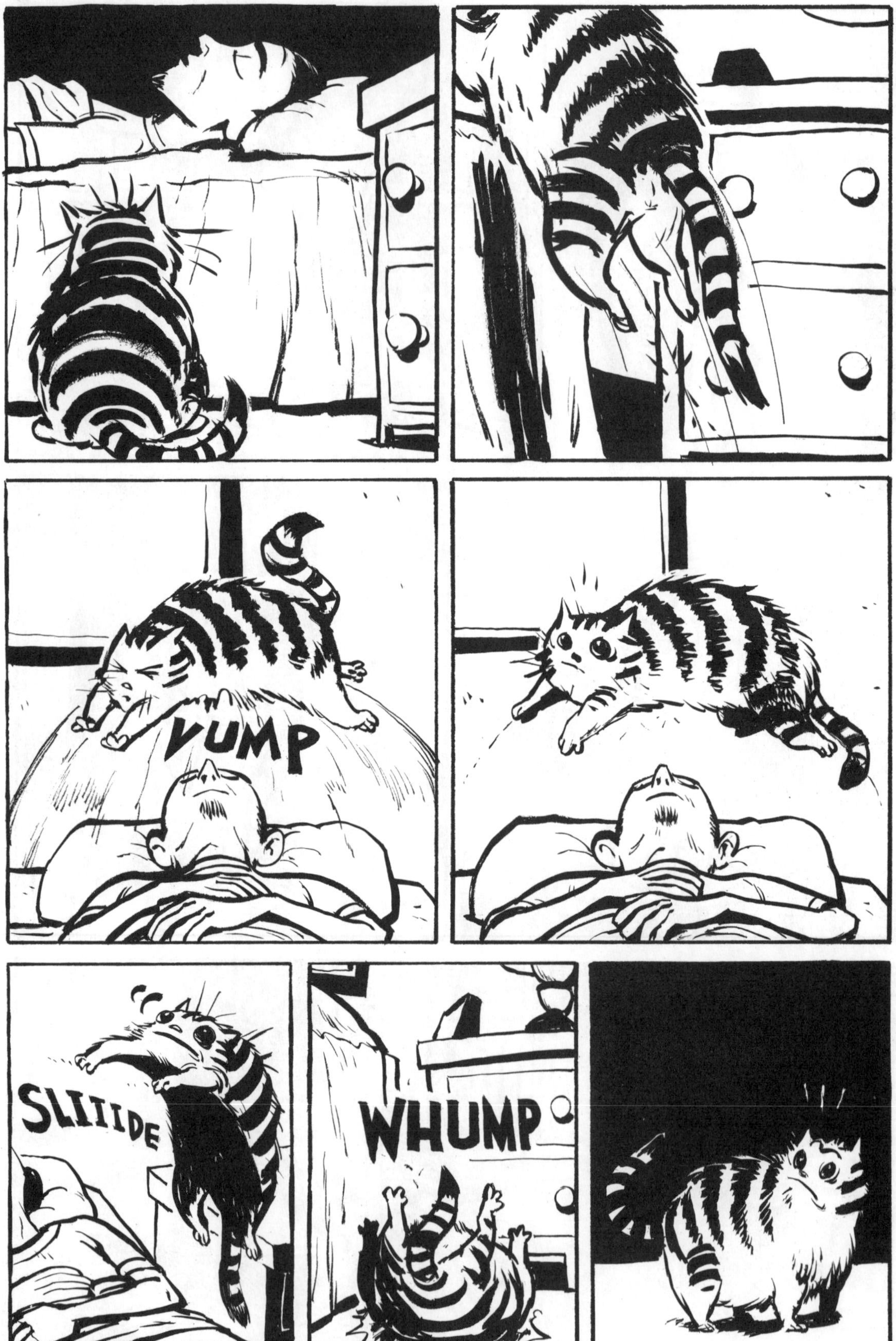
VUMP
SLIIIDE
WHUMP

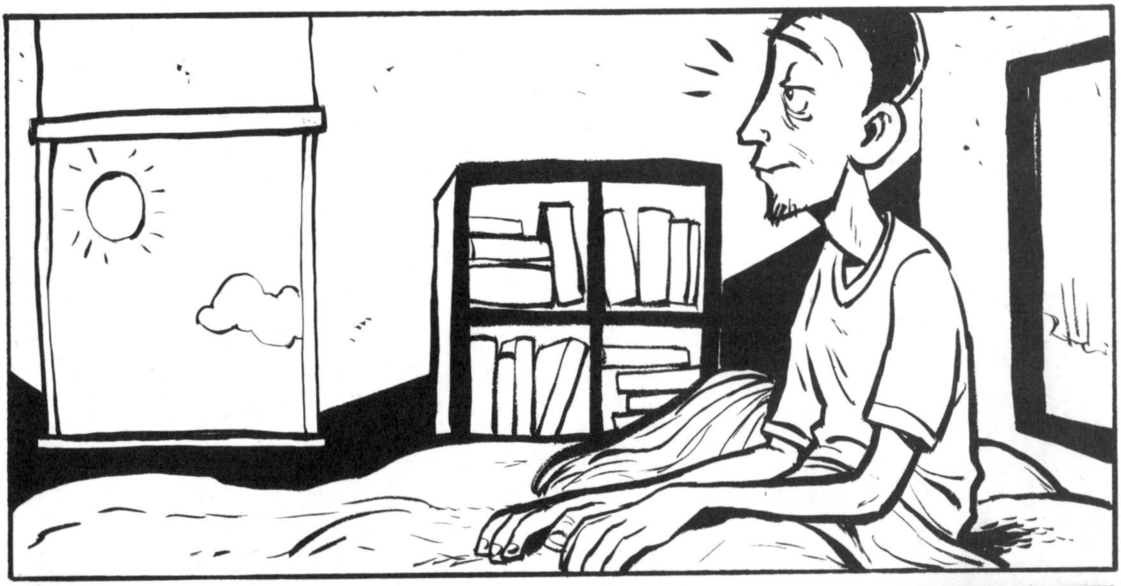

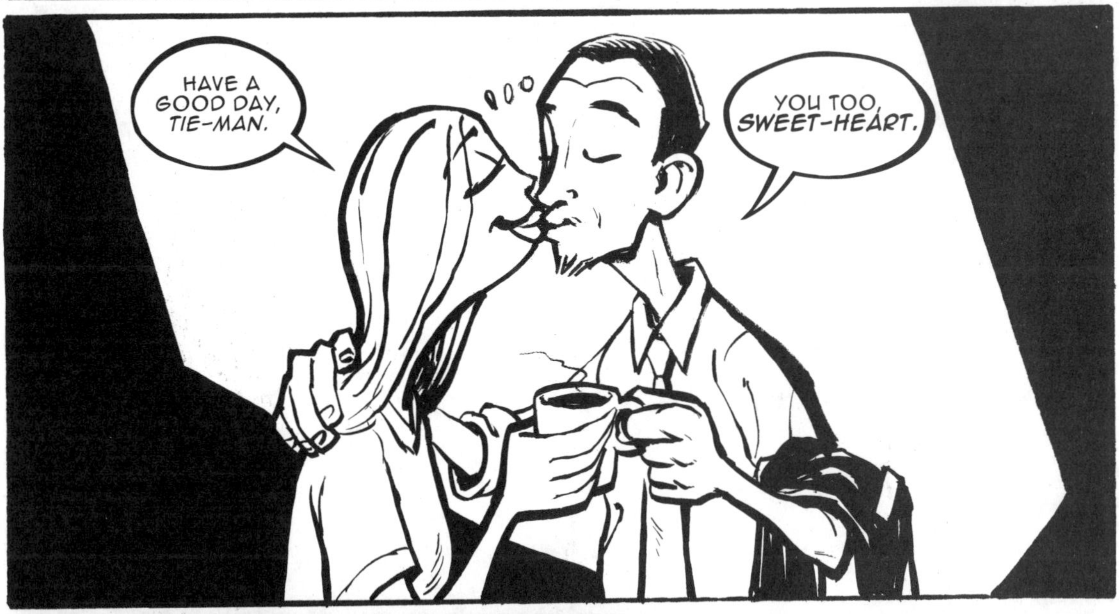
HAVE A GOOD DAY, TIE-MAN.
YOU TOO, SWEET-HEART.

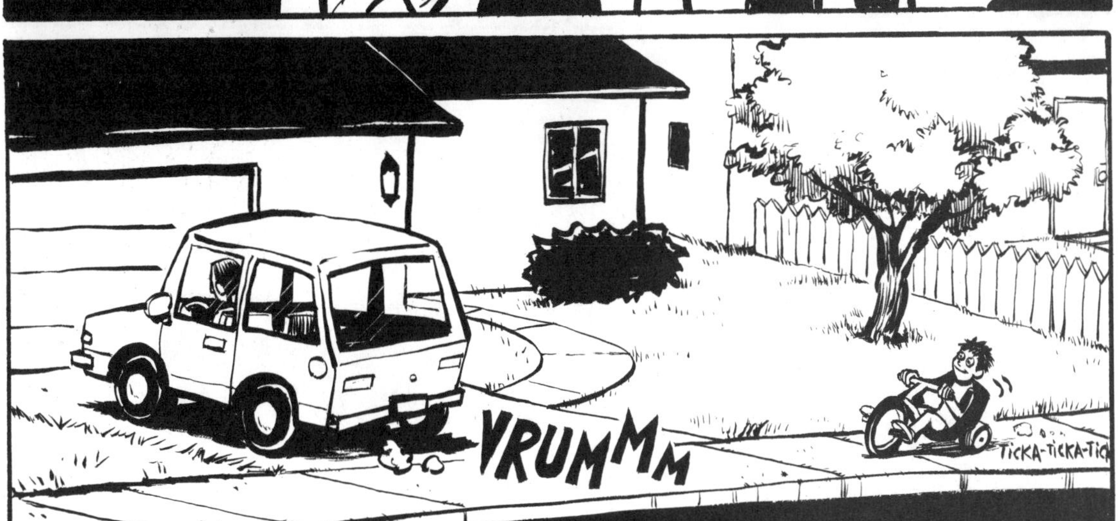
VRUMMM
TICKA-TICKA-TICK

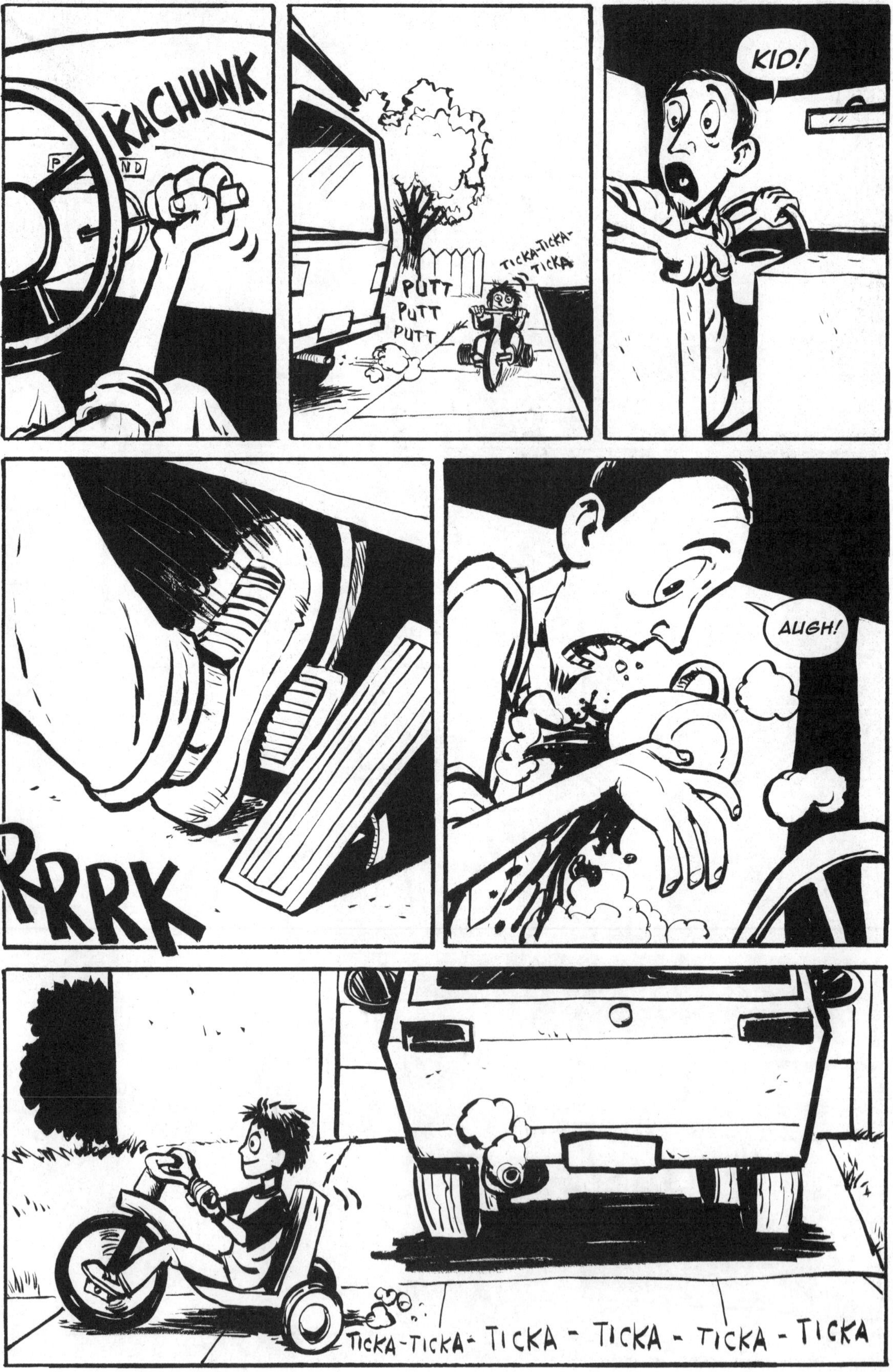
KACHUNK
P
ND
PUTT
PUTT
PUTT
TICKA-TICKA-
TICKA
KID!
RRRK
AUGH!
TICKA-TICKA- TICKA - TICKA - TICKA - TICKA

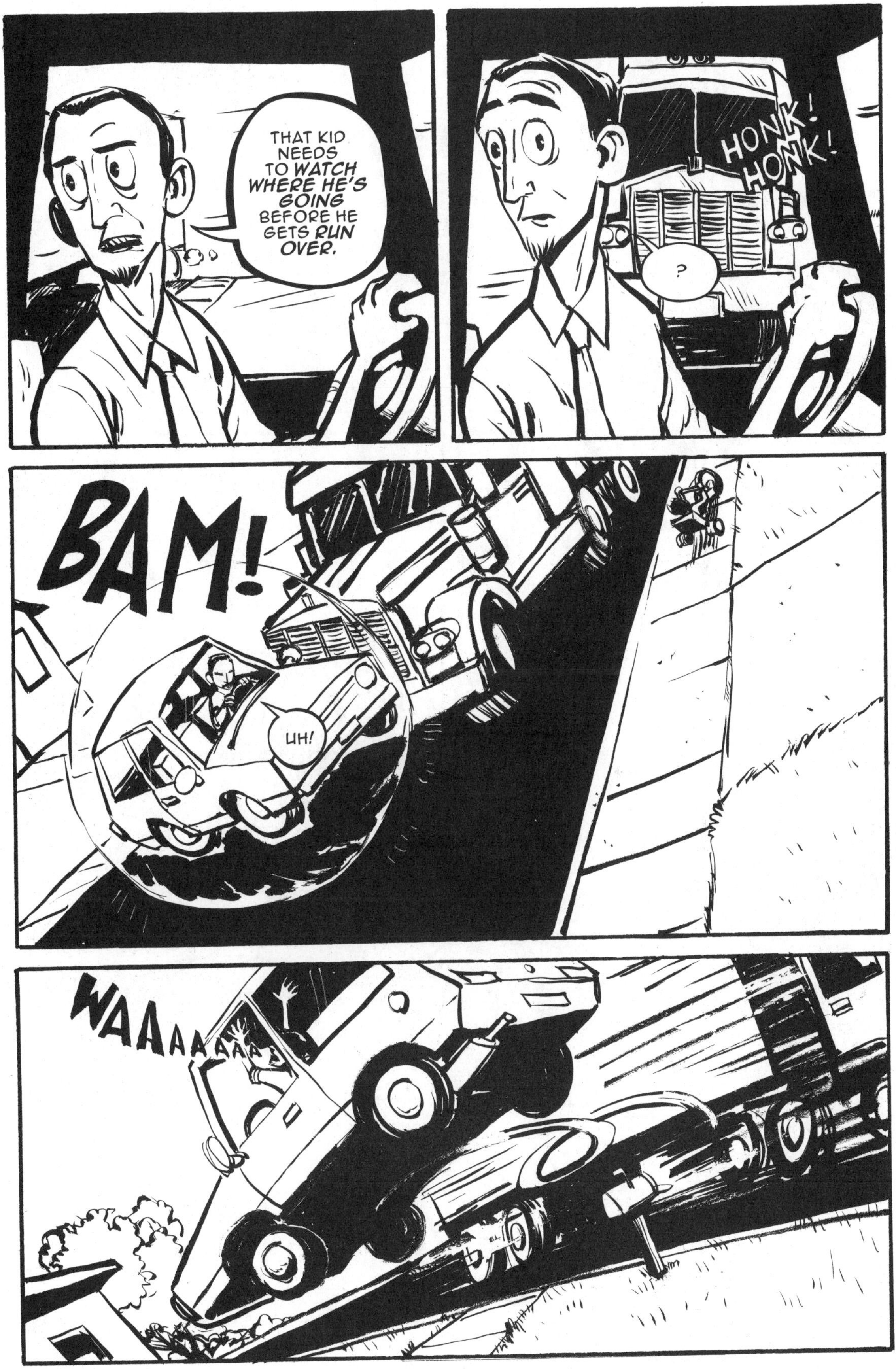
THAT KID NEEDS TO WATCH WHERE HE'S GOING BEFORE HE GETS RUN OVER.
HONK! HONK!
?
BAM!
UH!
WAAAAAAA

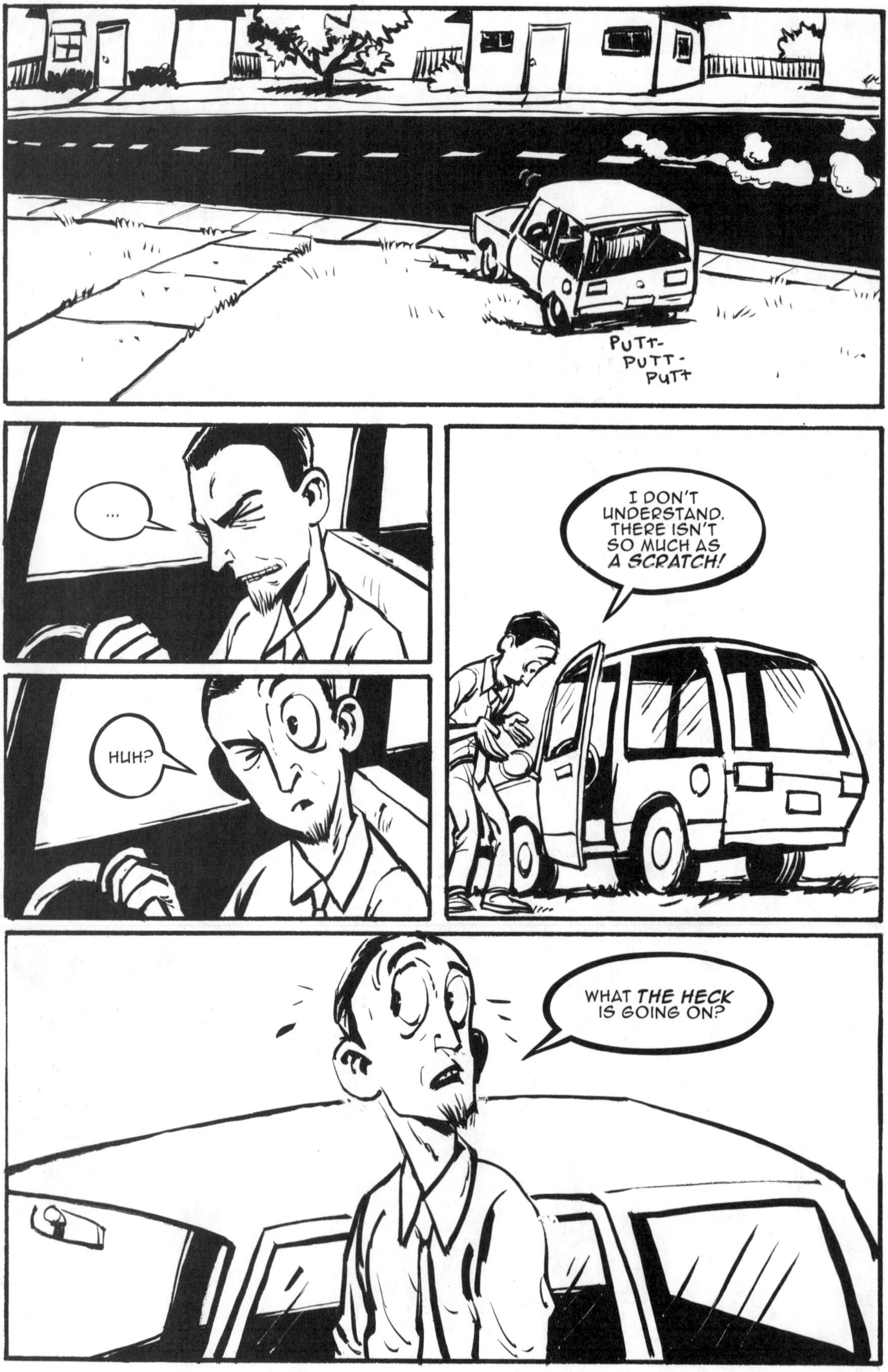
PUTT-
PUTT-
PUTT
...
HUH?
I DON'T UNDERSTAND. THERE ISN'T SO MUCH AS A *SCRATCH!*
WHAT *THE HECK* IS GOING ON?

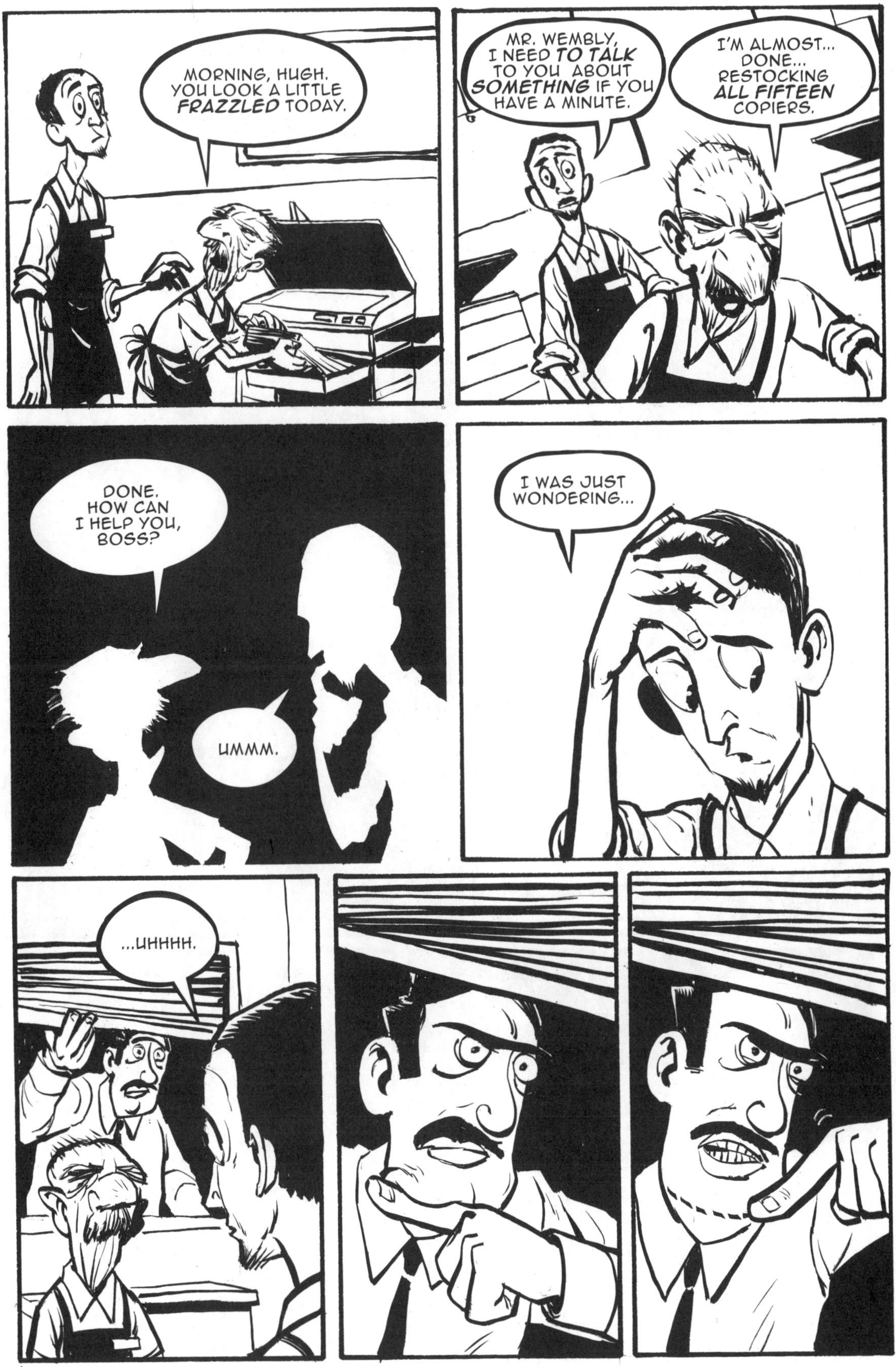
MORNING, HUGH. YOU LOOK A LITTLE FRAZZLED TODAY.
MR. WEMBLY, I NEED TO TALK TO YOU ABOUT SOMETHING IF YOU HAVE A MINUTE.
I'M ALMOST... DONE... RESTOCKING ALL FIFTEEN COPIERS.
DONE. HOW CAN I HELP YOU, BOSS?
UMMM.
I WAS JUST WONDERING...
...UHHHH.

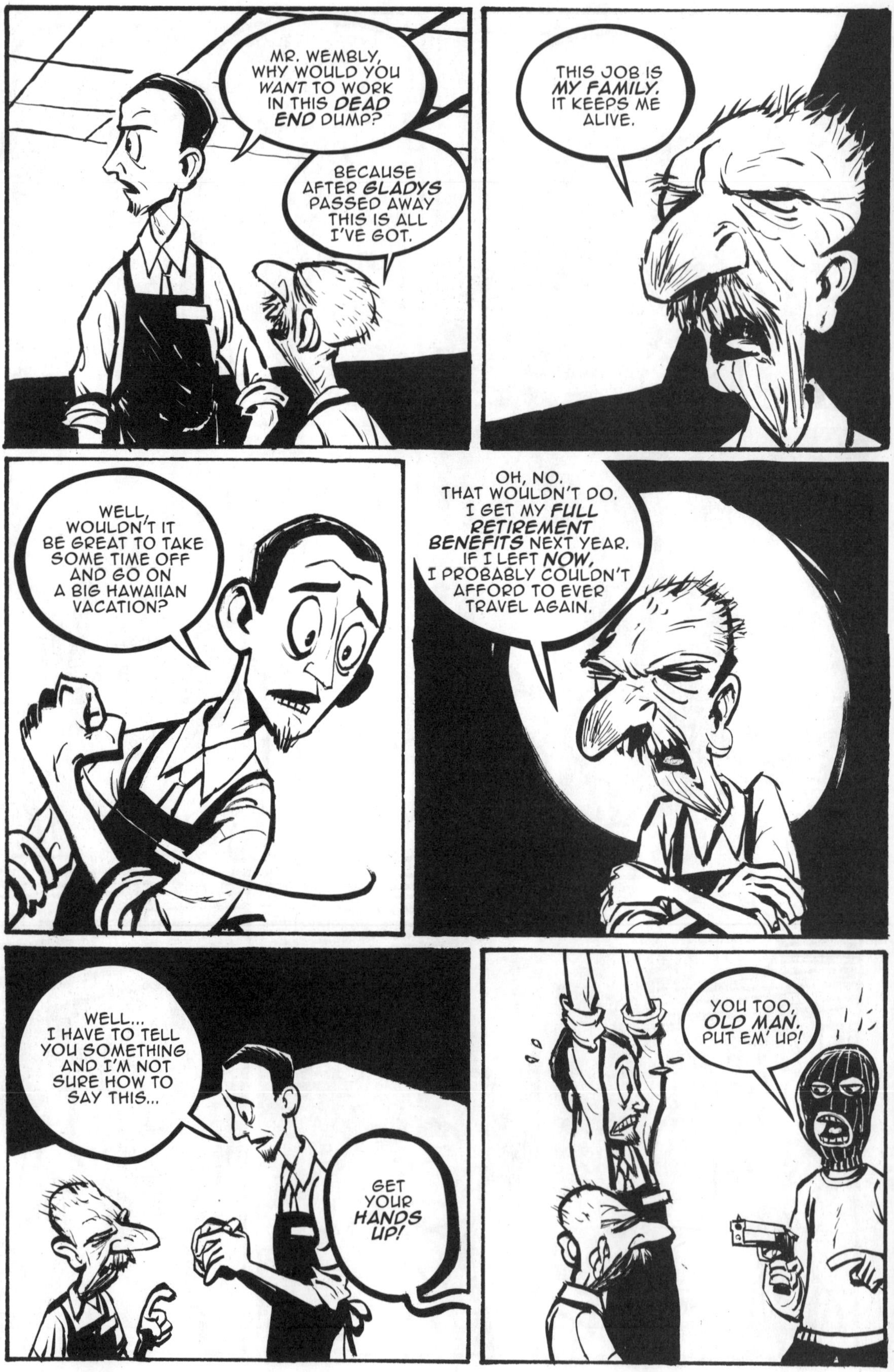
MR. WEMBLY, WHY WOULD YOU *WANT* TO WORK IN THIS ***DEAD END*** DUMP?
BECAUSE AFTER ***GLADYS*** PASSED AWAY THIS IS ALL I'VE GOT.
THIS JOB IS ***MY FAMILY.*** IT KEEPS ME ALIVE.
WELL, WOULDN'T IT BE GREAT TO TAKE SOME TIME OFF AND GO ON A BIG HAWAIIAN VACATION?
OH, NO. THAT WOULDN'T DO. I GET MY ***FULL RETIREMENT BENEFITS*** NEXT YEAR. IF I LEFT ***NOW,*** I PROBABLY COULDN'T AFFORD TO EVER TRAVEL AGAIN.
WELL... I HAVE TO TELL YOU SOMETHING AND I'M NOT SURE HOW TO SAY THIS...
GET YOUR ***HANDS UP!***
YOU TOO, ***OLD MAN.*** PUT EM' UP!

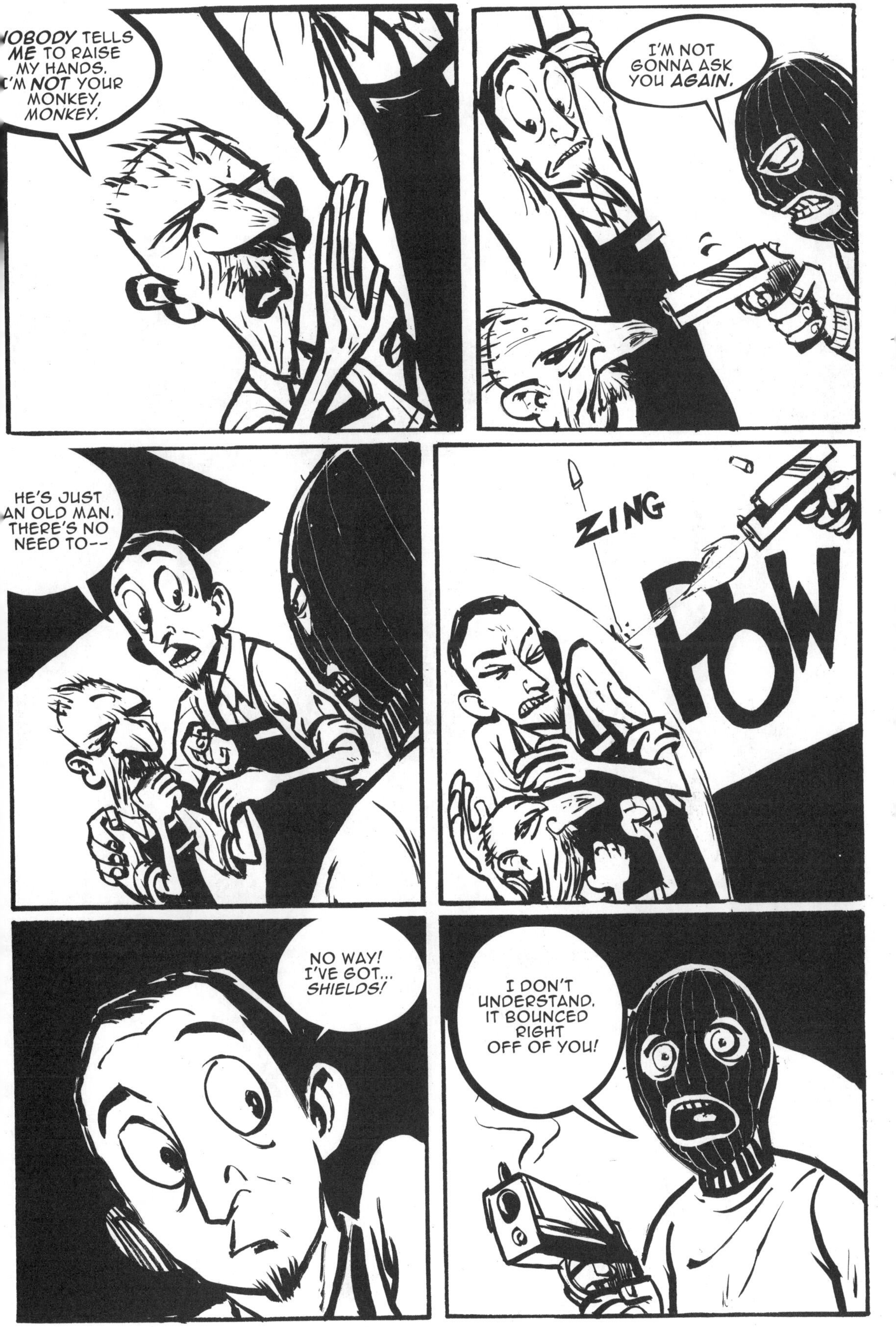
NOBODY TELLS ME TO RAISE MY HANDS. I'M NOT YOUR MONKEY, MONKEY.
I'M NOT GONNA ASK YOU AGAIN.
HE'S JUST AN OLD MAN. THERE'S NO NEED TO--
ZING
POW
NO WAY! I'VE GOT... SHIELDS!
I DON'T UNDERSTAND. IT BOUNCED RIGHT OFF OF YOU!

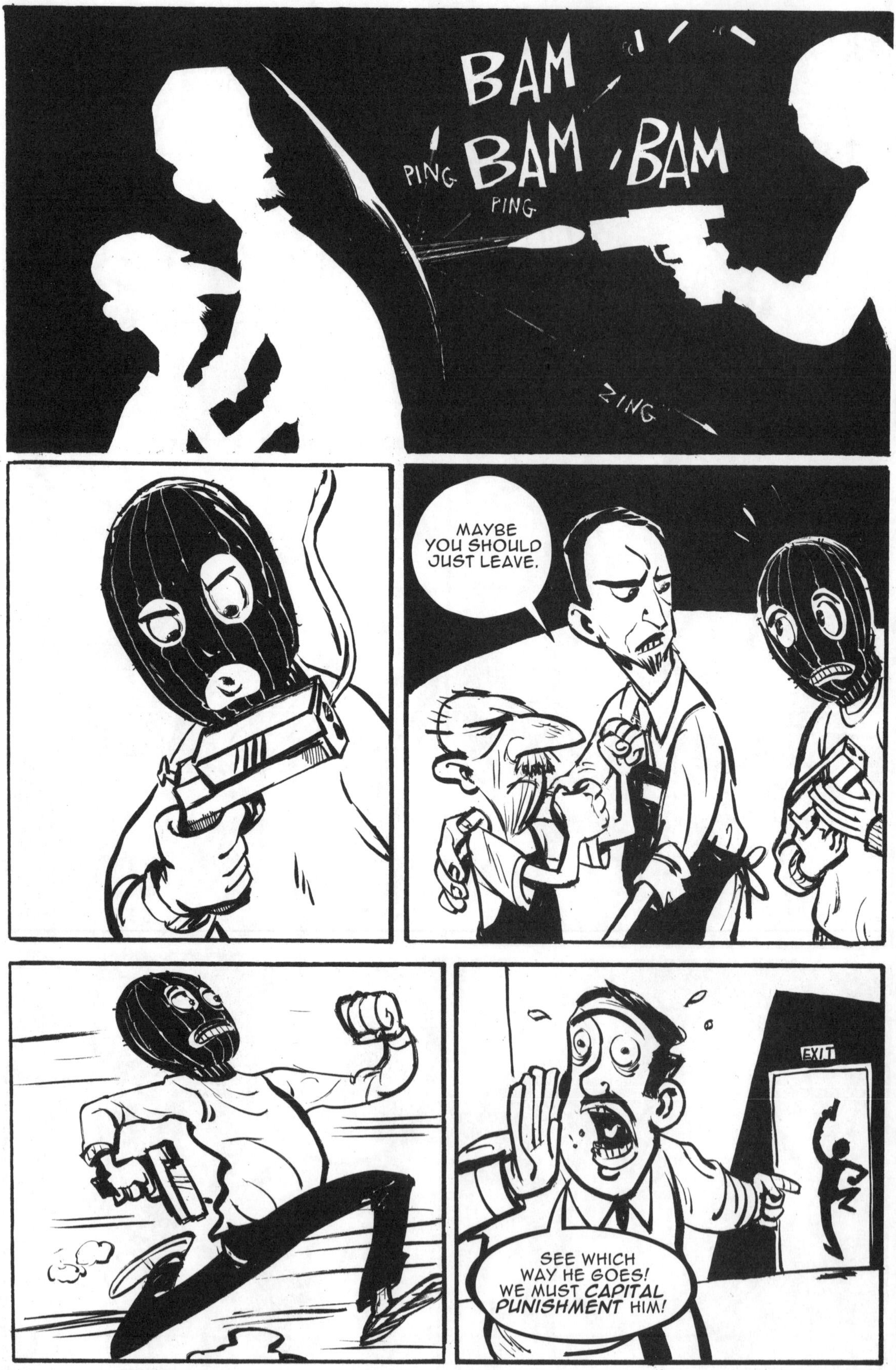
BAM
PING
BAM
BAM
PING
ZING
MAYBE YOU SHOULD JUST LEAVE.
EXIT
SEE WHICH WAY HE GOES! WE MUST *CAPITAL PUNISHMENT* HIM!

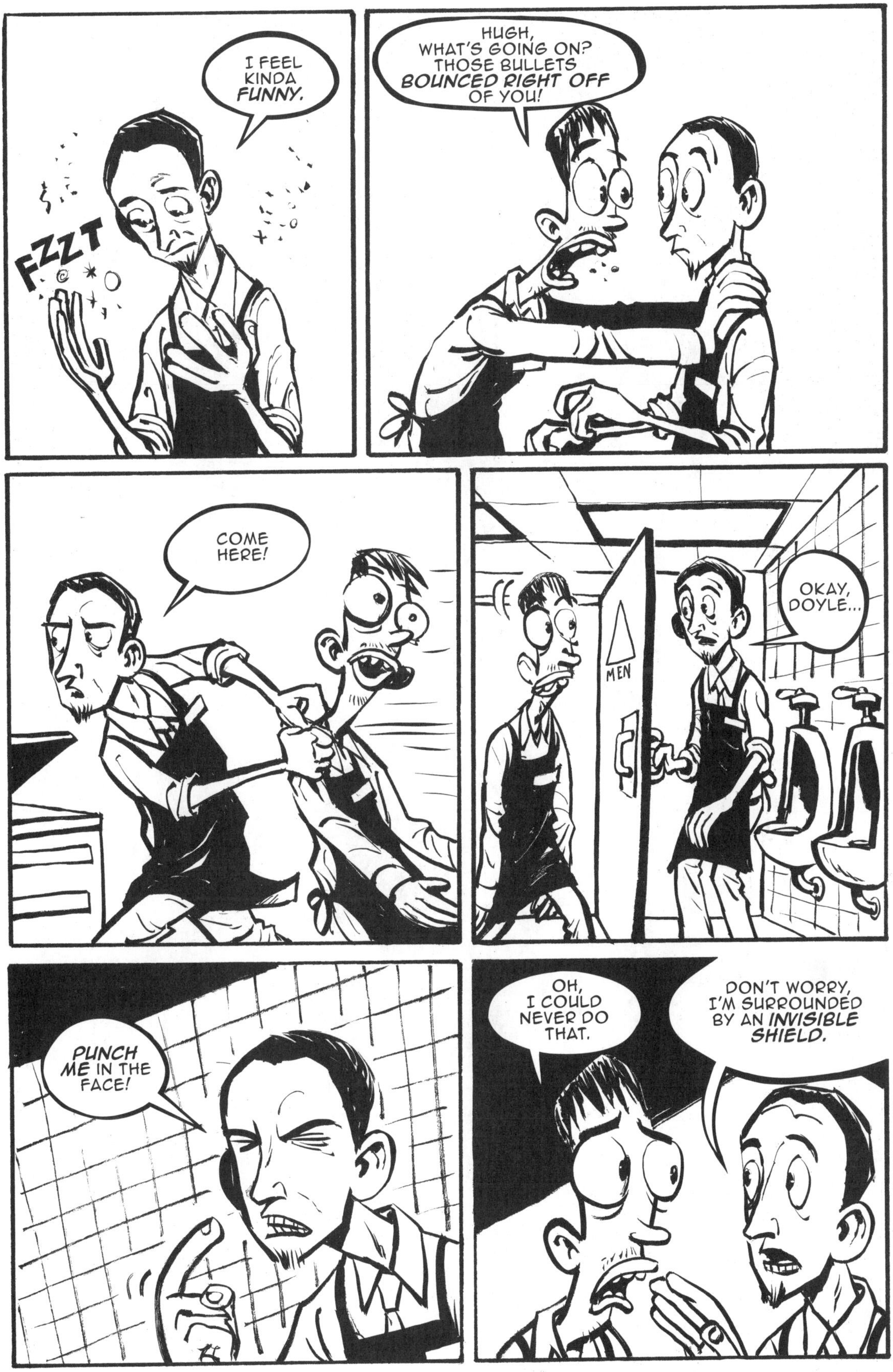
I FEEL KINDA FUNNY.
FZZT
HUGH, WHAT'S GOING ON? THOSE BULLETS BOUNCED RIGHT OFF OF YOU!
COME HERE!
MEN
OKAY, DOYLE...
PUNCH ME IN THE FACE!
OH, I COULD NEVER DO THAT.
DON'T WORRY, I'M SURROUNDED BY AN INVISIBLE SHIELD.

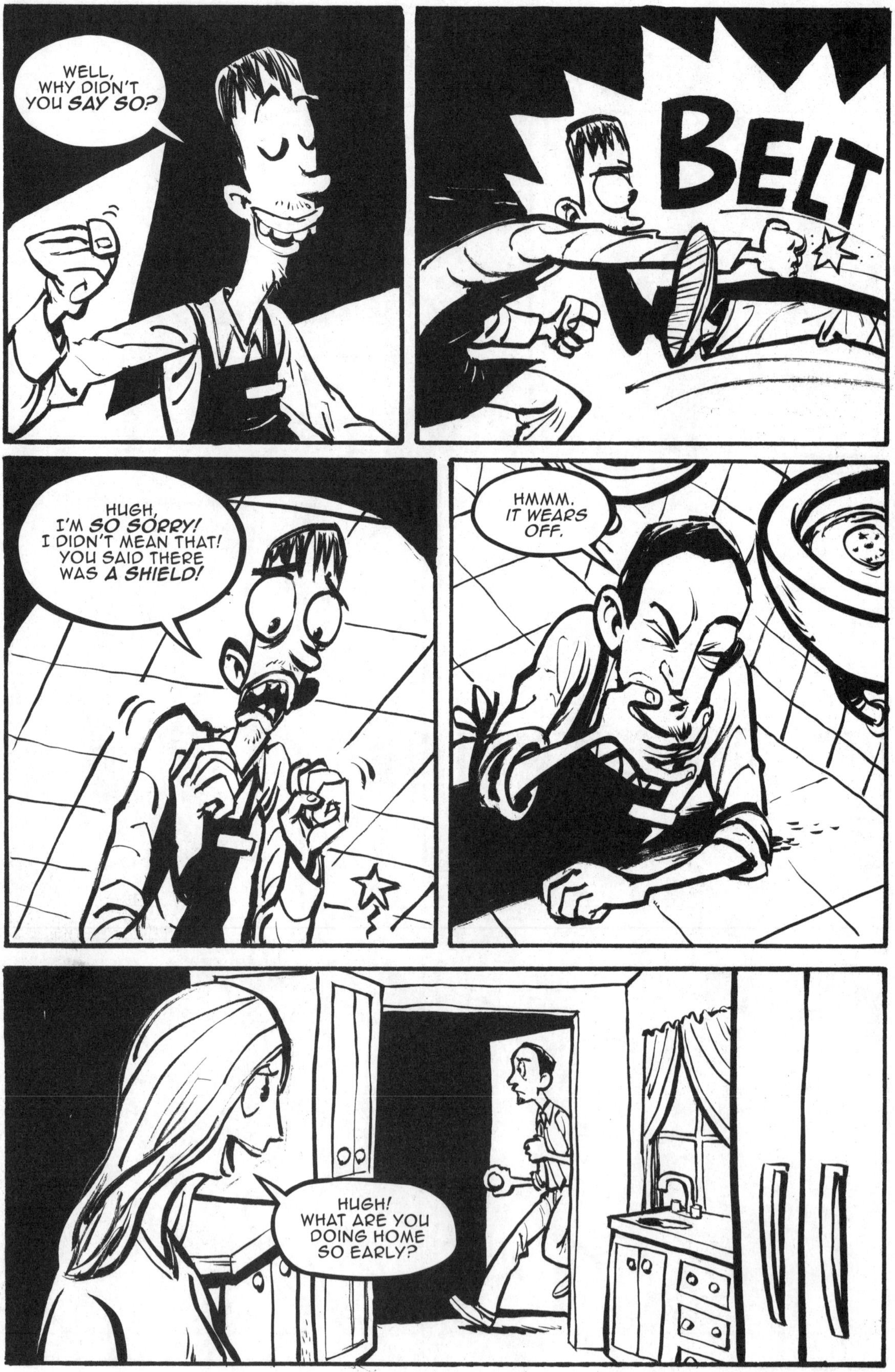
WELL, WHY DIDN'T YOU SAY SO?
BELT
HUGH, I'M SO SORRY! I DIDN'T MEAN THAT! YOU SAID THERE WAS A SHIELD!
HMMM. IT WEARS OFF.
HUGH! WHAT ARE YOU DOING HOME SO EARLY?

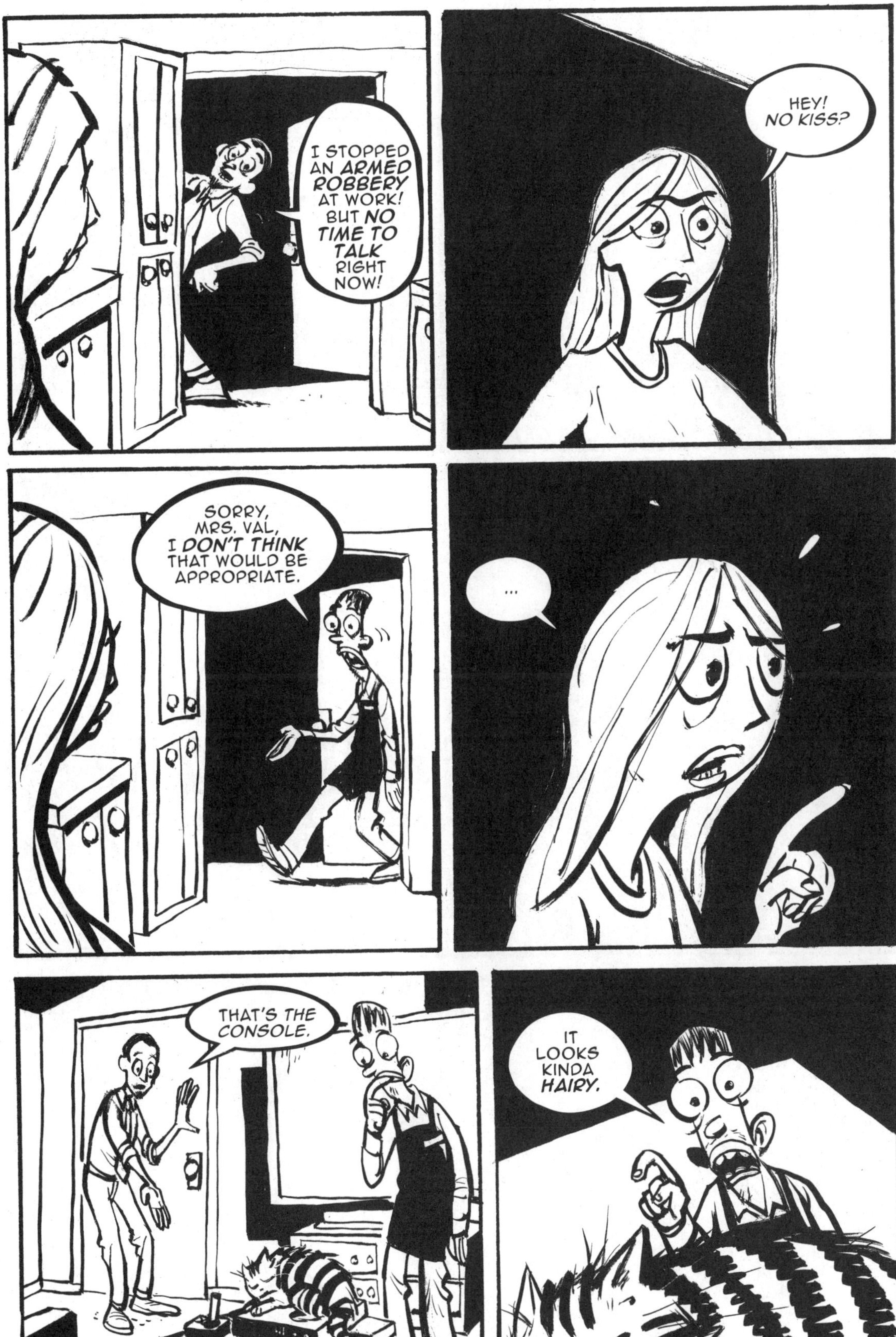
I STOPPED AN ARMED ROBBERY AT WORK! BUT NO TIME TO TALK RIGHT NOW!
HEY! NO KISS?
SORRY, MRS. VAL, I DON'T THINK THAT WOULD BE APPROPRIATE.
...
THAT'S THE CONSOLE.
IT LOOKS KINDA HAIRY.

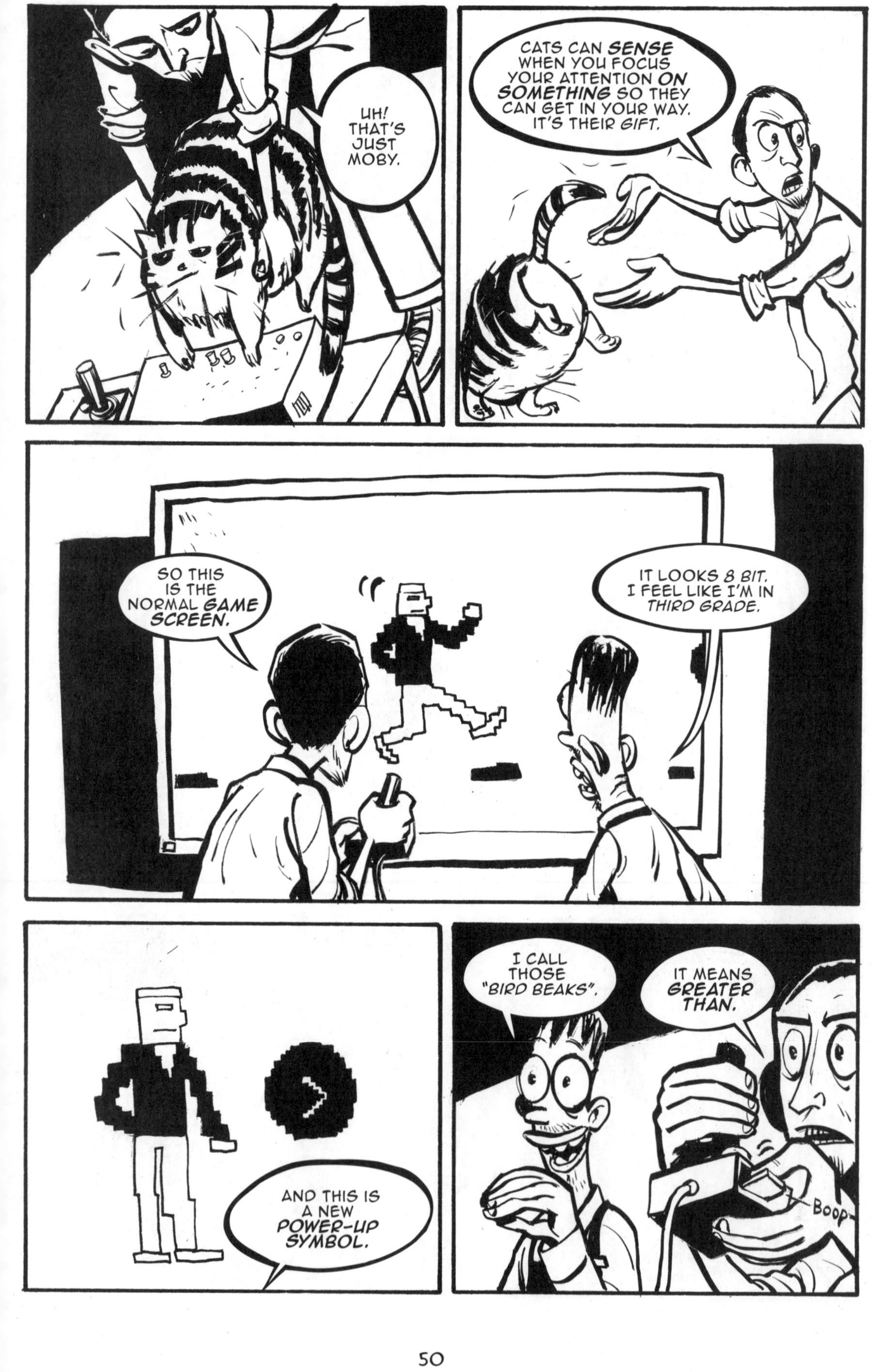
UH! THAT'S JUST MOBY.
CATS CAN SENSE WHEN YOU FOCUS YOUR ATTENTION ON SOMETHING SO THEY CAN GET IN YOUR WAY. IT'S THEIR GIFT.
SO THIS IS THE NORMAL GAME SCREEN.
IT LOOKS 8 BIT. I FEEL LIKE I'M IN THIRD GRADE.
AND THIS IS A NEW POWER-UP SYMBOL.
I CALL THOSE "BIRD BEAKS".
IT MEANS GREATER THAN.
Boop

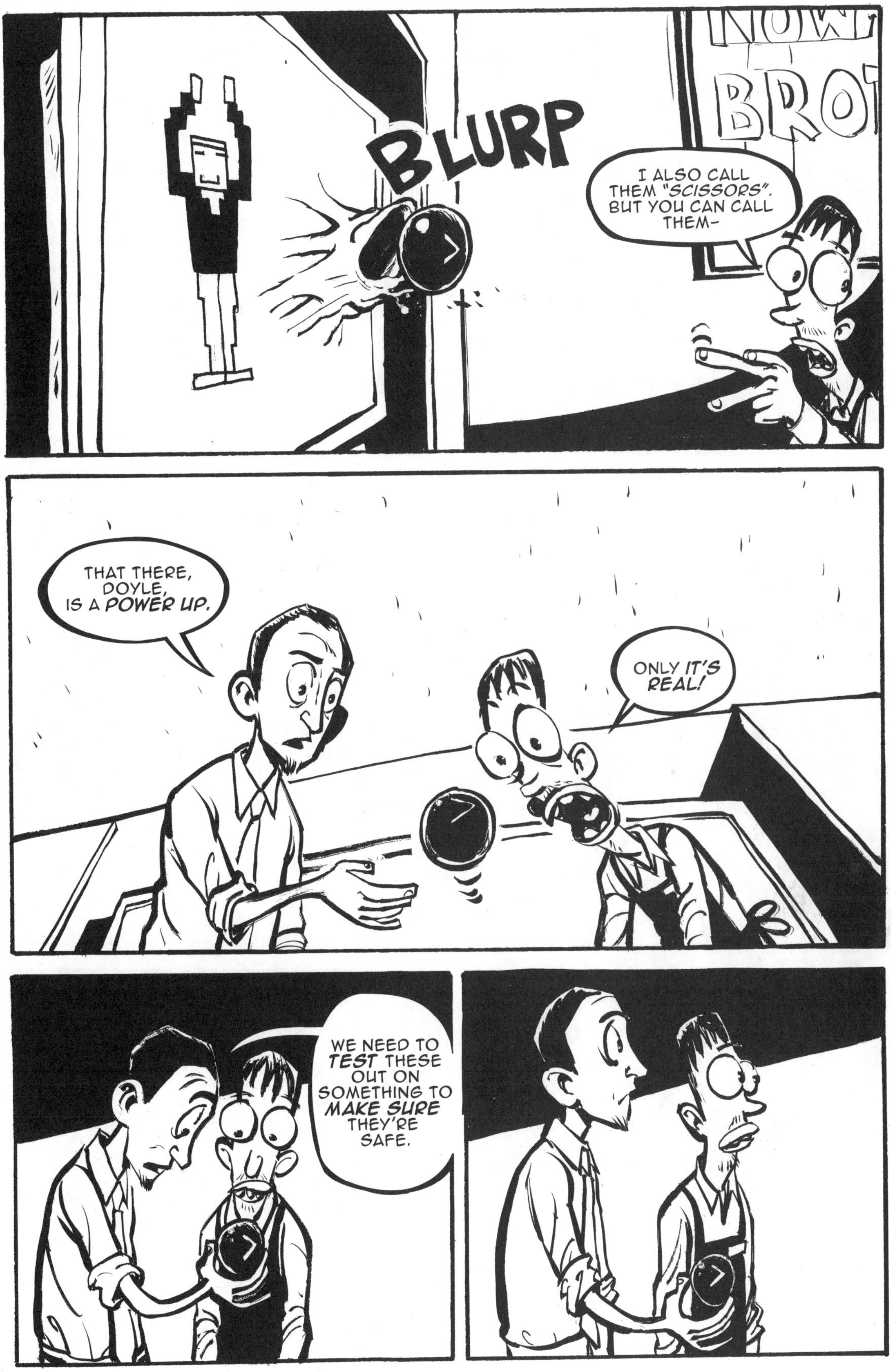
NOW
BRO
BLURP
I ALSO CALL THEM "SCISSORS". BUT YOU CAN CALL THEM-
THAT THERE, DOYLE, IS A POWER UP.
ONLY IT'S REAL!
WE NEED TO TEST THESE OUT ON SOMETHING TO MAKE SURE THEY'RE SAFE.

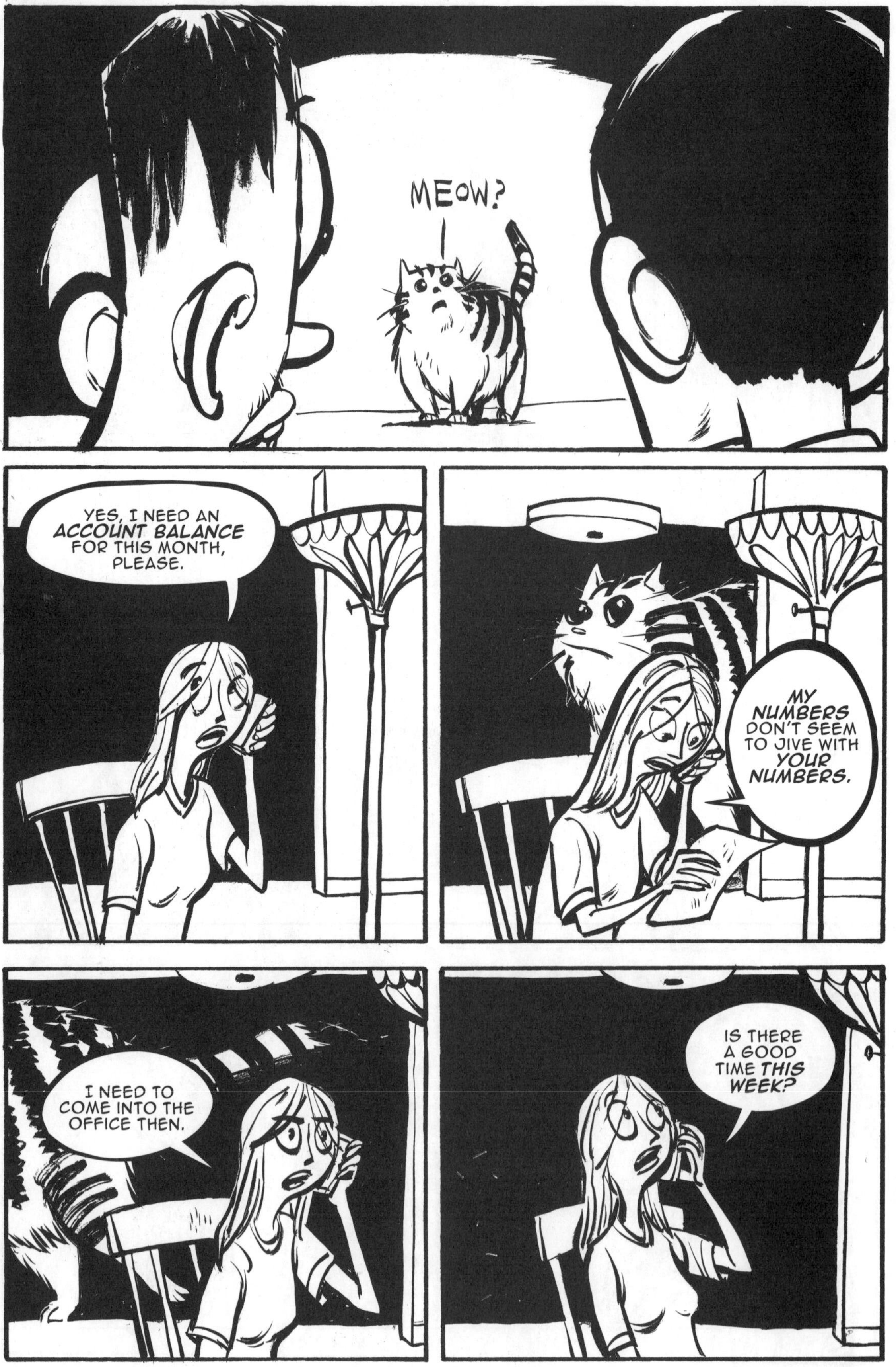
MEOW?
YES, I NEED AN ACCOUNT BALANCE FOR THIS MONTH, PLEASE.
MY NUMBERS DON'T SEEM TO JIVE WITH YOUR NUMBERS.
I NEED TO COME INTO THE OFFICE THEN.
IS THERE A GOOD TIME THIS WEEK?

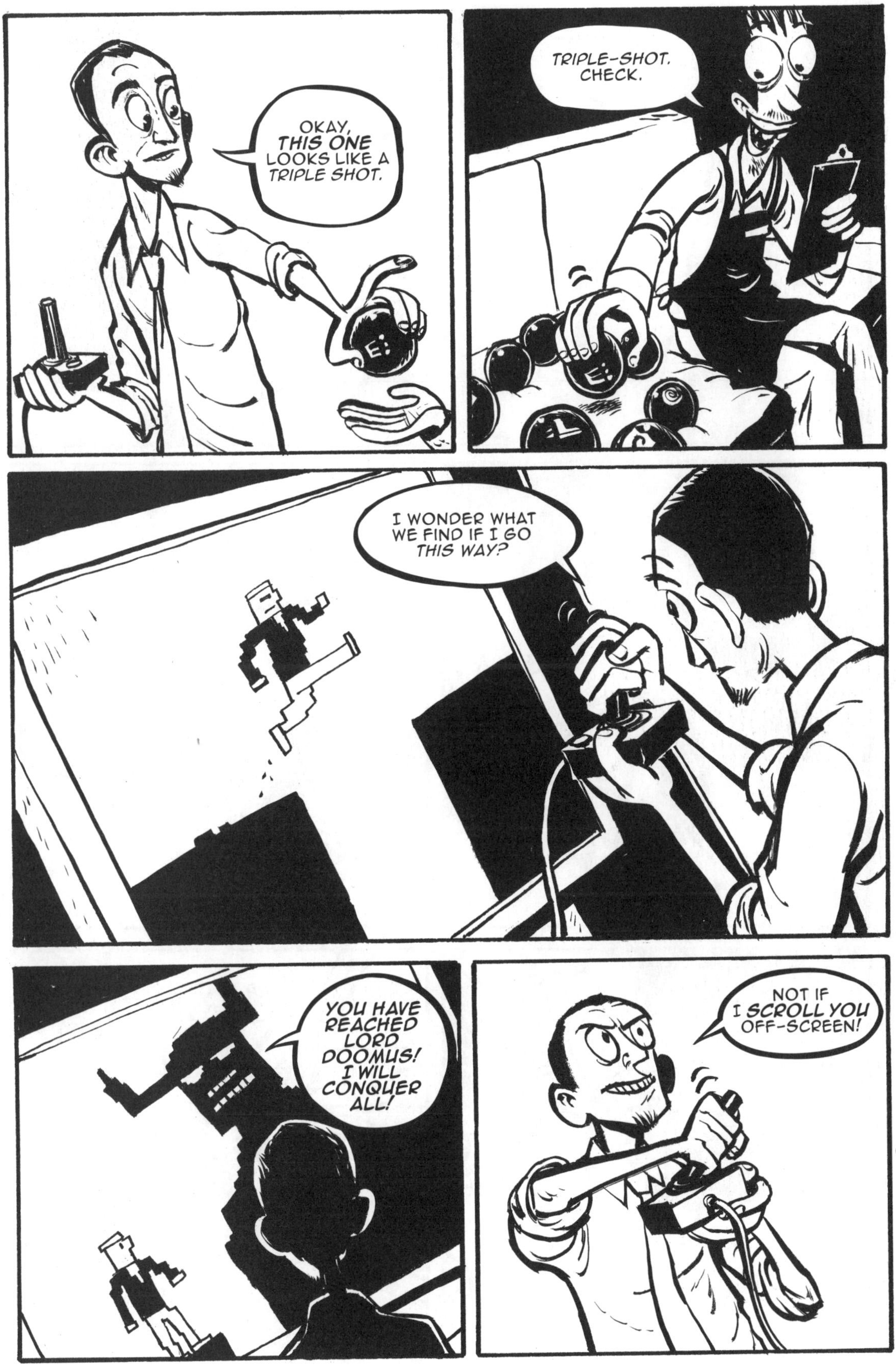
OKAY, THIS ONE LOOKS LIKE A TRIPLE SHOT.
TRIPLE-SHOT. CHECK.
I WONDER WHAT WE FIND IF I GO THIS WAY?
YOU HAVE REACHED LORD DOOMUS! I WILL CONQUER ALL!
NOT IF I SCROLL YOU OFF-SCREEN!

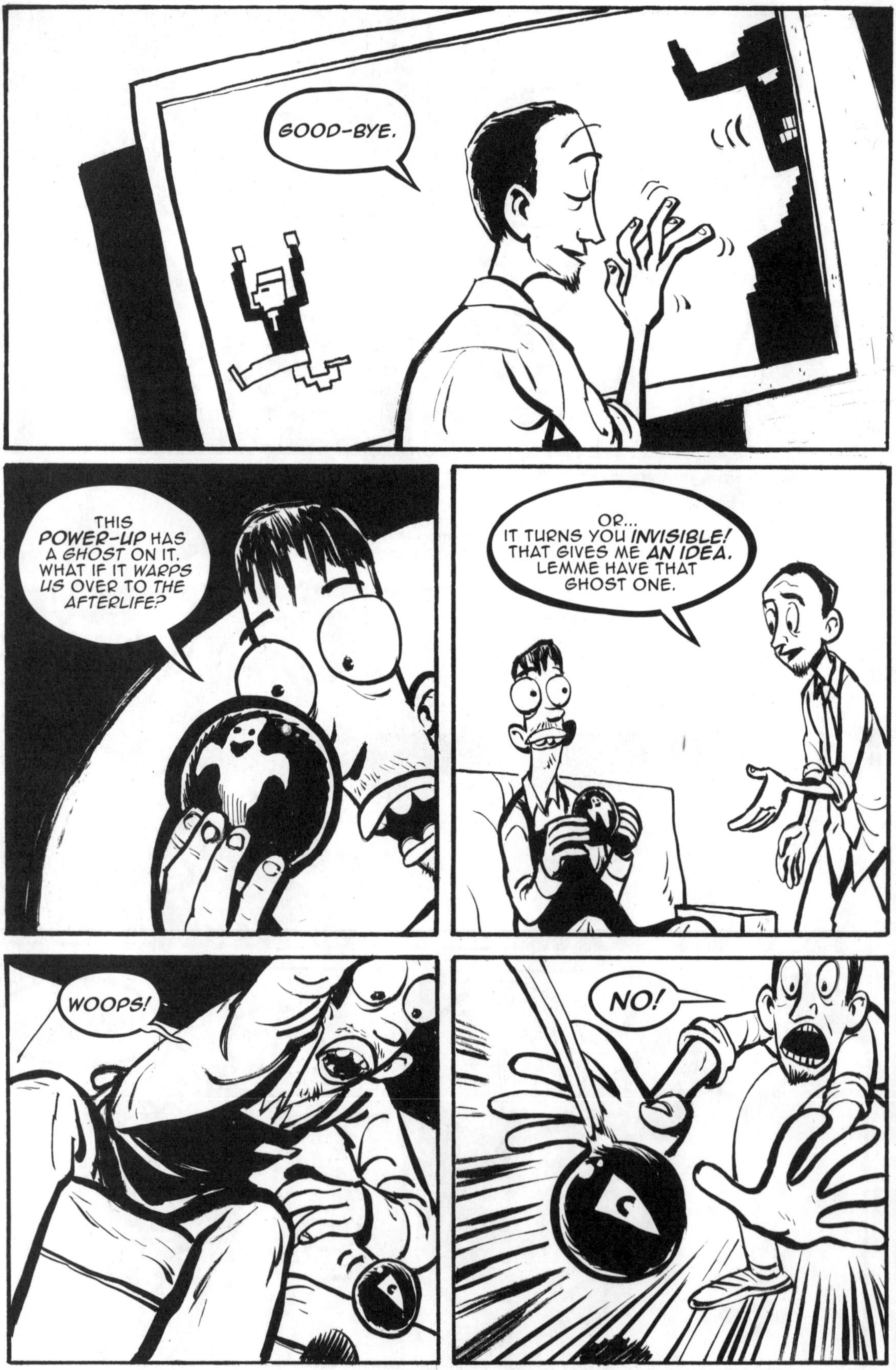
GOOD-BYE.
THIS POWER-UP HAS A GHOST ON IT. WHAT IF IT WARPS US OVER TO THE AFTERLIFE?
OR... IT TURNS YOU INVISIBLE! THAT GIVES ME AN IDEA. LEMME HAVE THAT GHOST ONE.
WOOPS!
NO!

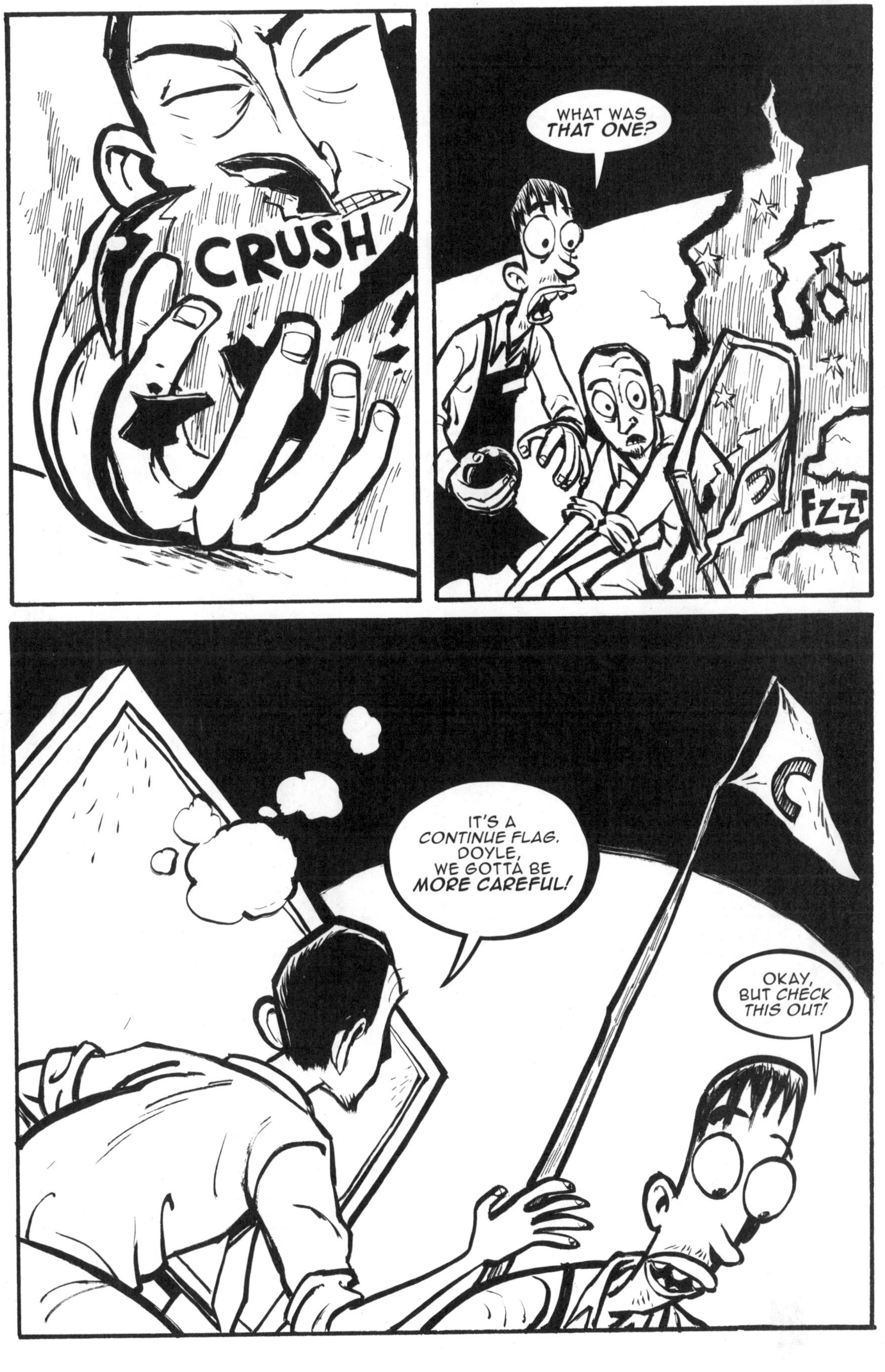
CRUSH
WHAT WAS THAT ONE?
FZZZT
IT'S A CONTINUE FLAG. DOYLE, WE GOTTA BE MORE CAREFUL!
OKAY, BUT CHECK THIS OUT!

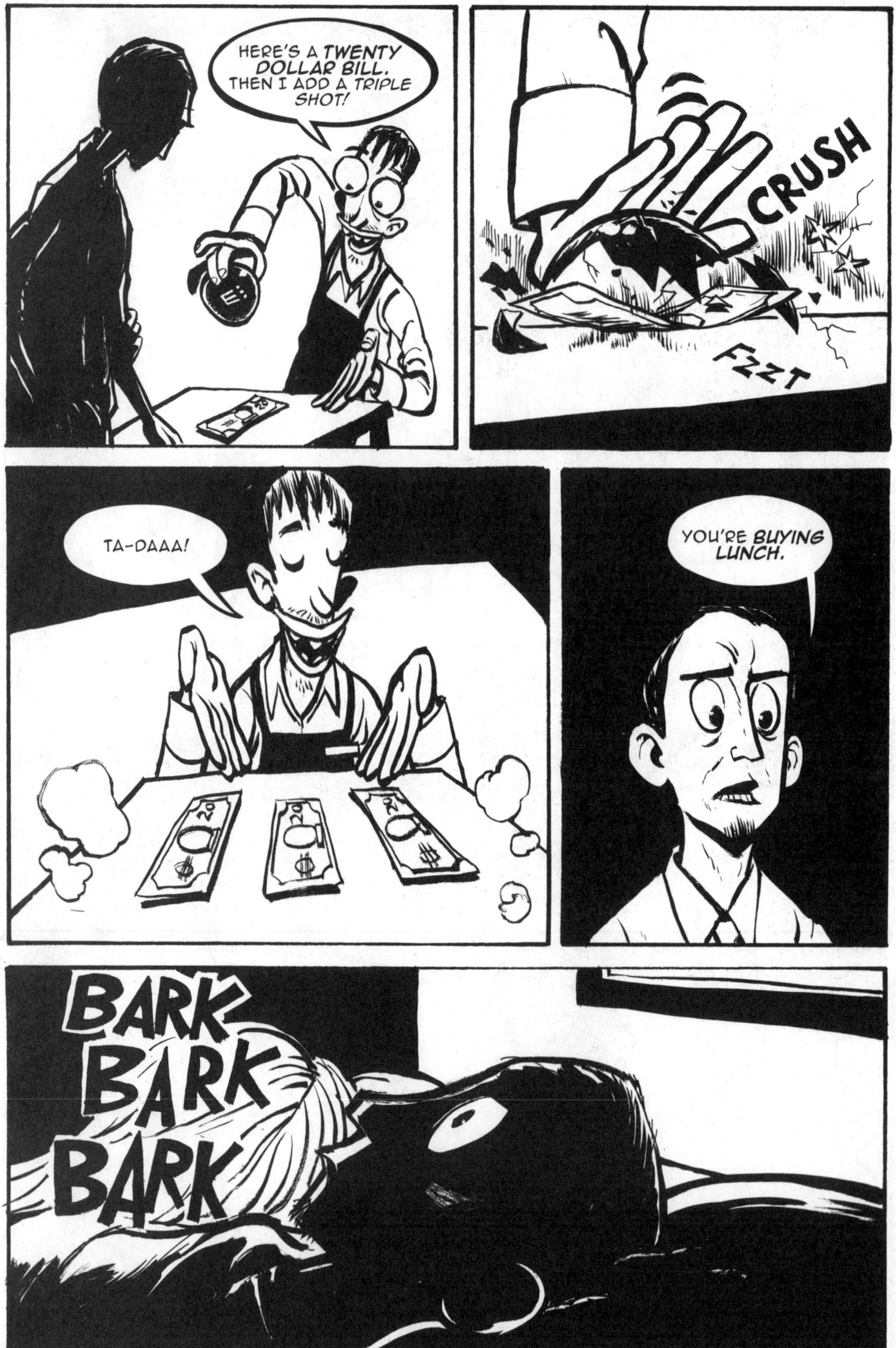
HERE'S A TWENTY DOLLAR BILL. THEN I ADD A TRIPLE SHOT!
CRUSH
FZZT
TA-DAAA!
YOU'RE BUYING LUNCH.
BARK
BARK
BARK

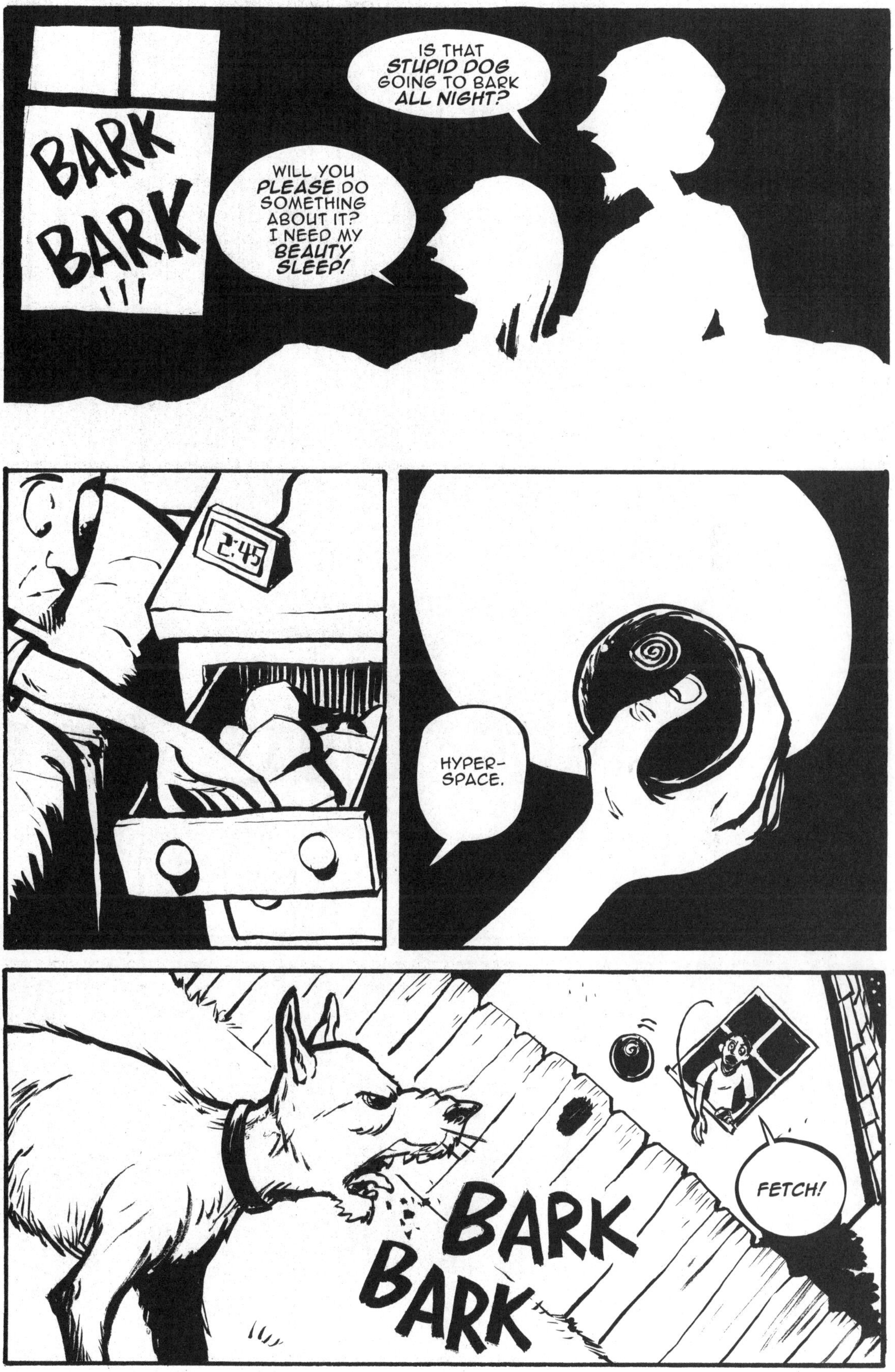
BARK
BARK
IS THAT STUPID DOG GOING TO BARK ALL NIGHT?
WILL YOU PLEASE DO SOMETHING ABOUT IT? I NEED MY BEAUTY SLEEP!
2:45
HYPER-SPACE.
FETCH!
BARK
BARK

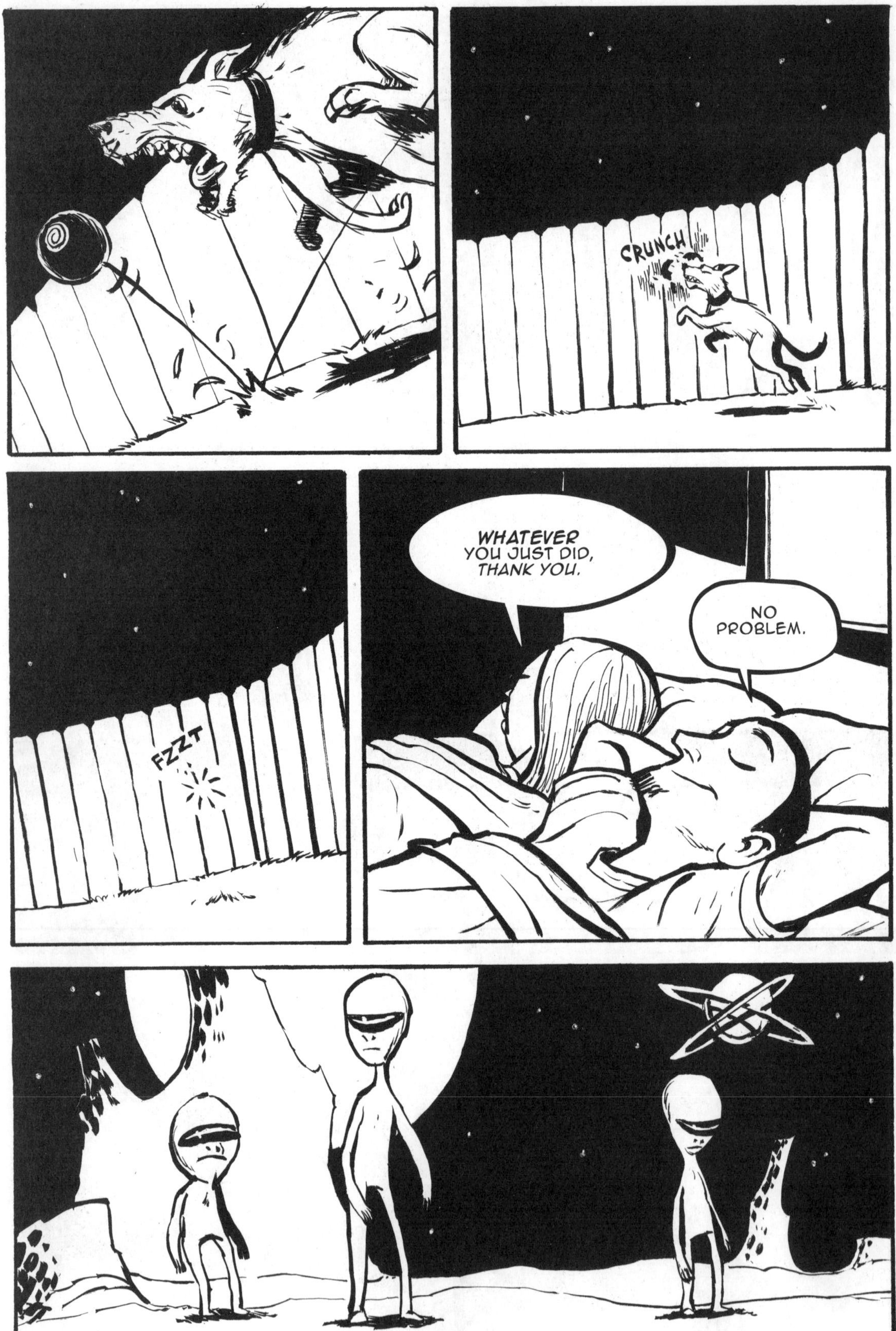
CRUNCH
FZZT
WHATEVER YOU JUST DID, THANK YOU.
NO PROBLEM.

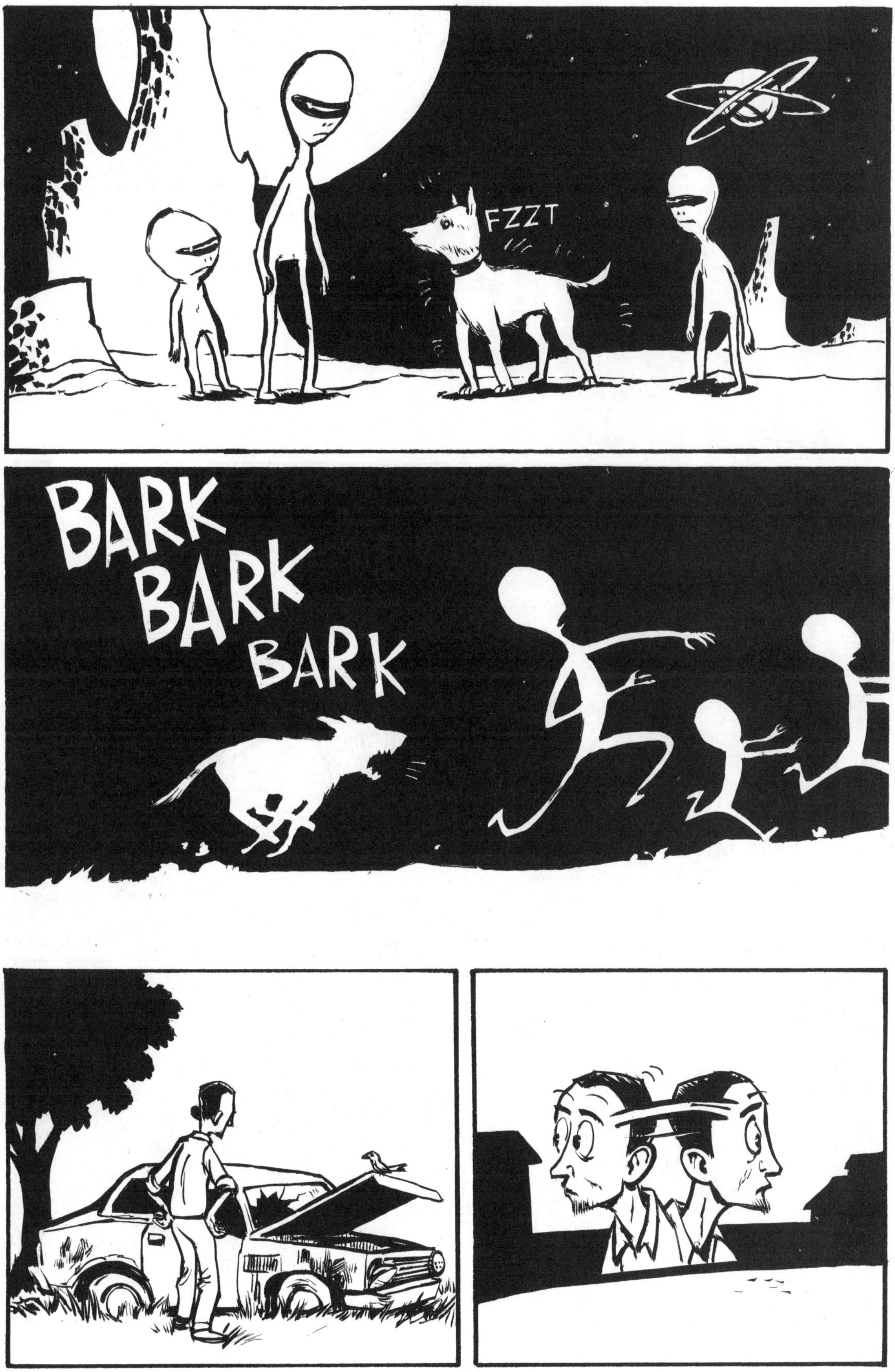
FZZT
BARK
BARK
BARK

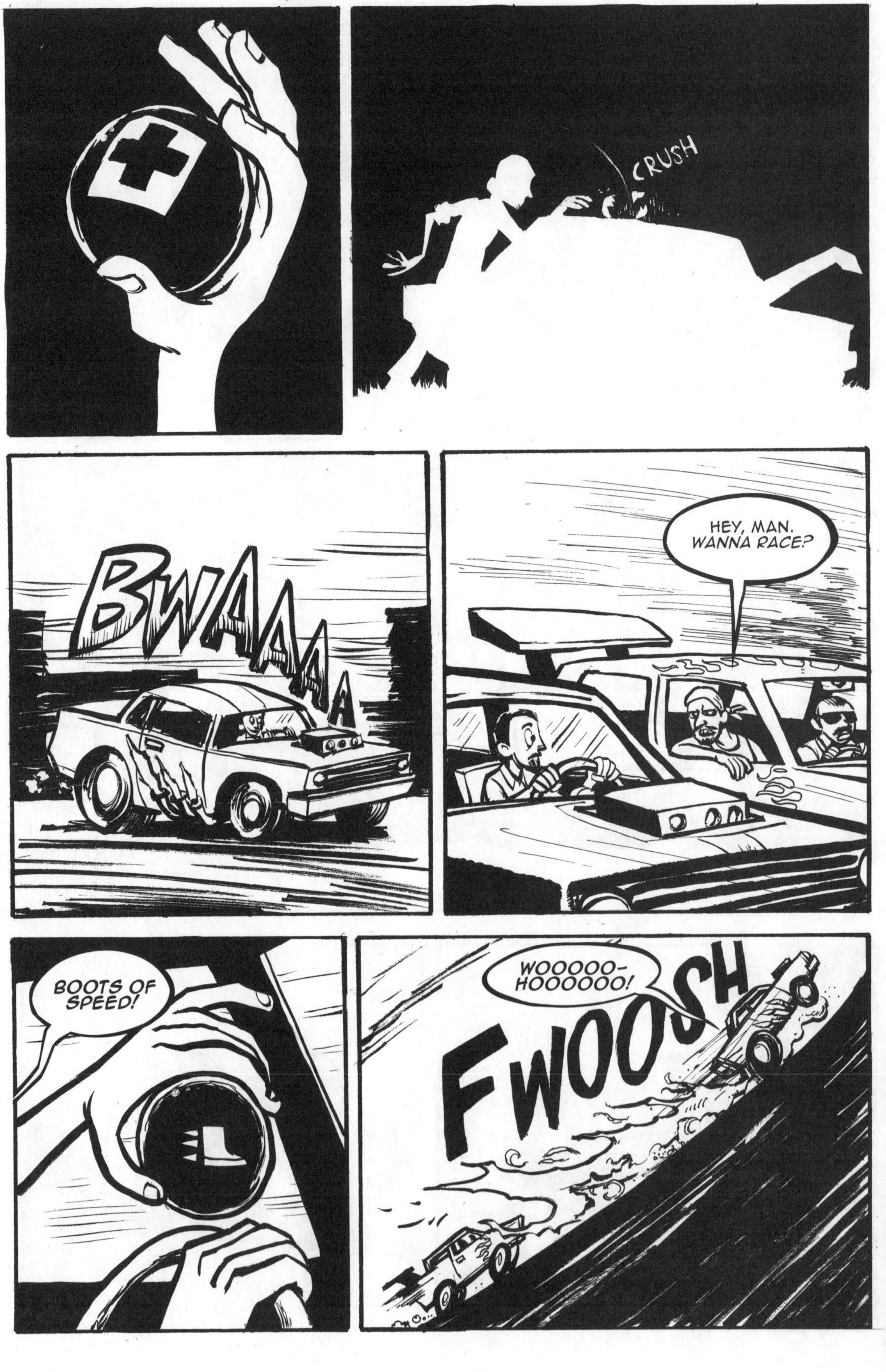
CRUSH
BWAAAAA
HEY, MAN. WANNA RACE?
BOOTS OF SPEED!
WOOOOO-HOOOOOO!
FWOOSH

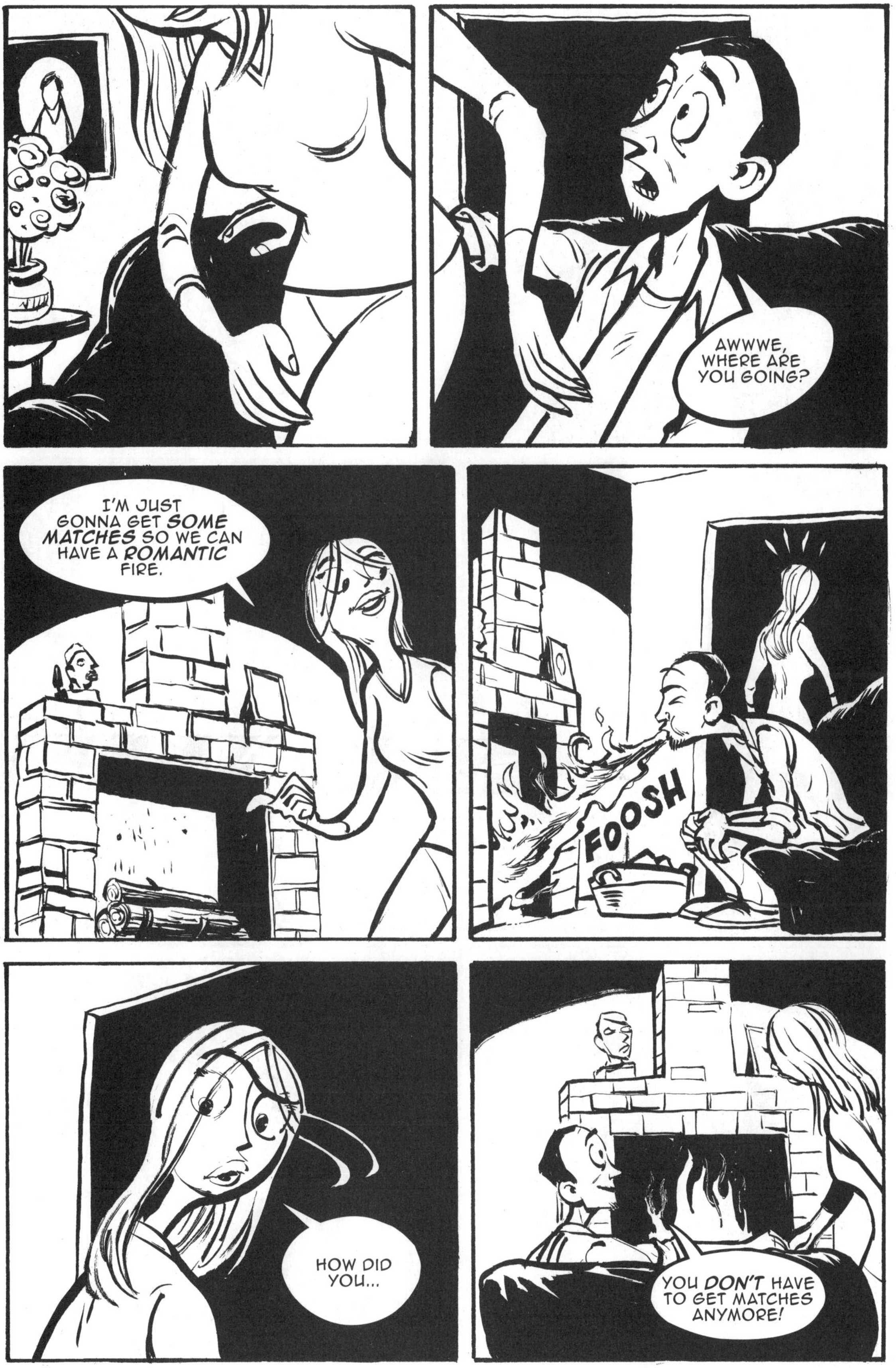
AWWWE, WHERE ARE YOU GOING?
I'M JUST GONNA GET SOME MATCHES SO WE CAN HAVE A ROMANTIC FIRE.
FOOSH
HOW DID YOU...
YOU DON'T HAVE TO GET MATCHES ANYMORE!

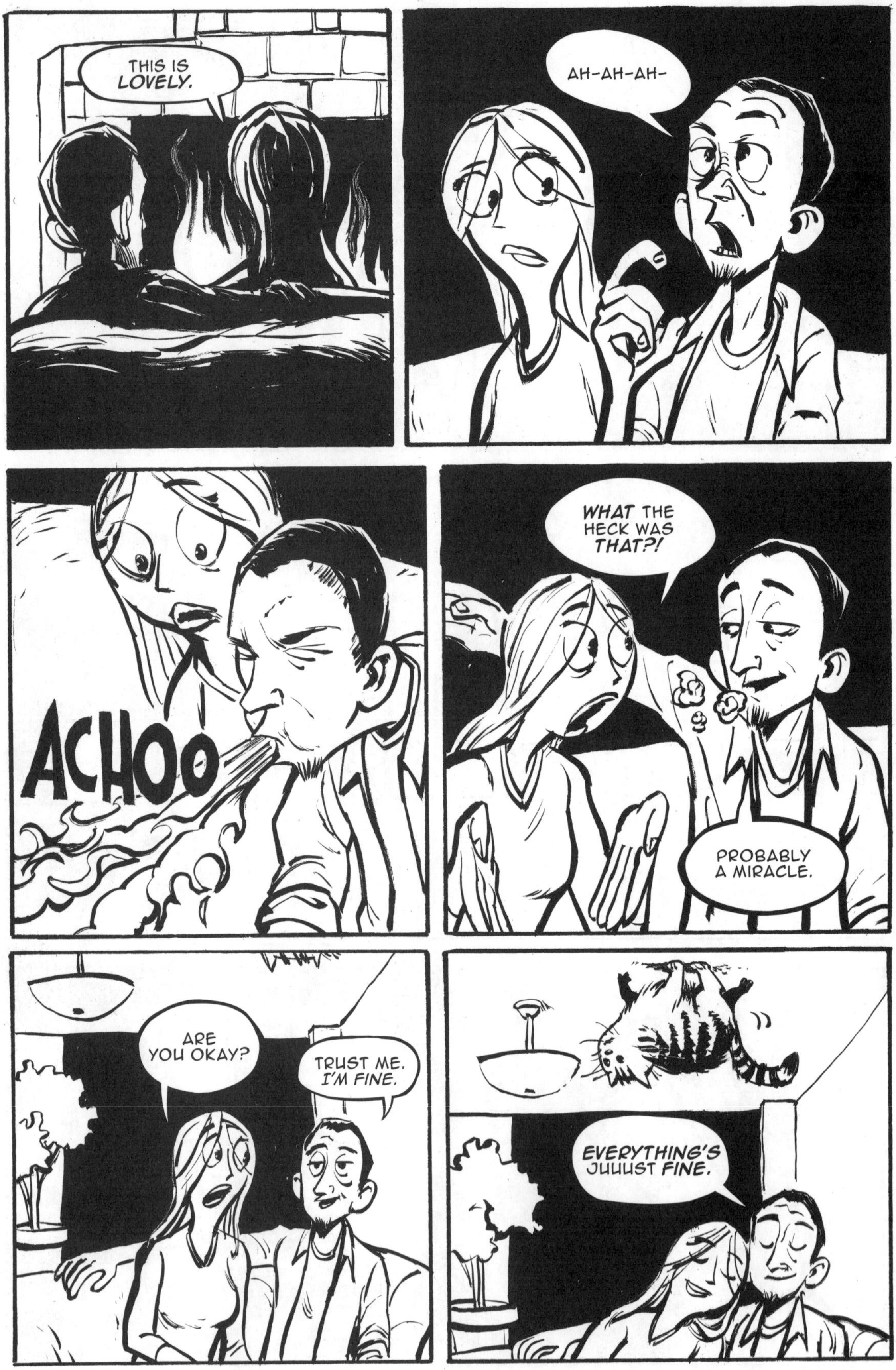
THIS IS LOVELY.
AH-AH-AH-
ACHOO
WHAT THE HECK WAS THAT?!
PROBABLY A MIRACLE.
ARE YOU OKAY?
TRUST ME. I'M FINE.
EVERYTHING'S JUUUST FINE.

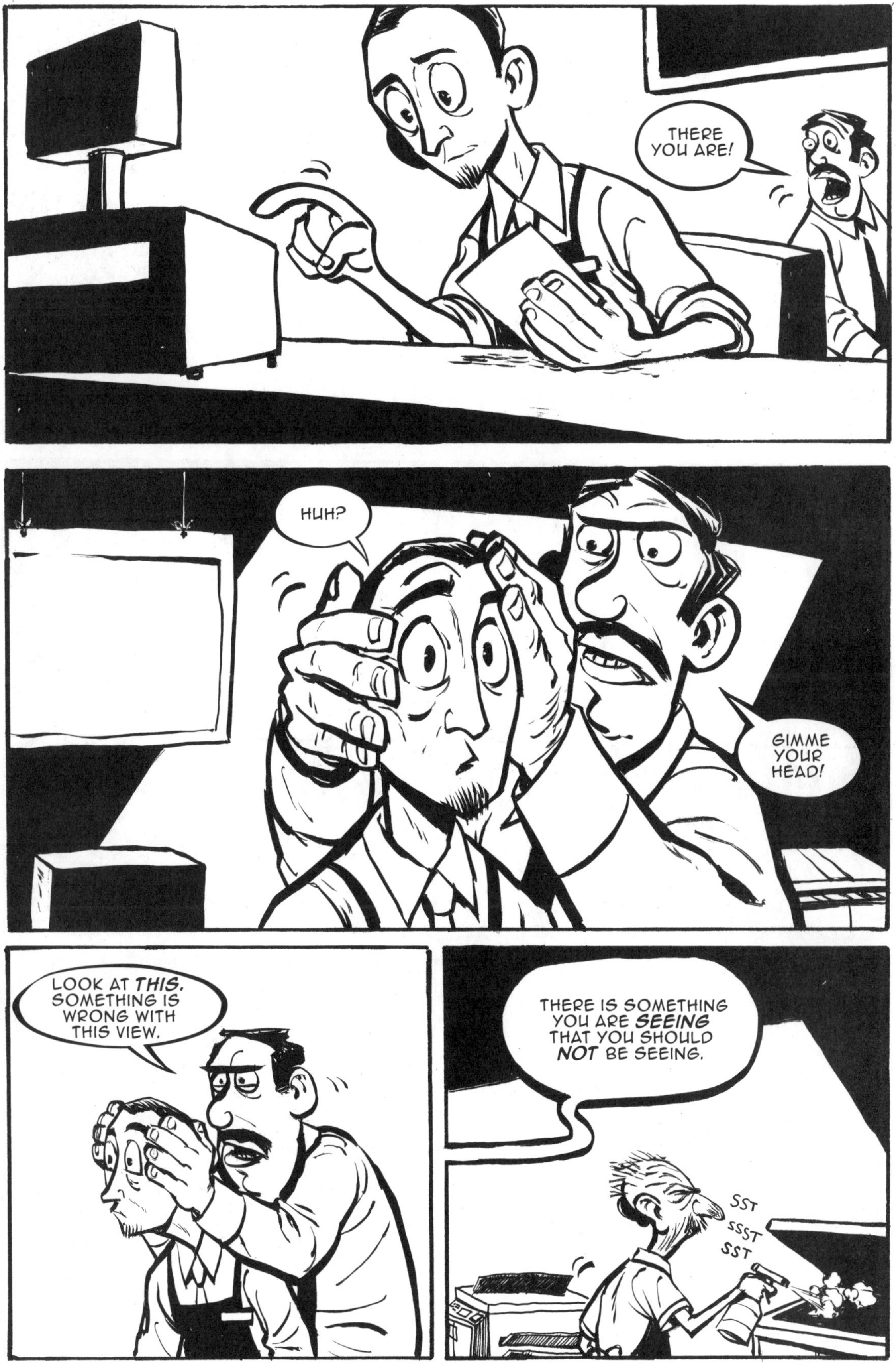
THERE YOU ARE!
HUH?
GIMME YOUR HEAD!
LOOK AT *THIS.* SOMETHING IS WRONG WITH THIS VIEW.
THERE IS SOMETHING YOU ARE *SEEING* THAT YOU SHOULD *NOT* BE SEEING.
SST
SSST
SST

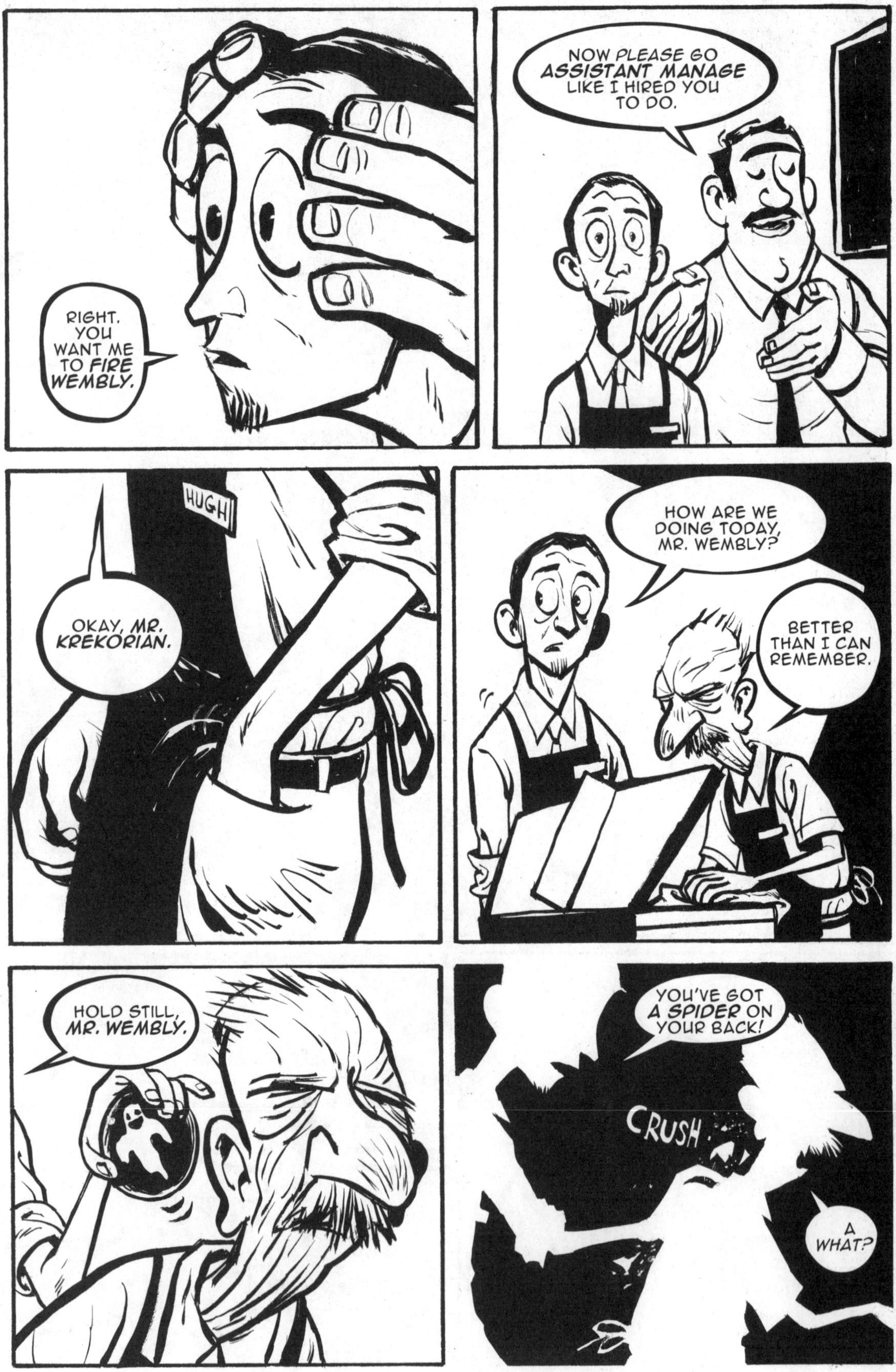
RIGHT. YOU WANT ME TO FIRE WEMBLY.
NOW PLEASE GO ASSISTANT MANAGE LIKE I HIRED YOU TO DO.
HUGH
OKAY, MR. KREKORIAN.
HOW ARE WE DOING TODAY, MR. WEMBLY?
BETTER THAN I CAN REMEMBER.
HOLD STILL, MR. WEMBLY.
YOU'VE GOT A SPIDER ON YOUR BACK!
CRUSH
A WHAT?

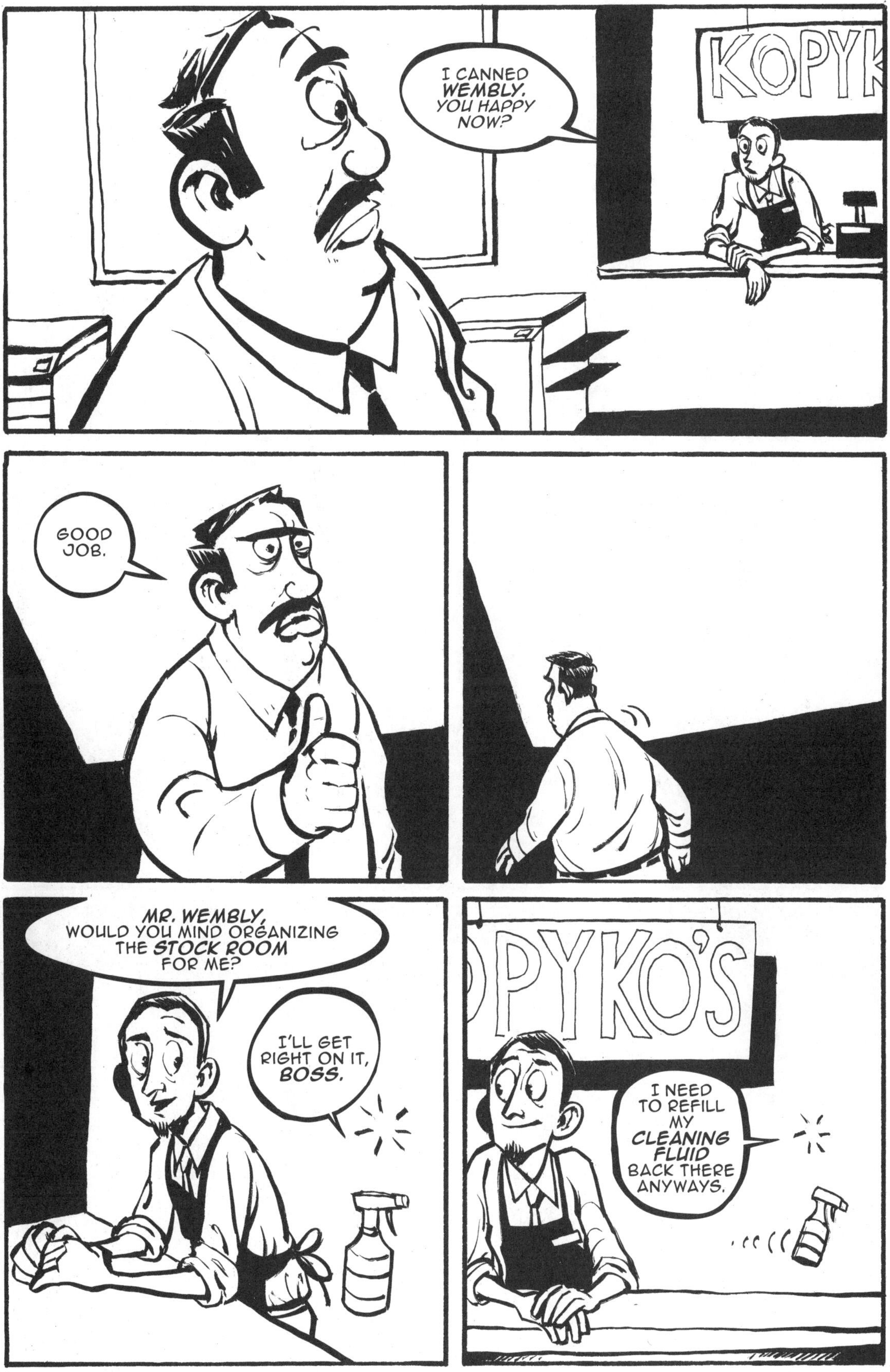
KOPYK
I CANNED WEMBLY. YOU HAPPY NOW?
GOOD JOB.
MR. WEMBLY, WOULD YOU MIND ORGANIZING THE STOCK ROOM FOR ME?
I'LL GET RIGHT ON IT, BOSS.
OPYKO'S
I NEED TO REFILL MY CLEANING FLUID BACK THERE ANYWAYS.

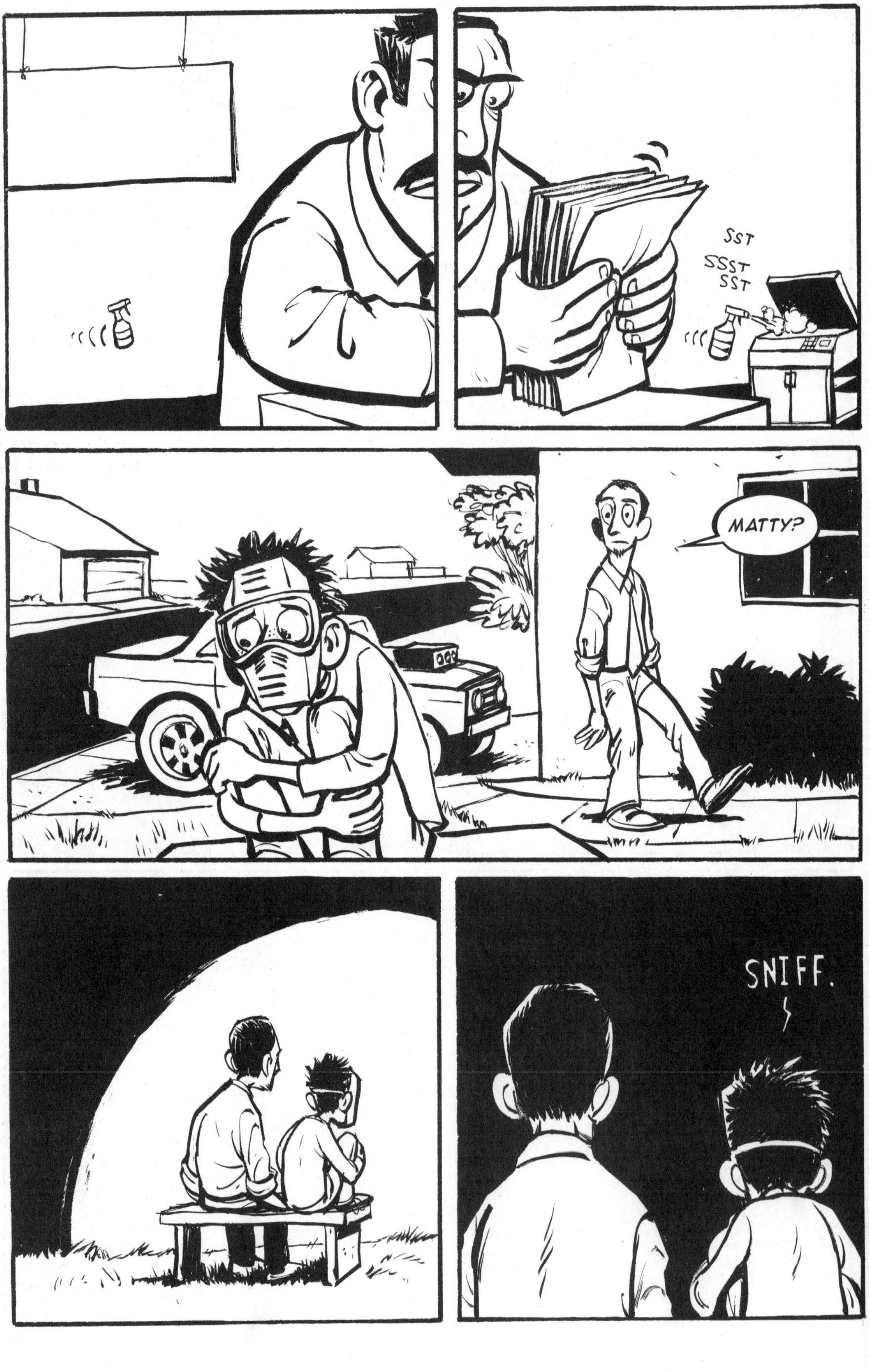
SST
SSST
SST
MATTY?
SNIFF.

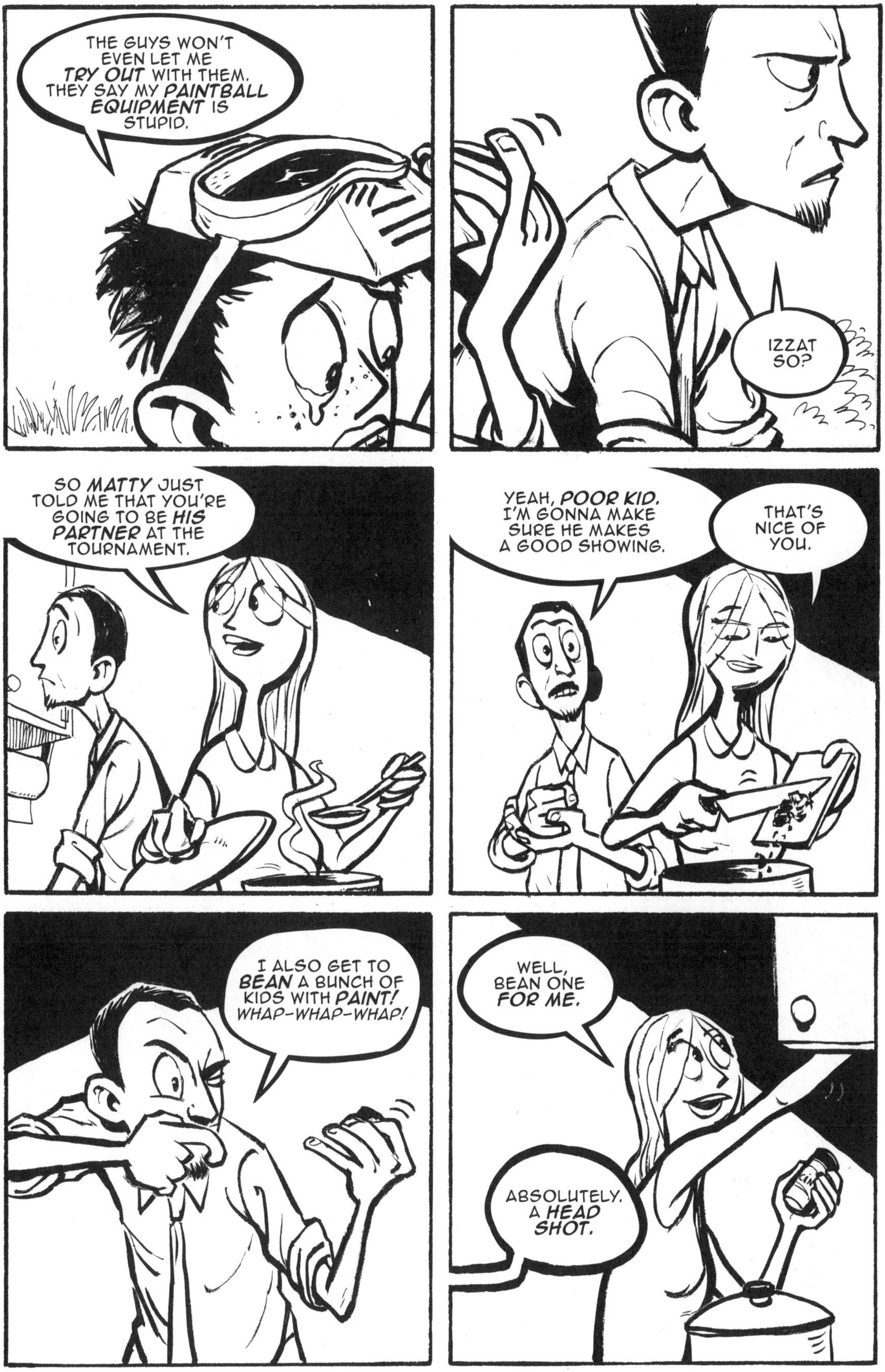
THE GUYS WON'T EVEN LET ME TRY OUT WITH THEM. THEY SAY MY PAINTBALL EQUIPMENT IS STUPID.
IZZAT SO?
SO MATTY JUST TOLD ME THAT YOU'RE GOING TO BE HIS PARTNER AT THE TOURNAMENT.
YEAH, POOR KID. I'M GONNA MAKE SURE HE MAKES A GOOD SHOWING.
THAT'S NICE OF YOU.
I ALSO GET TO BEAN A BUNCH OF KIDS WITH PAINT! WHAP-WHAP-WHAP!
WELL, BEAN ONE FOR ME.
ABSOLUTELY. A HEAD SHOT.

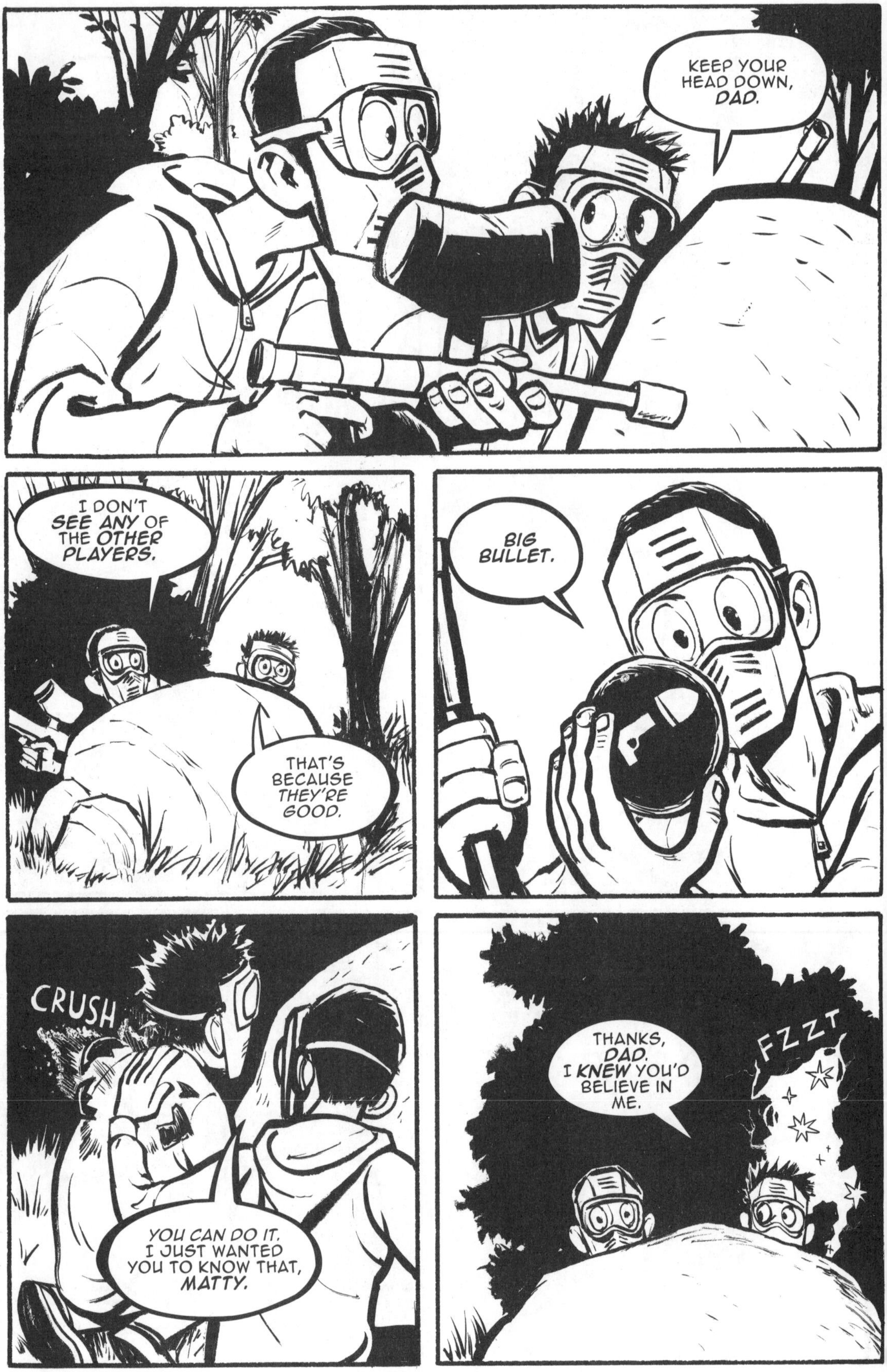
KEEP YOUR HEAD DOWN, DAD.
I DON'T SEE ANY OF THE OTHER PLAYERS.
THAT'S BECAUSE THEY'RE GOOD.
BIG BULLET.
CRUSH
YOU CAN DO IT. I JUST WANTED YOU TO KNOW THAT, MATTY.
THANKS, DAD. I KNEW YOU'D BELIEVE IN ME.
FZZT

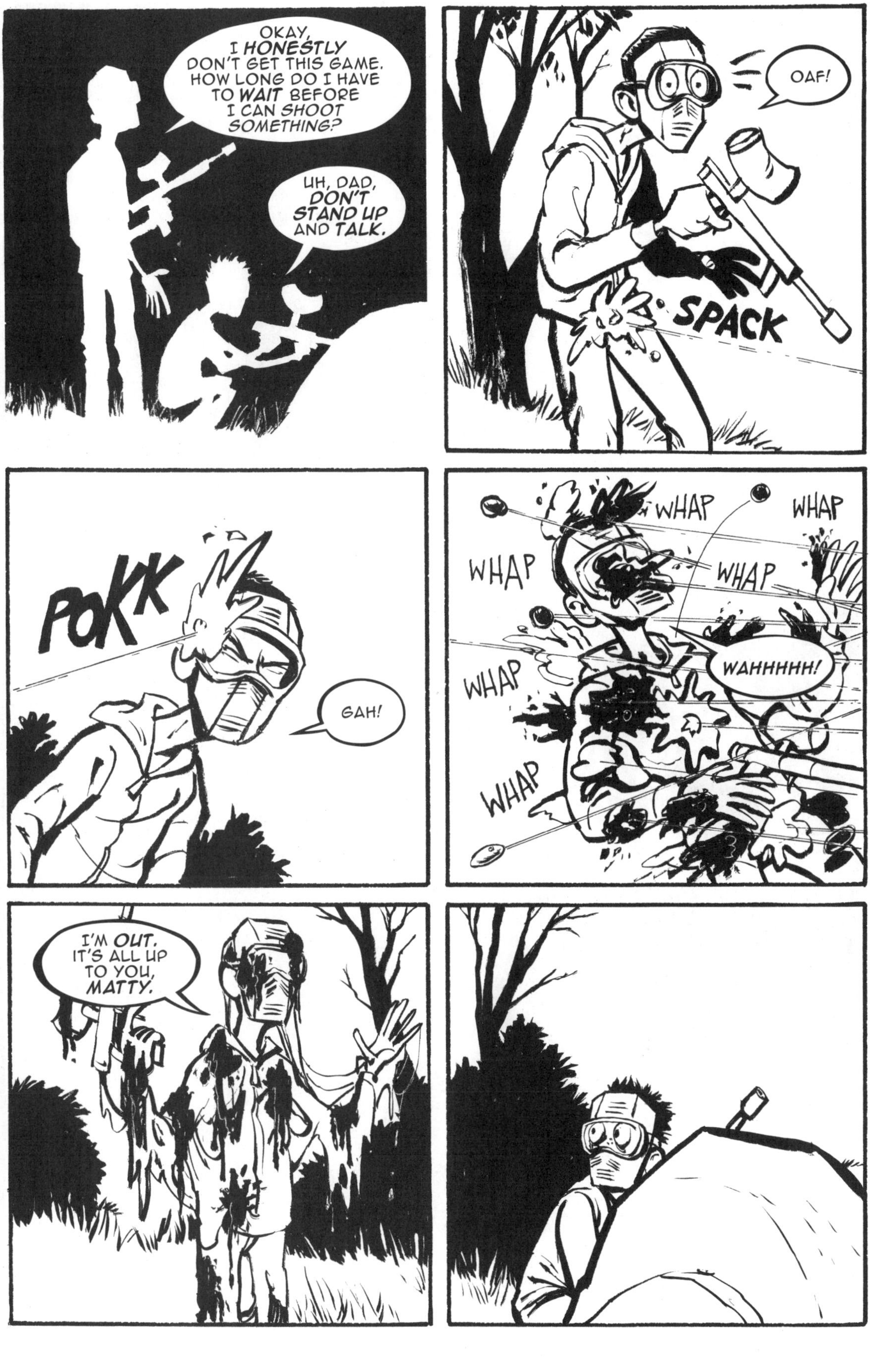
OKAY, I HONESTLY DON'T GET THIS GAME. HOW LONG DO I HAVE TO WAIT BEFORE I CAN SHOOT SOMETHING?
UH, DAD, DON'T STAND UP AND TALK.
OAF!
SPACK
POKK
GAH!
WHAP
WHAP
WHAP
WHAP
WHAP
WHAP
WAHHHHH!
I'M OUT. IT'S ALL UP TO YOU, MATTY.

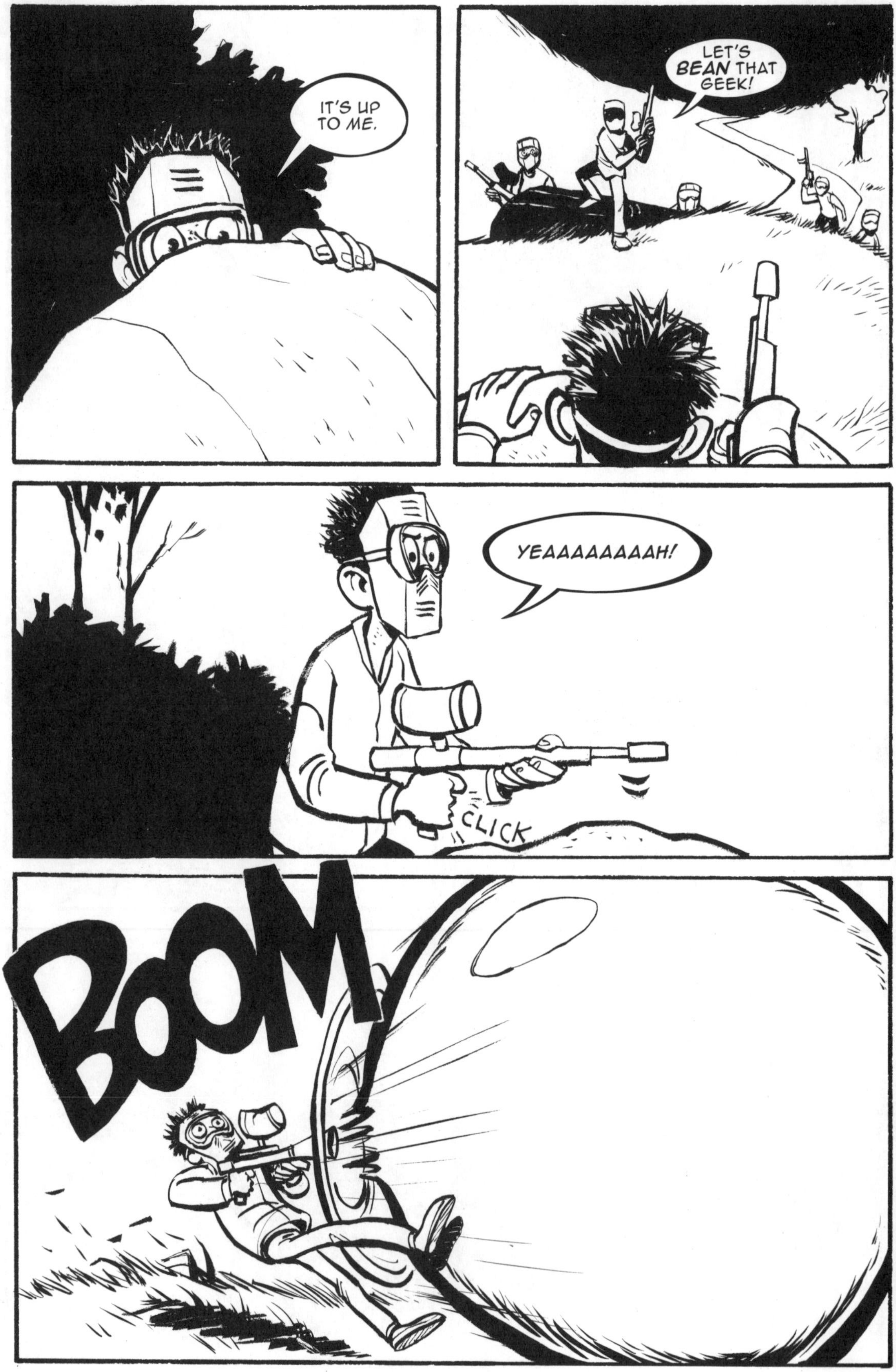
IT'S UP TO ME.
LET'S BEAN THAT GEEK!
YEAAAAAAAAH!
CLICK
BOOM

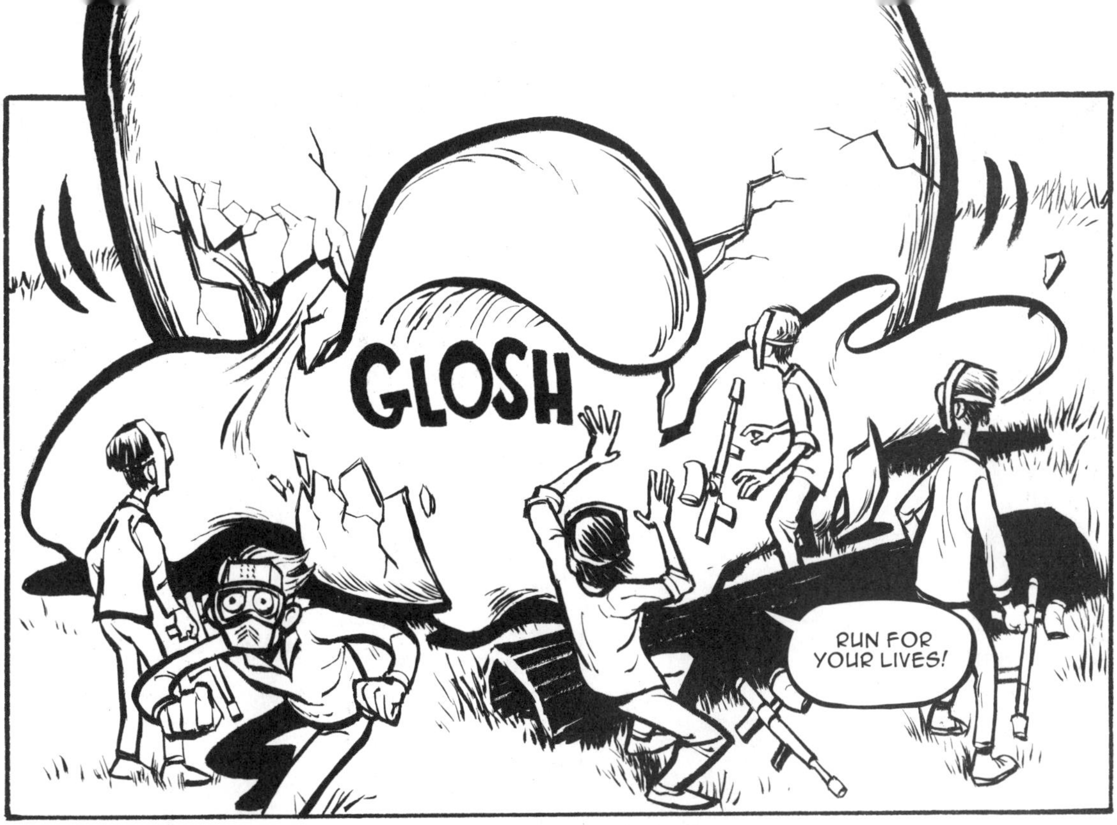
GLOSH
RUN FOR YOUR LIVES!

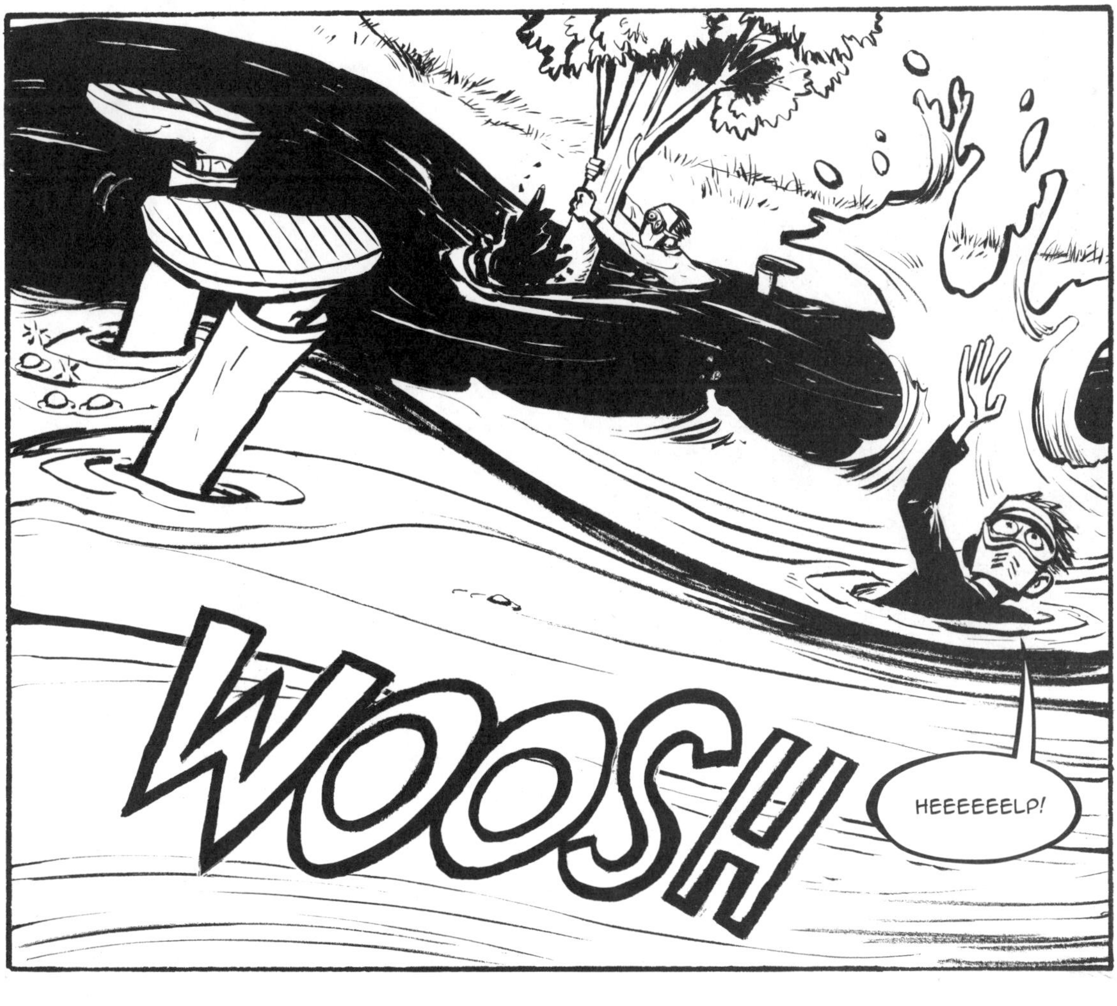
WOOSH
HEEEEEELP!

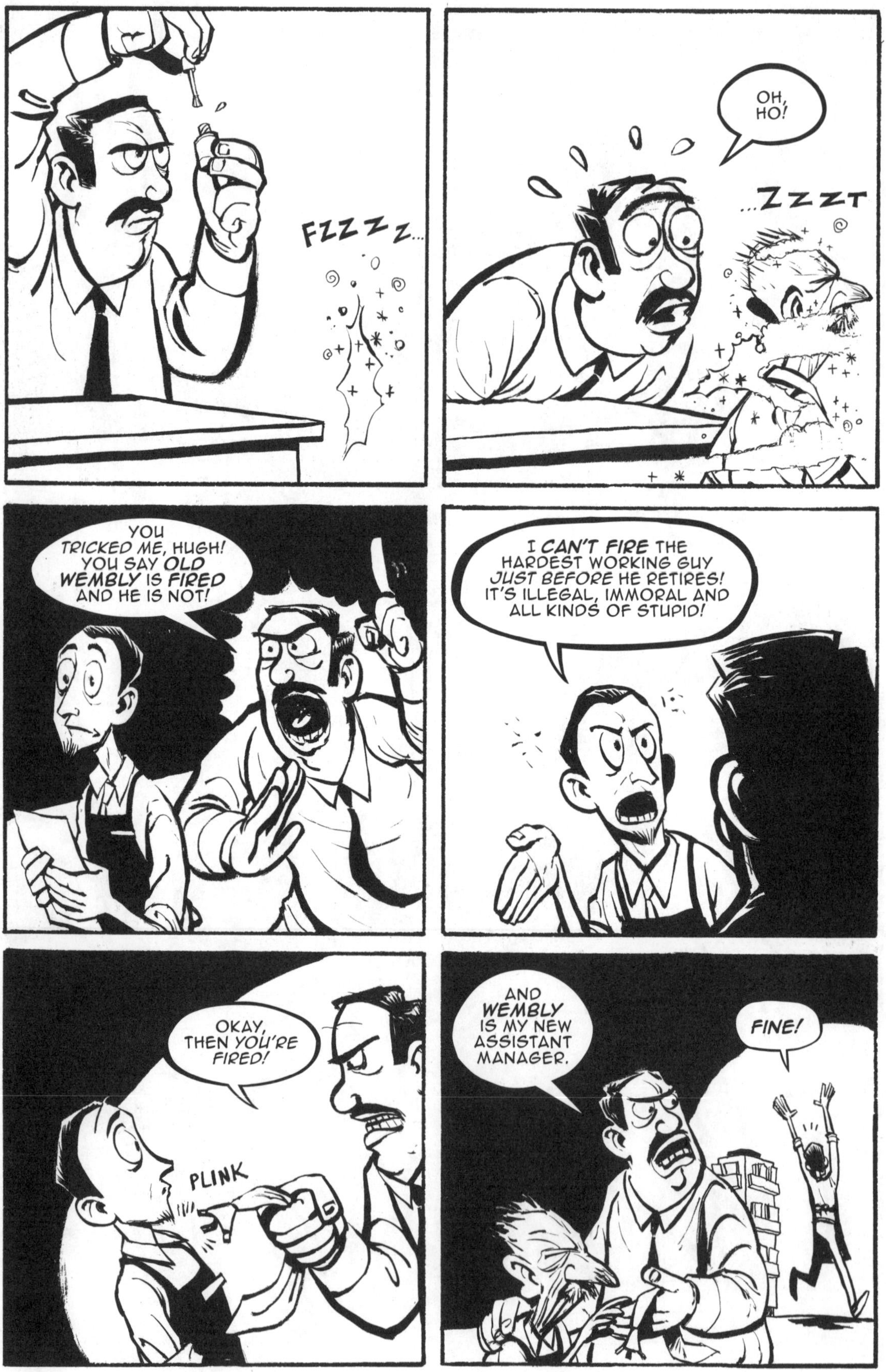
FZZZZ...
OH, HO!
...ZZZT
YOU TRICKED ME, HUGH! YOU SAY OLD WEMBLY IS FIRED AND HE IS NOT!
I CAN'T FIRE THE HARDEST WORKING GUY JUST BEFORE HE RETIRES! IT'S ILLEGAL, IMMORAL AND ALL KINDS OF STUPID!
OKAY, THEN YOU'RE FIRED!
PLINK
AND WEMBLY IS MY NEW ASSISTANT MANAGER.
FINE!

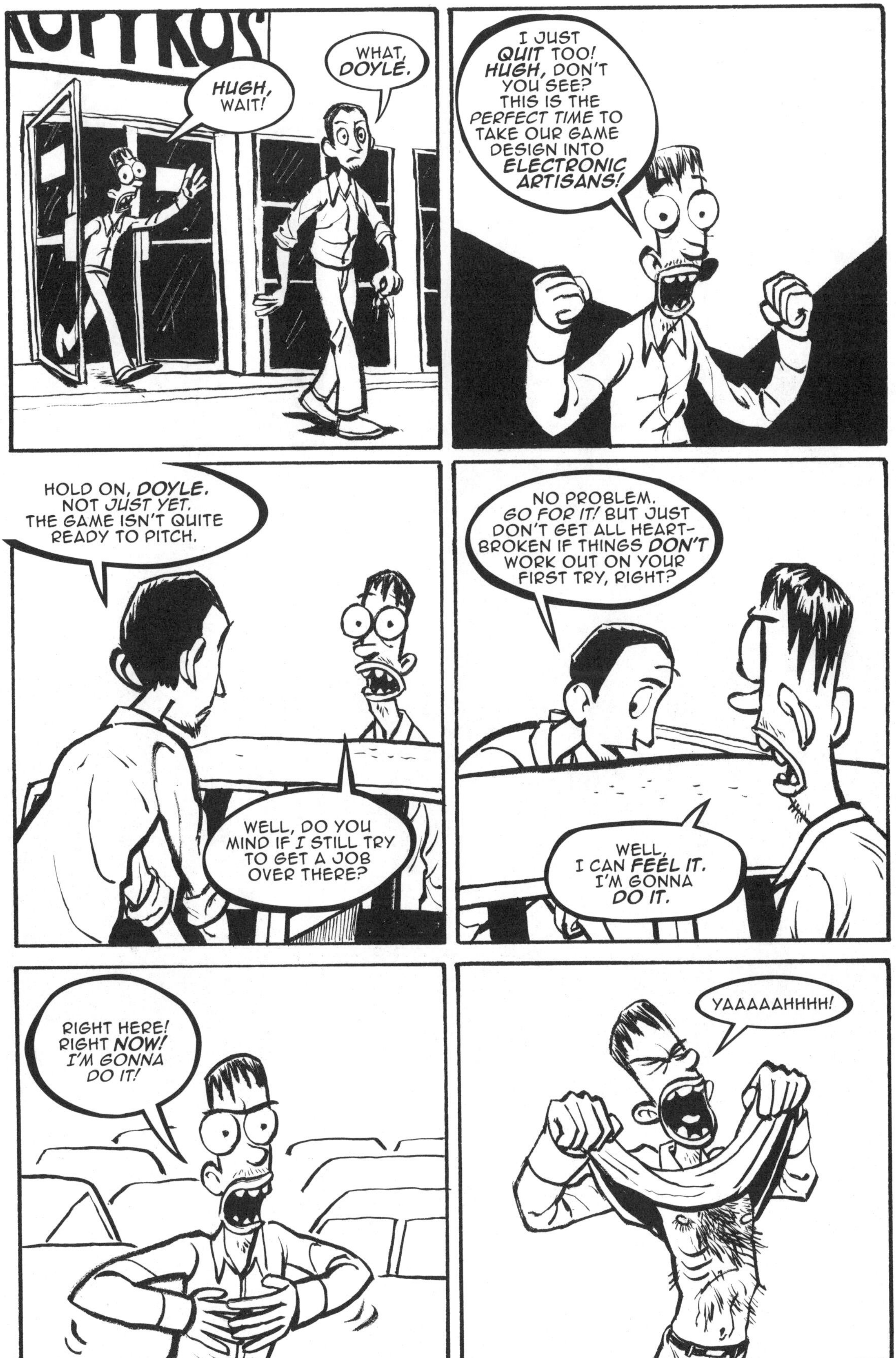
HUGH, WAIT!
WHAT, DOYLE.
I JUST QUIT TOO! HUGH, DON'T YOU SEE? THIS IS THE PERFECT TIME TO TAKE OUR GAME DESIGN INTO ELECTRONIC ARTISANS!
HOLD ON, DOYLE. NOT JUST YET. THE GAME ISN'T QUITE READY TO PITCH.
WELL, DO YOU MIND IF I STILL TRY TO GET A JOB OVER THERE?
NO PROBLEM. GO FOR IT! BUT JUST DON'T GET ALL HEART-BROKEN IF THINGS DON'T WORK OUT ON YOUR FIRST TRY, RIGHT?
WELL, I CAN FEEL IT. I'M GONNA DO IT.
RIGHT HERE! RIGHT NOW! I'M GONNA DO IT!
YAAAAAHHHH!

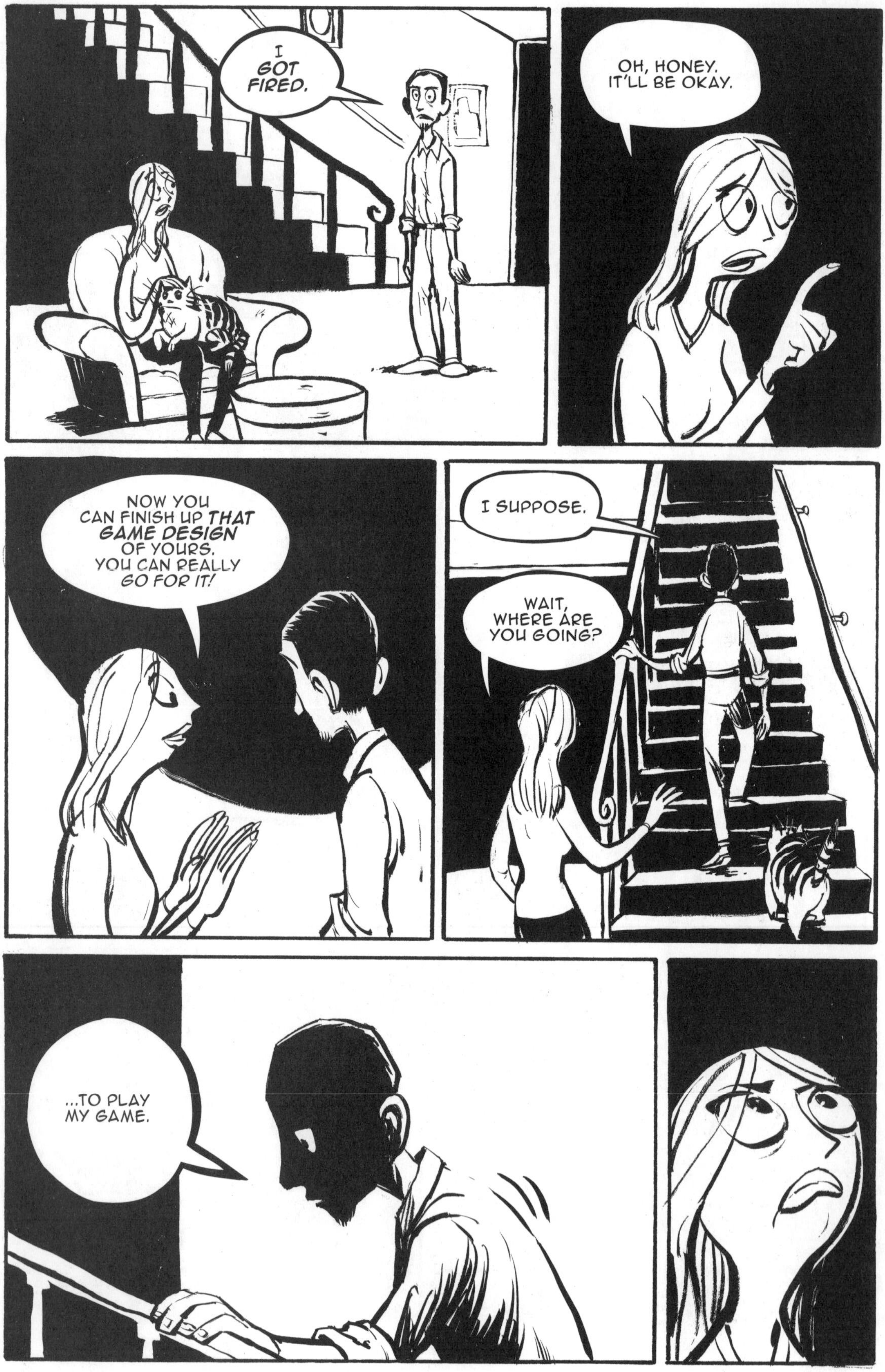
I *GOT FIRED.*
OH, HONEY. IT'LL BE OKAY.
NOW YOU CAN FINISH UP *THAT GAME DESIGN* OF YOURS. YOU CAN REALLY *GO FOR IT!*
I SUPPOSE.
WAIT, WHERE ARE YOU GOING?
...TO PLAY MY GAME.

WHAT ARE WE GONNA DO, MOBY?

BLEEP BLOOP

DADDY DOESN'T HAVE A JOB, AND HE KNOWS NOBODY WOULD EVER REALLY BUY HIS GAME DESIGN.

DADDY NEEDS A NEW JOB. BUT WHAT AM I GOOD AT? I CAN'T REALLY DO ANYTHING.

$

WAIT. A. MINUTE.

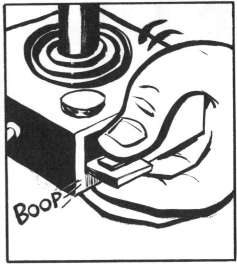

BOOP

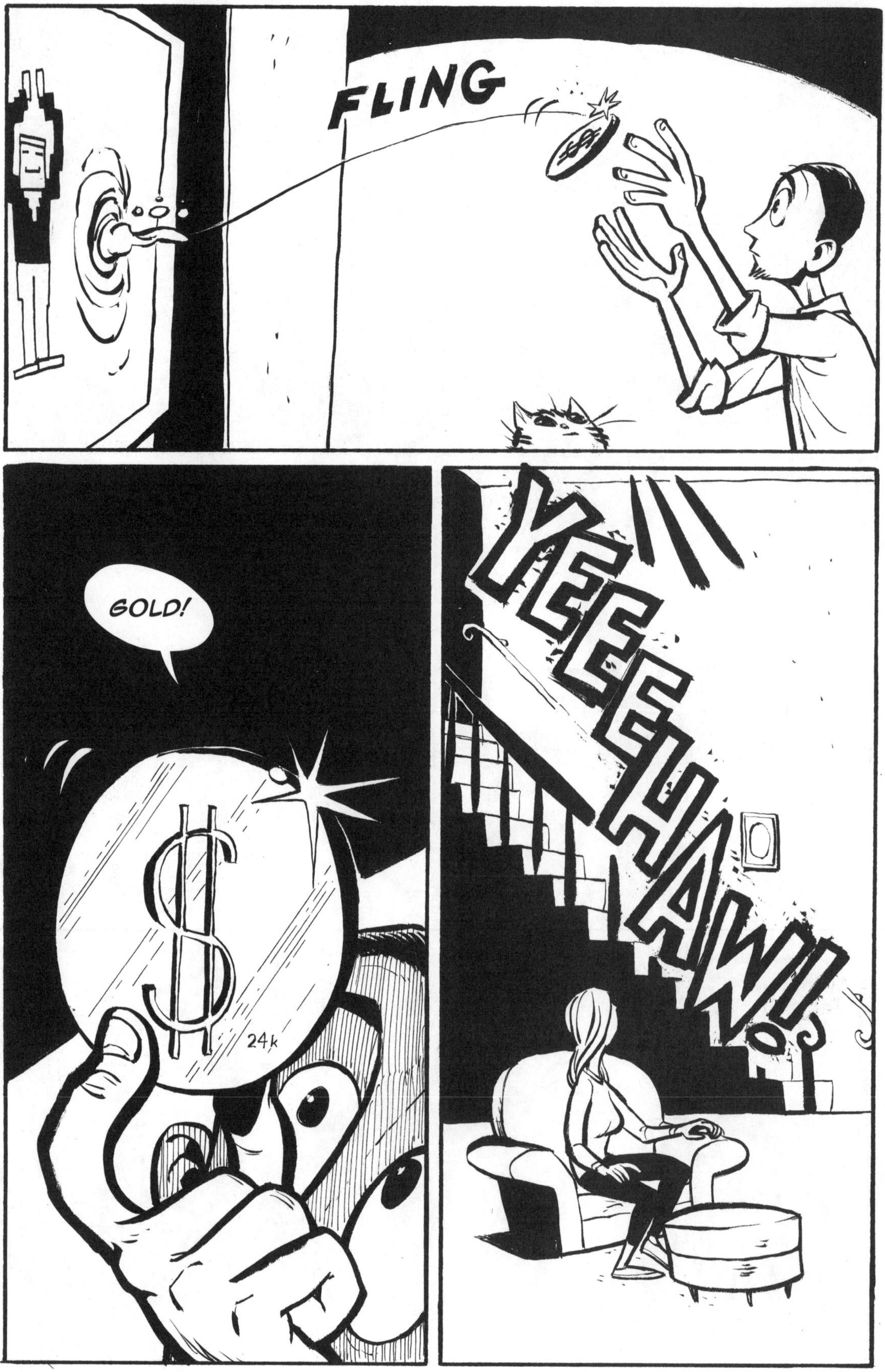
FLING
GOLD!
24k
YEEEHAW!

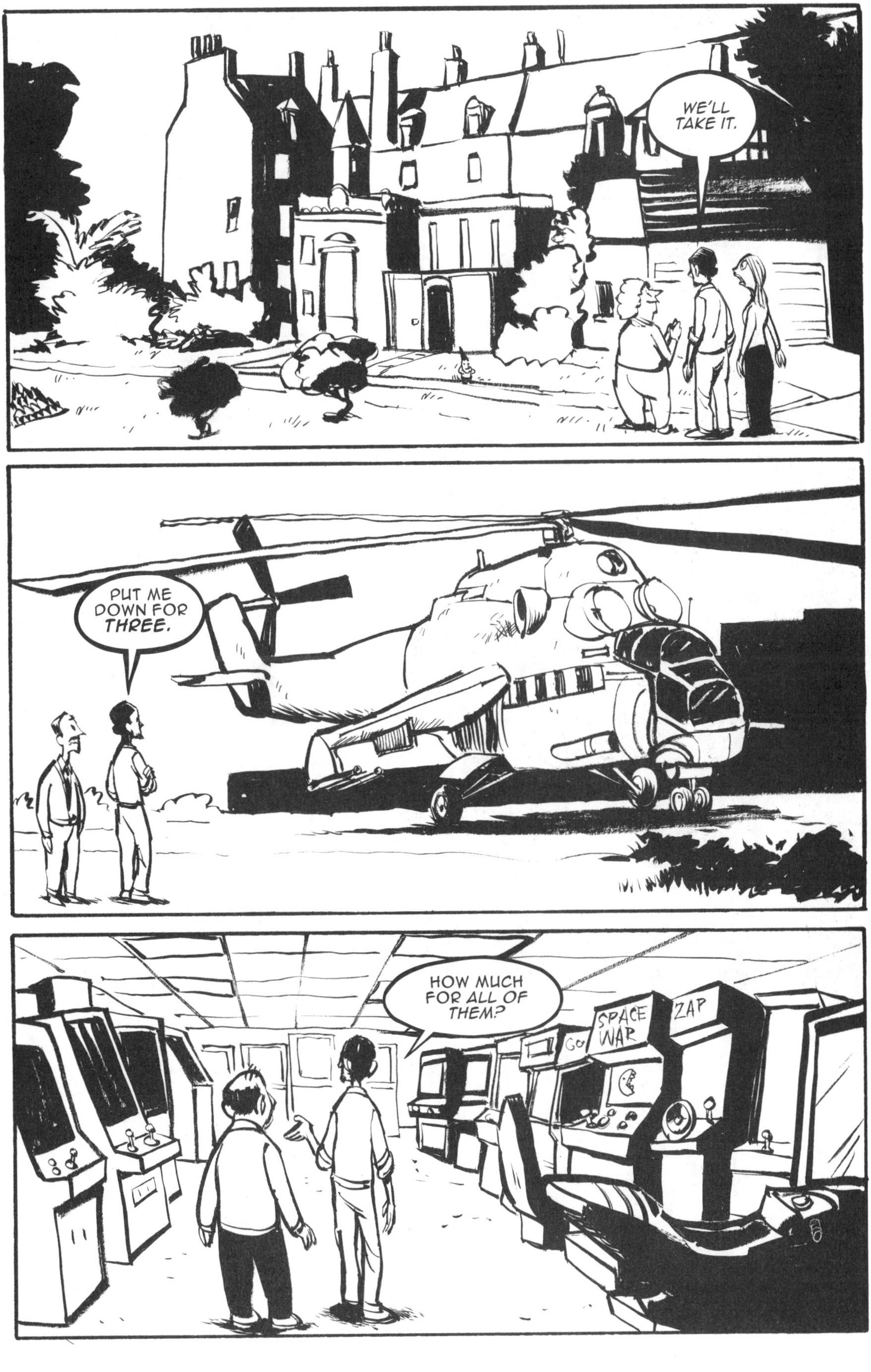
WE'LL TAKE IT.
PUT ME DOWN FOR THREE.
HOW MUCH FOR ALL OF THEM?
SPACE WAR
ZAP
GO

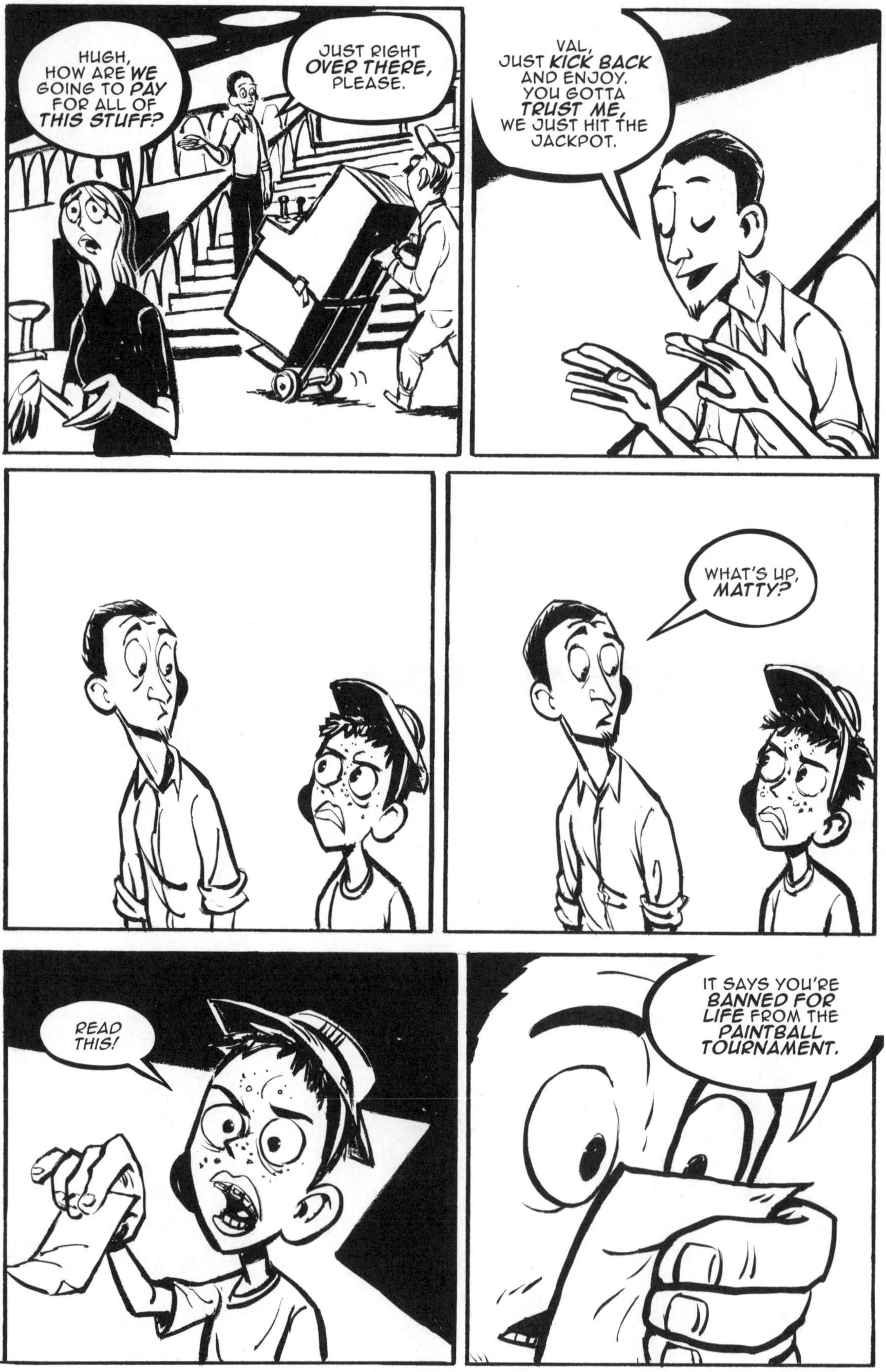
HUGH, HOW ARE WE GOING TO PAY FOR ALL OF THIS STUFF?
JUST RIGHT OVER THERE, PLEASE.
VAL, JUST KICK BACK AND ENJOY. YOU GOTTA TRUST ME, WE JUST HIT THE JACKPOT.
WHAT'S UP, MATTY?
READ THIS!
IT SAYS YOU'RE BANNED FOR LIFE FROM THE PAINTBALL TOURNAMENT.

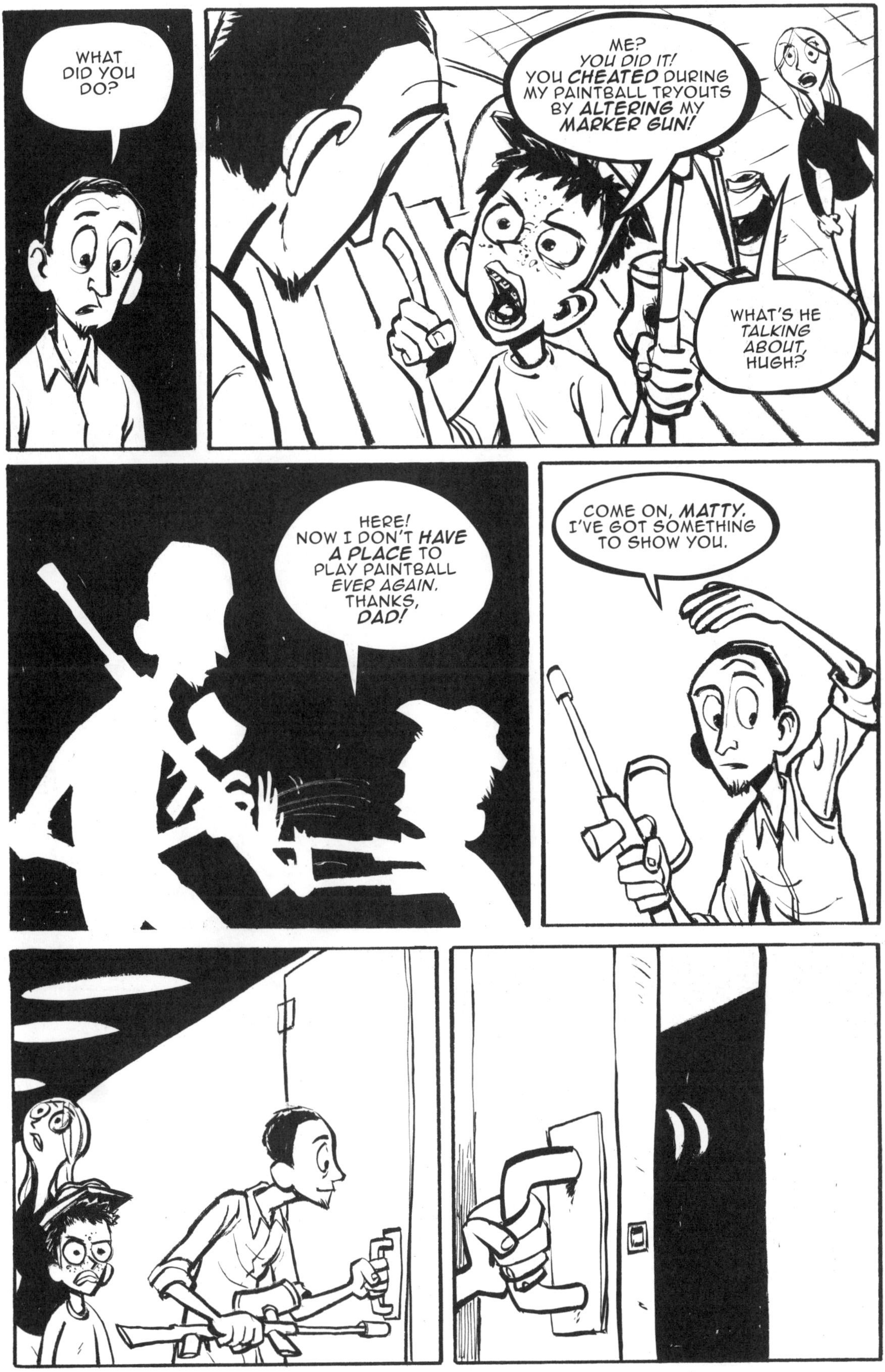
WHAT DID YOU DO?
ME? YOU DID IT! YOU CHEATED DURING MY PAINTBALL TRYOUTS BY ALTERING MY MARKER GUN!
WHAT'S HE TALKING ABOUT, HUGH?
HERE! NOW I DON'T HAVE A PLACE TO PLAY PAINTBALL EVER AGAIN. THANKS, DAD!
COME ON, MATTY. I'VE GOT SOMETHING TO SHOW YOU.

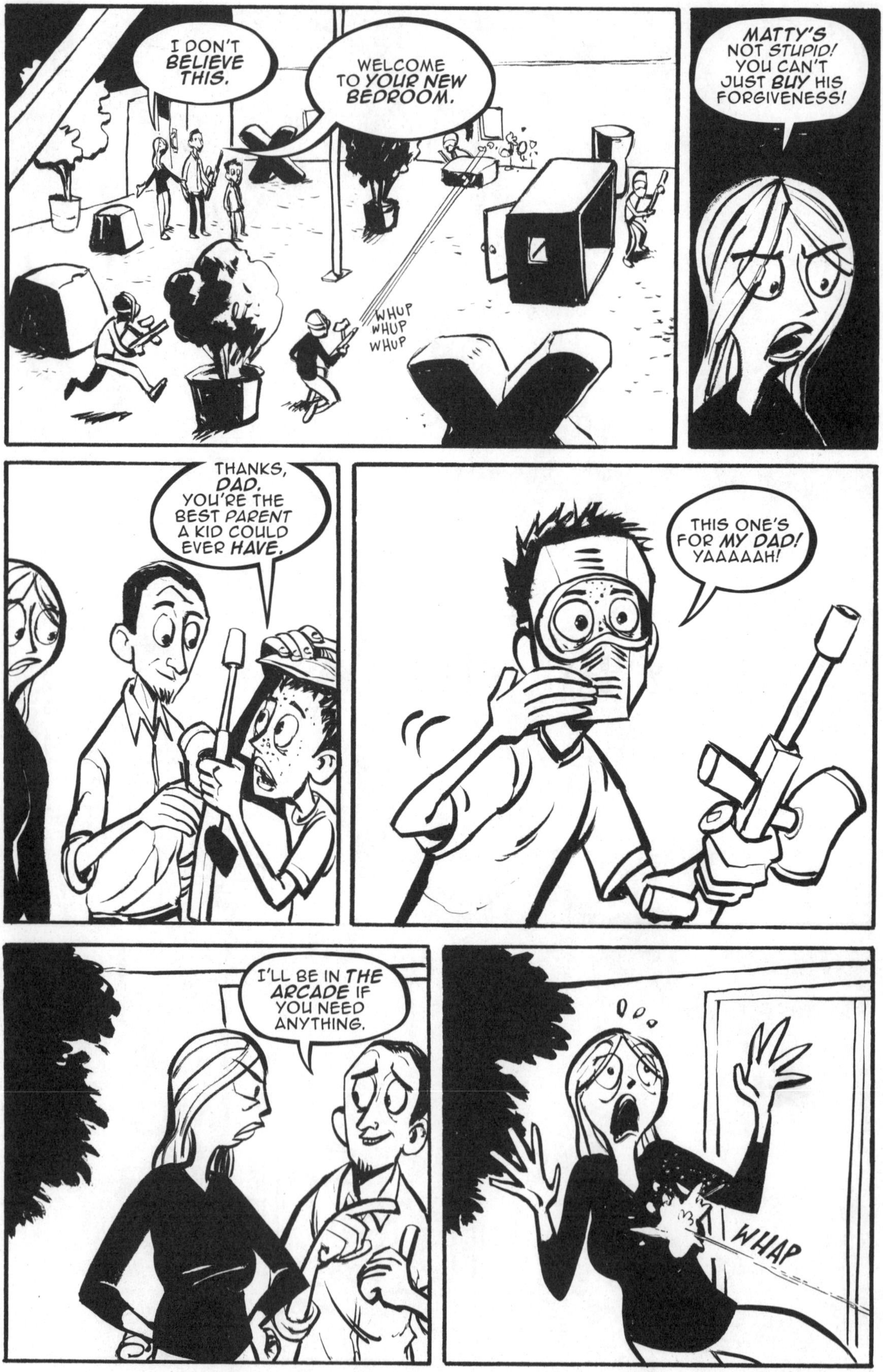
I DON'T BELIEVE THIS.
WELCOME TO YOUR NEW BEDROOM.
WHUP WHUP WHUP
MATTY'S NOT STUPID! YOU CAN'T JUST BUY HIS FORGIVENESS!
THANKS, DAD. YOU'RE THE BEST PARENT A KID COULD EVER HAVE.
THIS ONE'S FOR MY DAD! YAAAAAH!
I'LL BE IN THE ARCADE IF YOU NEED ANYTHING.
WHAP

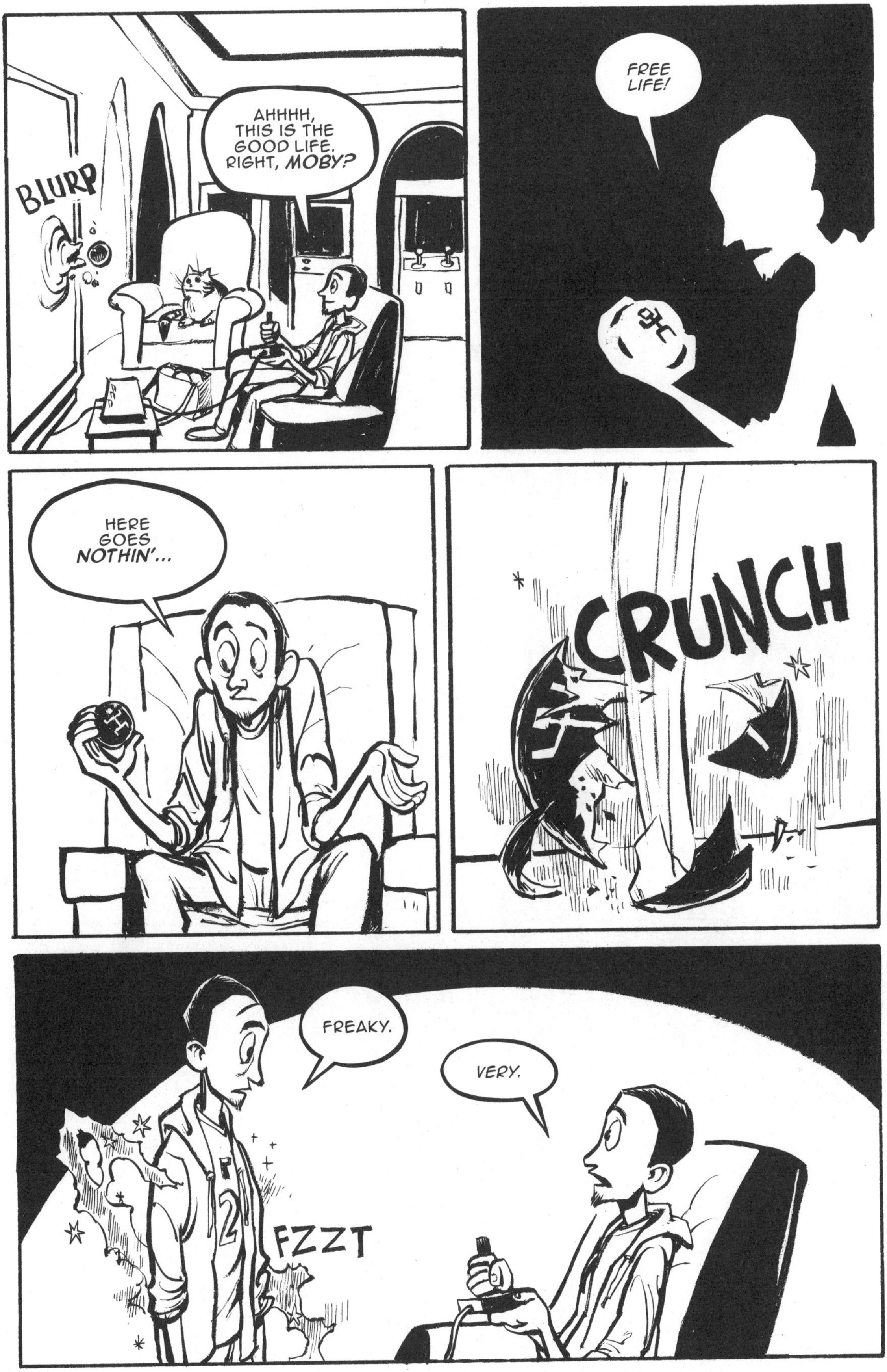
BLURP
AHHHH, THIS IS THE GOOD LIFE. RIGHT, MOBY?
FREE LIFE!
HERE GOES NOTHIN'...
CRUNCH
FREAKY.
VERY.
FZZT

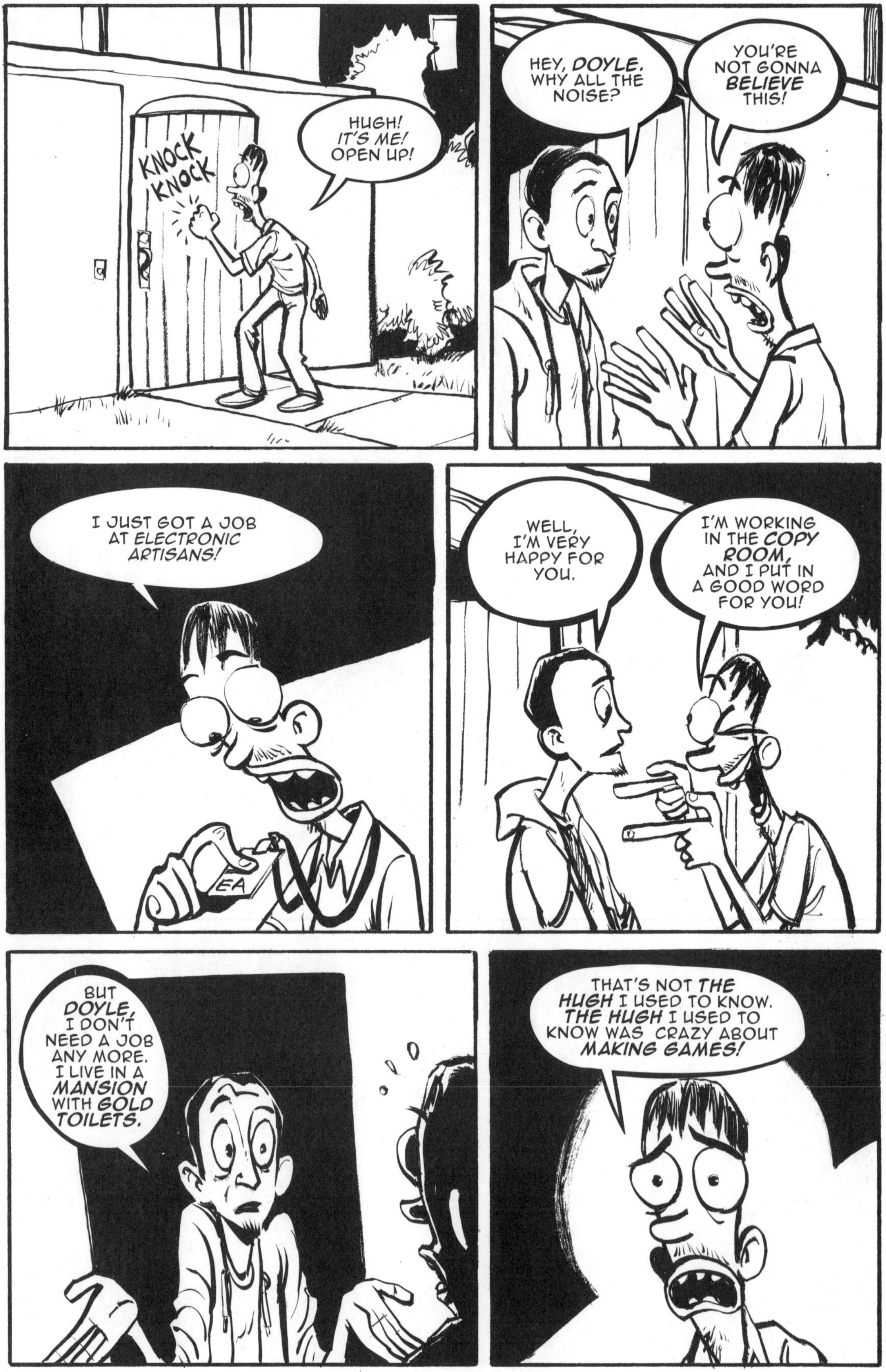
KNOCK KNOCK
HUGH! IT'S ME! OPEN UP!
HEY, DOYLE. WHY ALL THE NOISE?
YOU'RE NOT GONNA BELIEVE THIS!
I JUST GOT A JOB AT ELECTRONIC ARTISANS!
EA
WELL, I'M VERY HAPPY FOR YOU.
I'M WORKING IN THE COPY ROOM, AND I PUT IN A GOOD WORD FOR YOU!
BUT DOYLE, I DON'T NEED A JOB ANY MORE. I LIVE IN A MANSION WITH GOLD TOILETS.
THAT'S NOT THE HUGH I USED TO KNOW. THE HUGH I USED TO KNOW WAS CRAZY ABOUT MAKING GAMES!

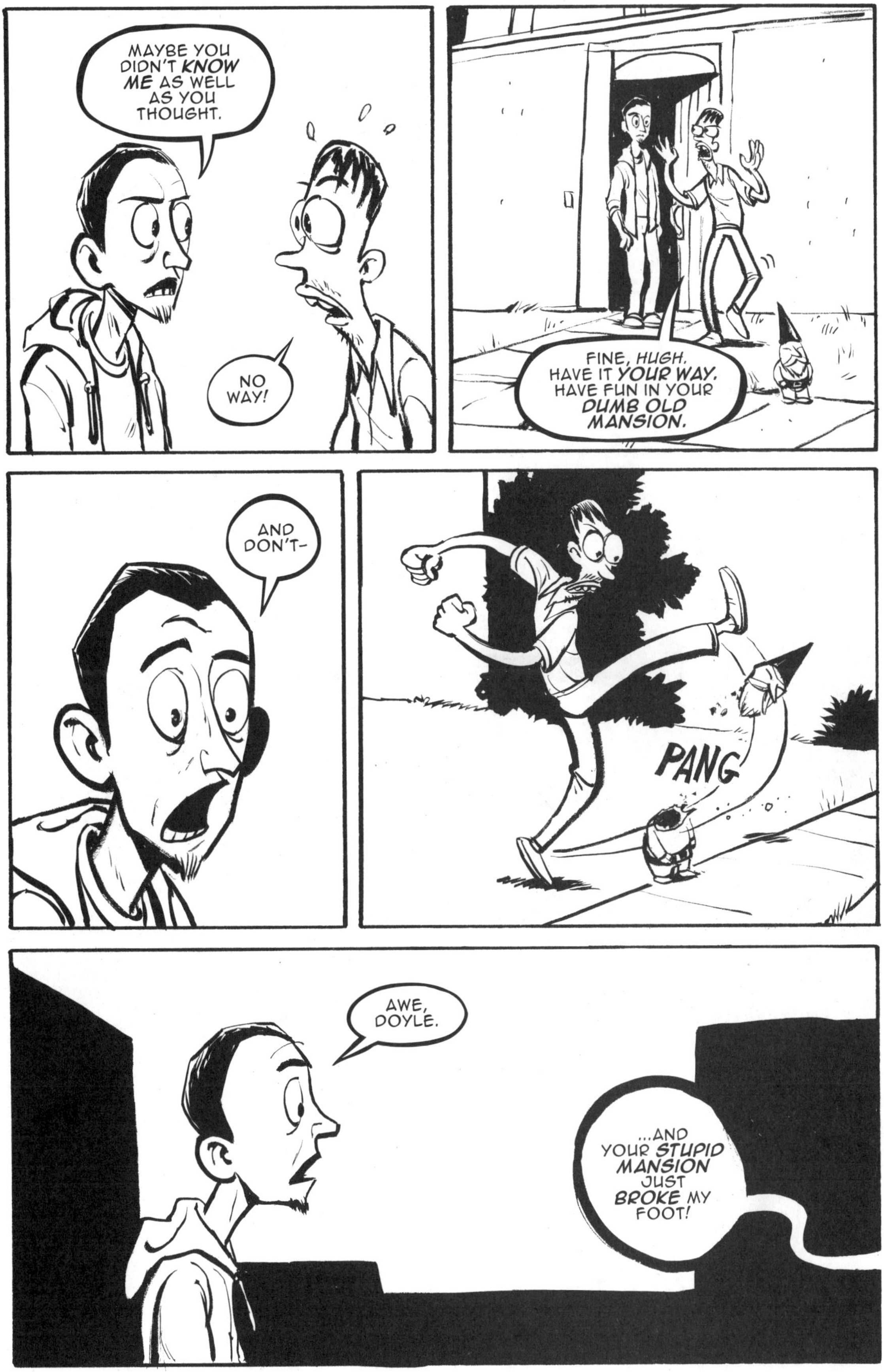
MAYBE YOU DIDN'T KNOW ME AS WELL AS YOU THOUGHT.
NO WAY!
FINE, HUGH. HAVE IT YOUR WAY. HAVE FUN IN YOUR DUMB OLD MANSION.
AND DON'T-
PANG
AWE, DOYLE.
...AND YOUR STUPID MANSION JUST BROKE MY FOOT!

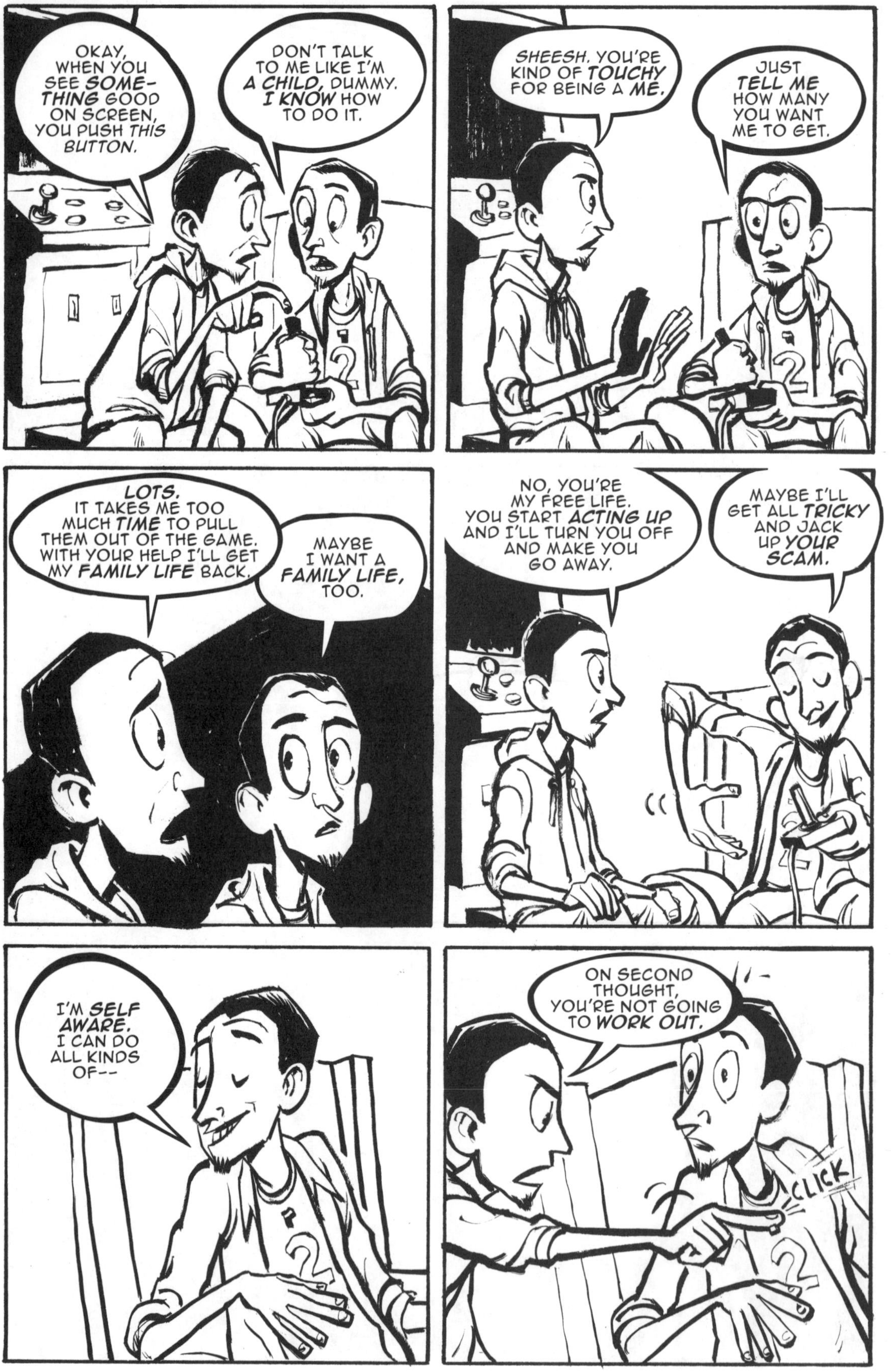

OKAY, WHEN YOU SEE SOMETHING GOOD ON SCREEN, YOU PUSH THIS BUTTON.
DON'T TALK TO ME LIKE I'M A CHILD, DUMMY. I KNOW HOW TO DO IT.
SHEESH. YOU'RE KIND OF TOUCHY FOR BEING A ME.
JUST TELL ME HOW MANY YOU WANT ME TO GET.
LOTS. IT TAKES ME TOO MUCH TIME TO PULL THEM OUT OF THE GAME. WITH YOUR HELP I'LL GET MY FAMILY LIFE BACK.
MAYBE I WANT A FAMILY LIFE, TOO.
NO, YOU'RE MY FREE LIFE. YOU START ACTING UP AND I'LL TURN YOU OFF AND MAKE YOU GO AWAY.
MAYBE I'LL GET ALL TRICKY AND JACK UP YOUR SCAM.
I'M SELF AWARE. I CAN DO ALL KINDS OF--
ON SECOND THOUGHT, YOU'RE NOT GOING TO WORK OUT.
CLICK

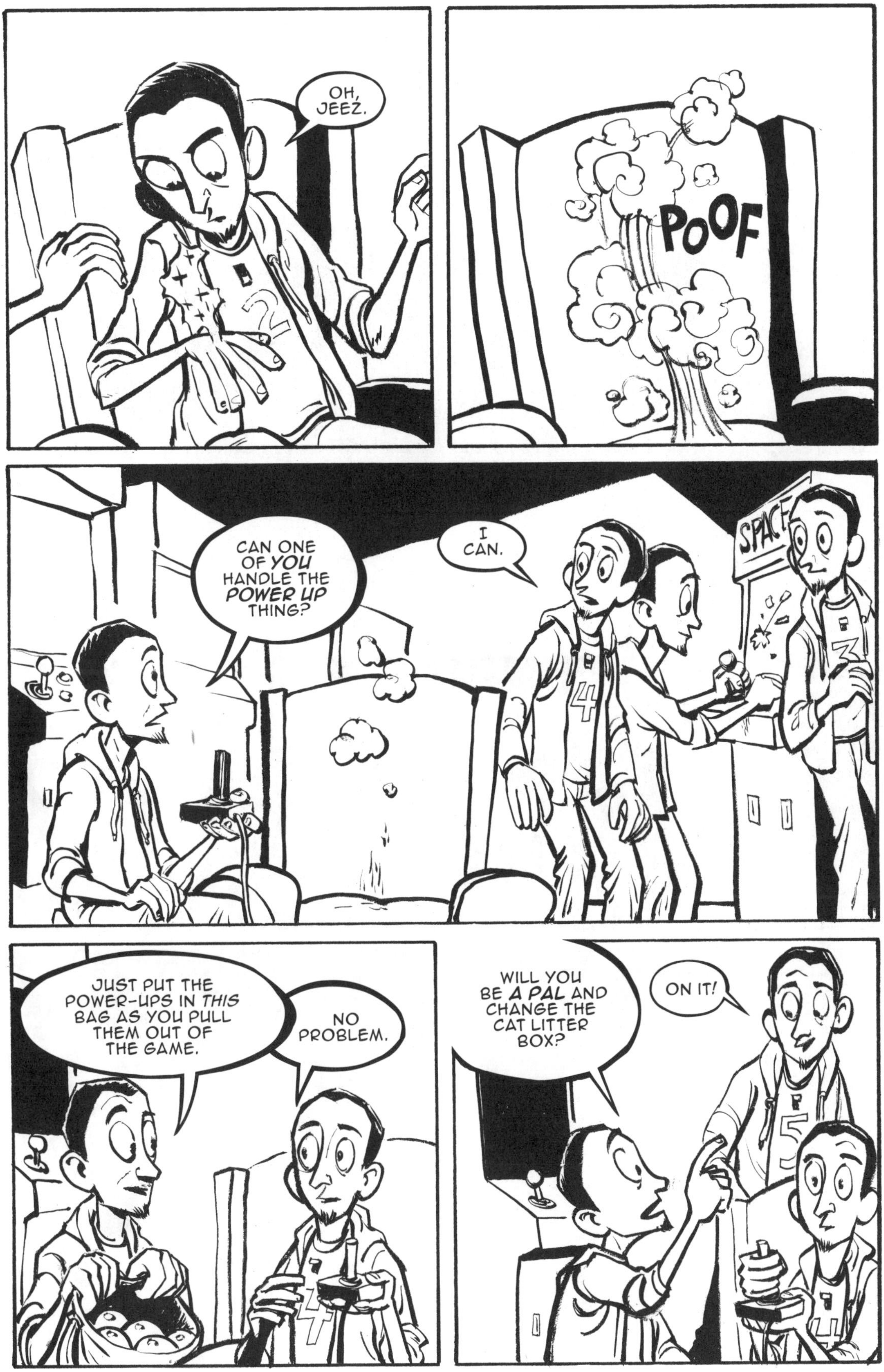
OH, JEEZ.
POOF
CAN ONE OF YOU HANDLE THE POWER UP THING?
I CAN.
SPACE
JUST PUT THE POWER-UPS IN THIS BAG AS YOU PULL THEM OUT OF THE GAME.
NO PROBLEM.
WILL YOU BE A PAL AND CHANGE THE CAT LITTER BOX?
ON IT!

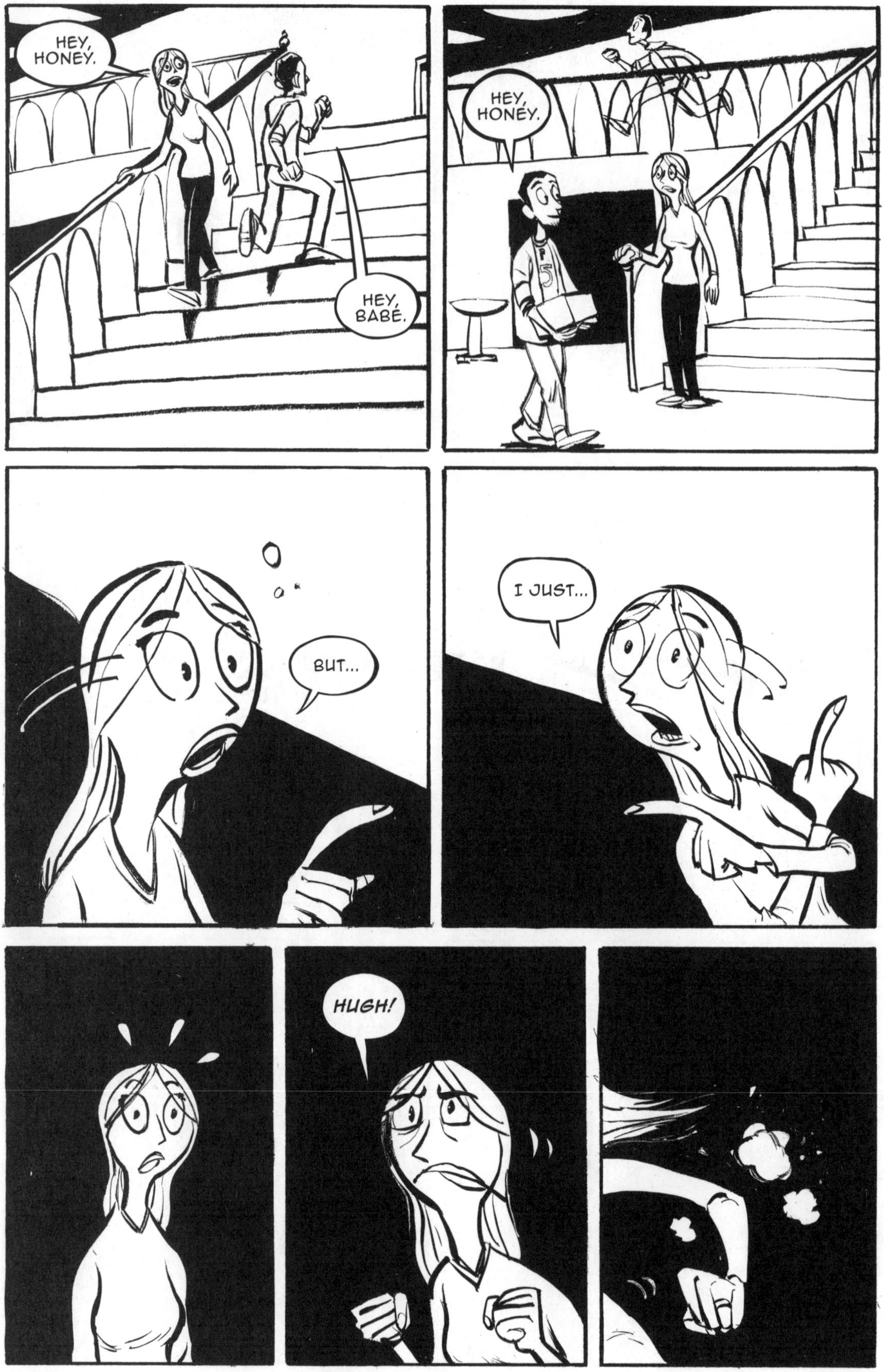
HEY, HONEY.
HEY, BABE.
HEY, HONEY.
BUT...
I JUST...
HUGH!

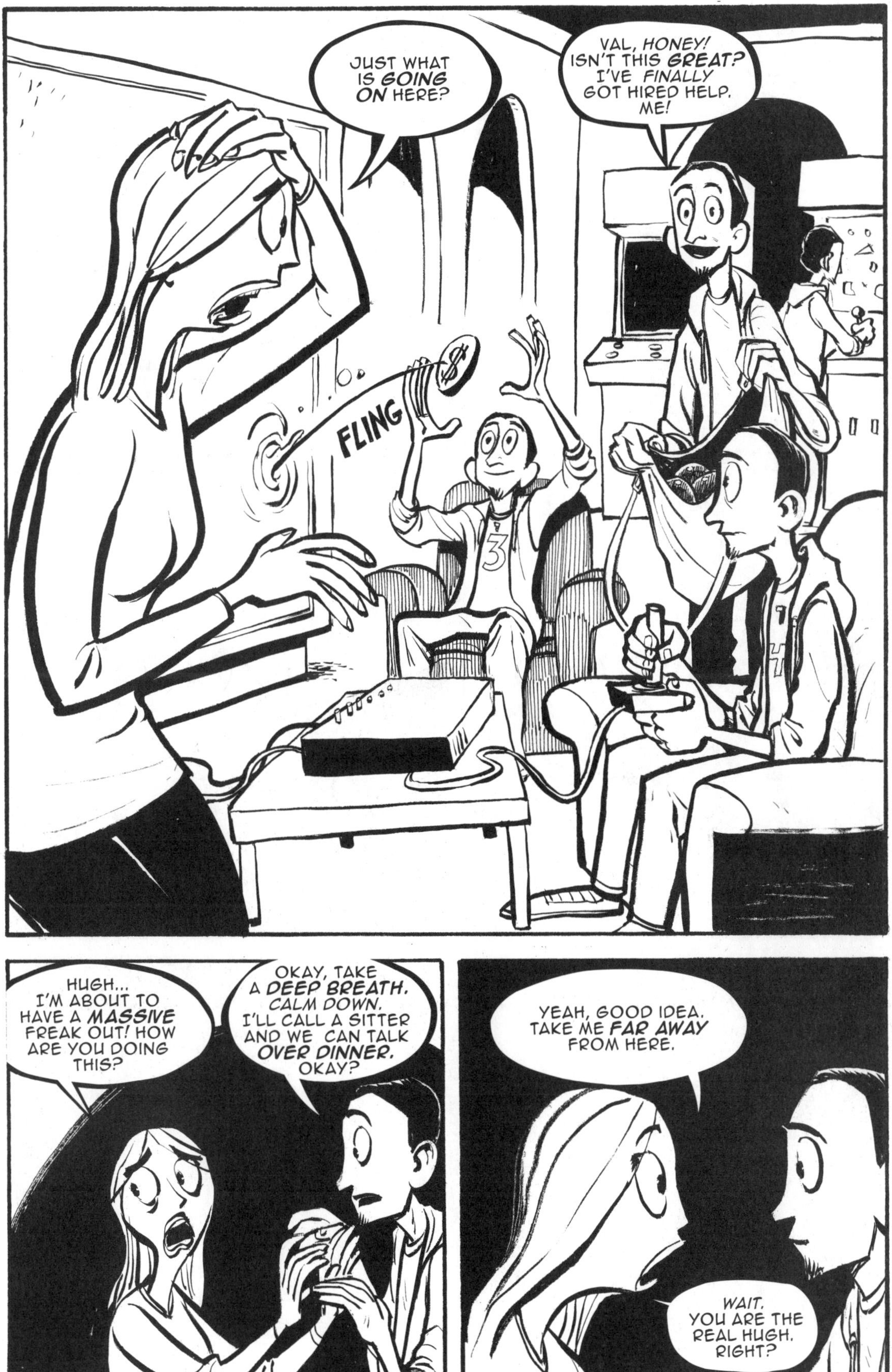
JUST WHAT IS GOING ON HERE?
VAL, HONEY! ISN'T THIS GREAT? I'VE FINALLY GOT HIRED HELP. ME!
FLING
HUGH... I'M ABOUT TO HAVE A MASSIVE FREAK OUT! HOW ARE YOU DOING THIS?
OKAY, TAKE A DEEP BREATH. CALM DOWN. I'LL CALL A SITTER AND WE CAN TALK OVER DINNER. OKAY?
YEAH, GOOD IDEA. TAKE ME FAR AWAY FROM HERE.
WAIT. YOU ARE THE REAL HUGH, RIGHT?

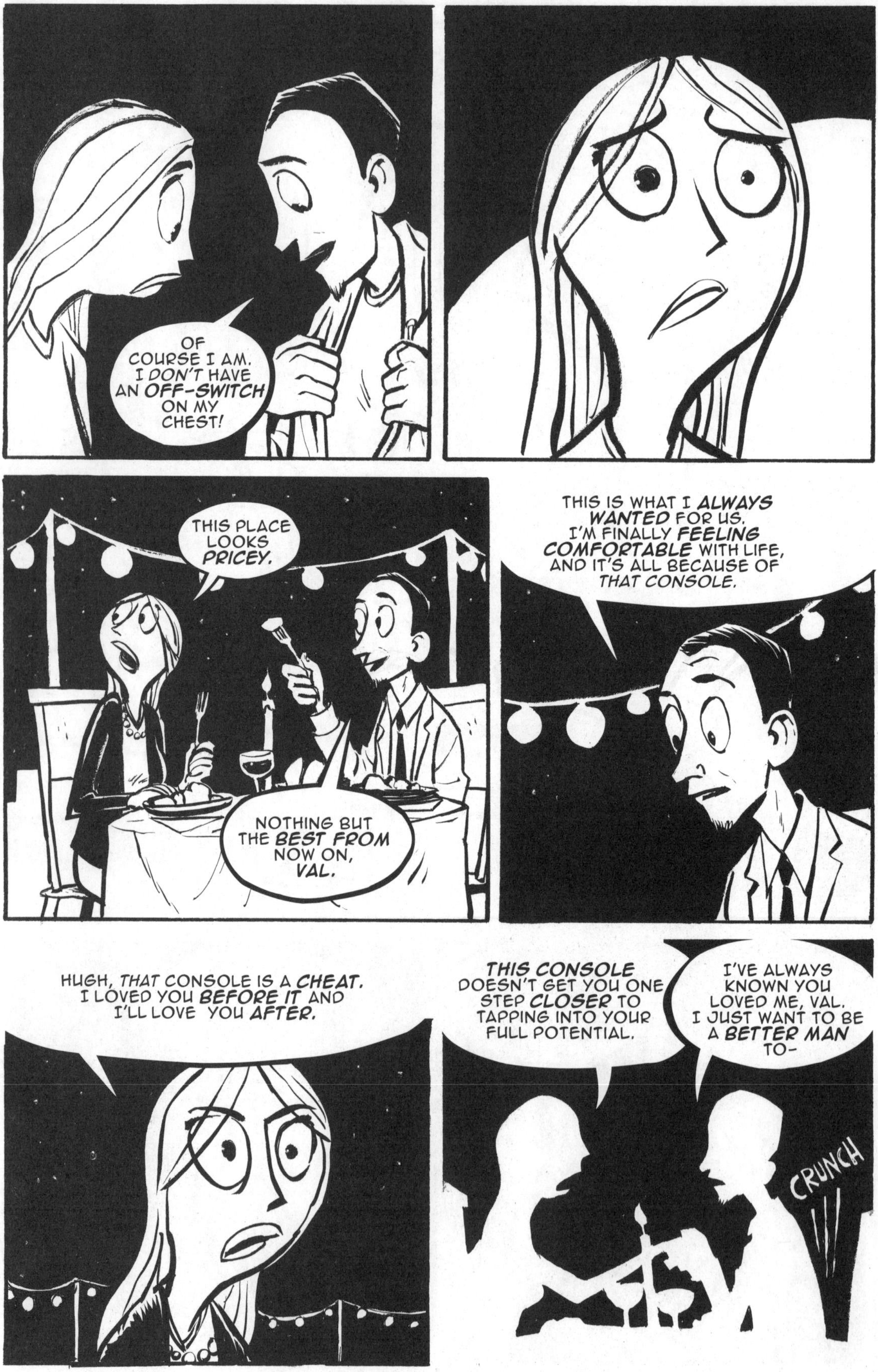
OF COURSE I AM. I DON'T HAVE AN OFF-SWITCH ON MY CHEST!
THIS PLACE LOOKS PRICEY.
NOTHING BUT THE BEST FROM NOW ON, VAL.
THIS IS WHAT I ALWAYS WANTED FOR US. I'M FINALLY FEELING COMFORTABLE WITH LIFE, AND IT'S ALL BECAUSE OF THAT CONSOLE.
HUGH, THAT CONSOLE IS A CHEAT. I LOVED YOU BEFORE IT AND I'LL LOVE YOU AFTER.
THIS CONSOLE DOESN'T GET YOU ONE STEP CLOSER TO TAPPING INTO YOUR FULL POTENTIAL.
I'VE ALWAYS KNOWN YOU LOVED ME, VAL. I JUST WANT TO BE A BETTER MAN TO-
CRUNCH

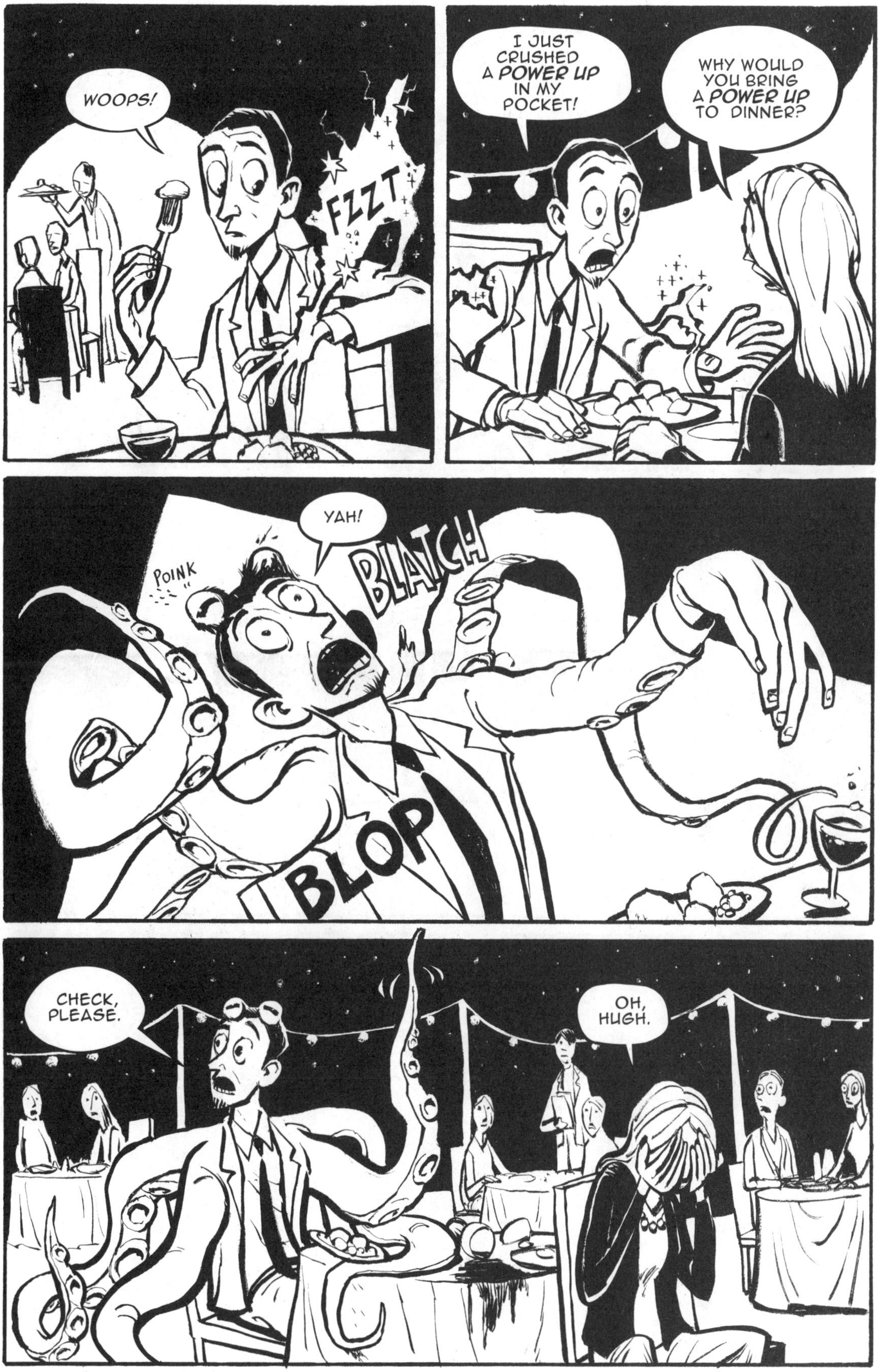
WOOPS!
FZZT
I JUST CRUSHED A POWER UP IN MY POCKET!
WHY WOULD YOU BRING A POWER UP TO DINNER?
YAH!
POINK
BLATCH
BLOP
CHECK, PLEASE.
OH, HUGH.

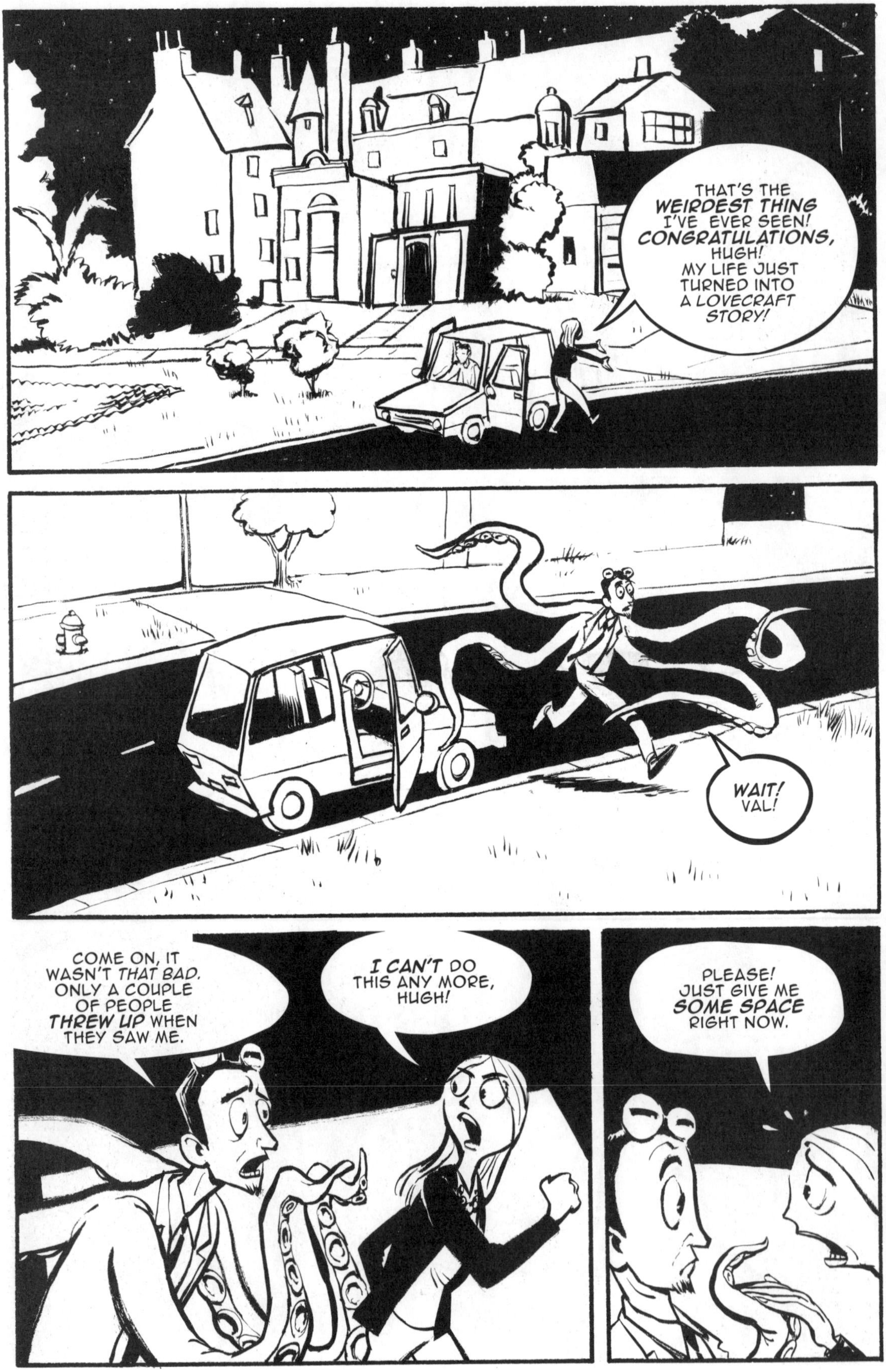
THAT'S THE WEIRDEST THING I'VE EVER SEEN! CONGRATULATIONS, HUGH! MY LIFE JUST TURNED INTO A LOVECRAFT STORY!
WAIT! VAL!
COME ON, IT WASN'T THAT BAD. ONLY A COUPLE OF PEOPLE THREW UP WHEN THEY SAW ME.
I CAN'T DO THIS ANY MORE, HUGH!
PLEASE! JUST GIVE ME SOME SPACE RIGHT NOW.

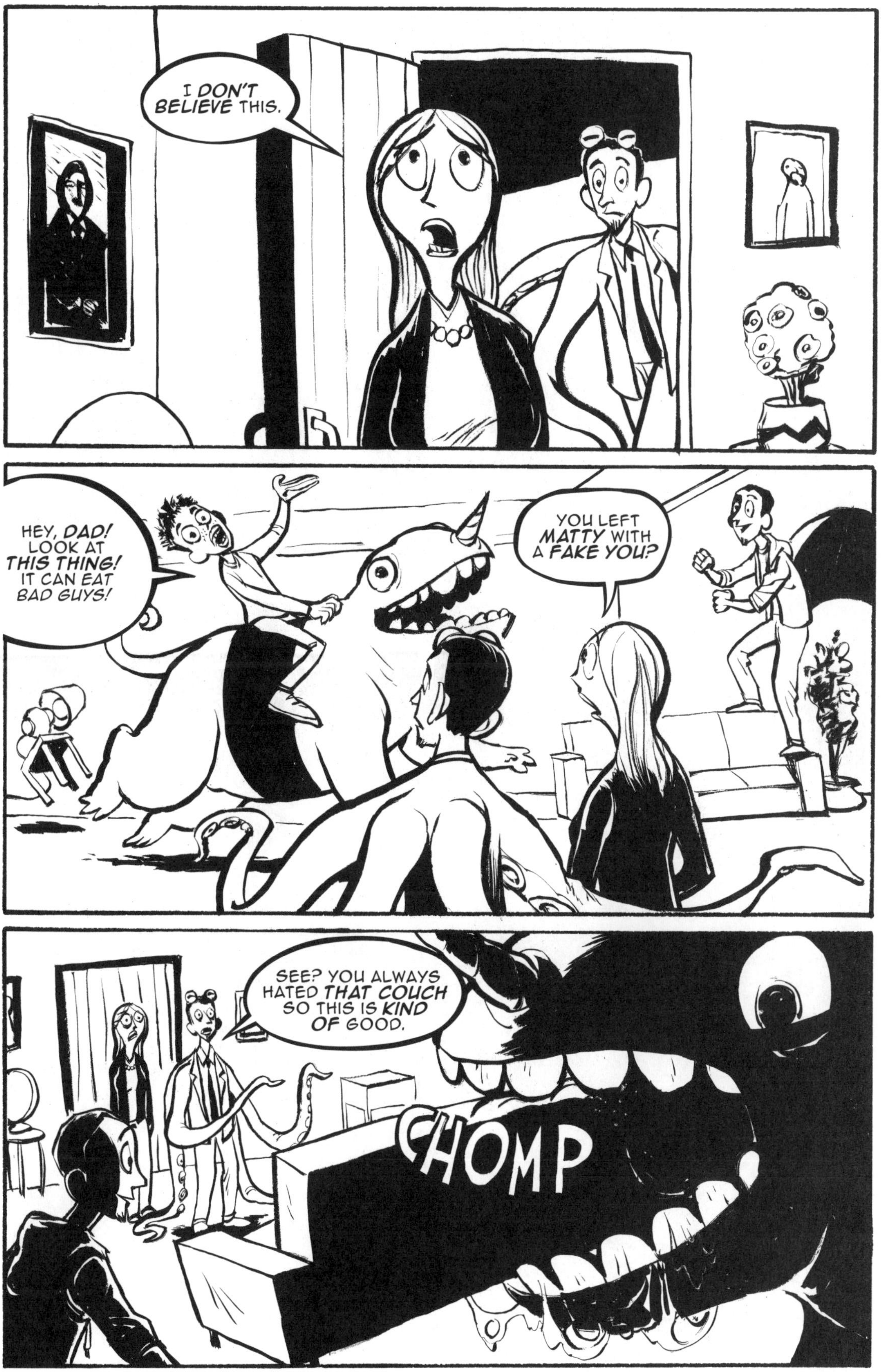
I DON'T BELIEVE THIS.
HEY, DAD! LOOK AT THIS THING! IT CAN EAT BAD GUYS!
YOU LEFT MATTY WITH A FAKE YOU?
SEE? YOU ALWAYS HATED THAT COUCH SO THIS IS KIND OF GOOD.
CHOMP

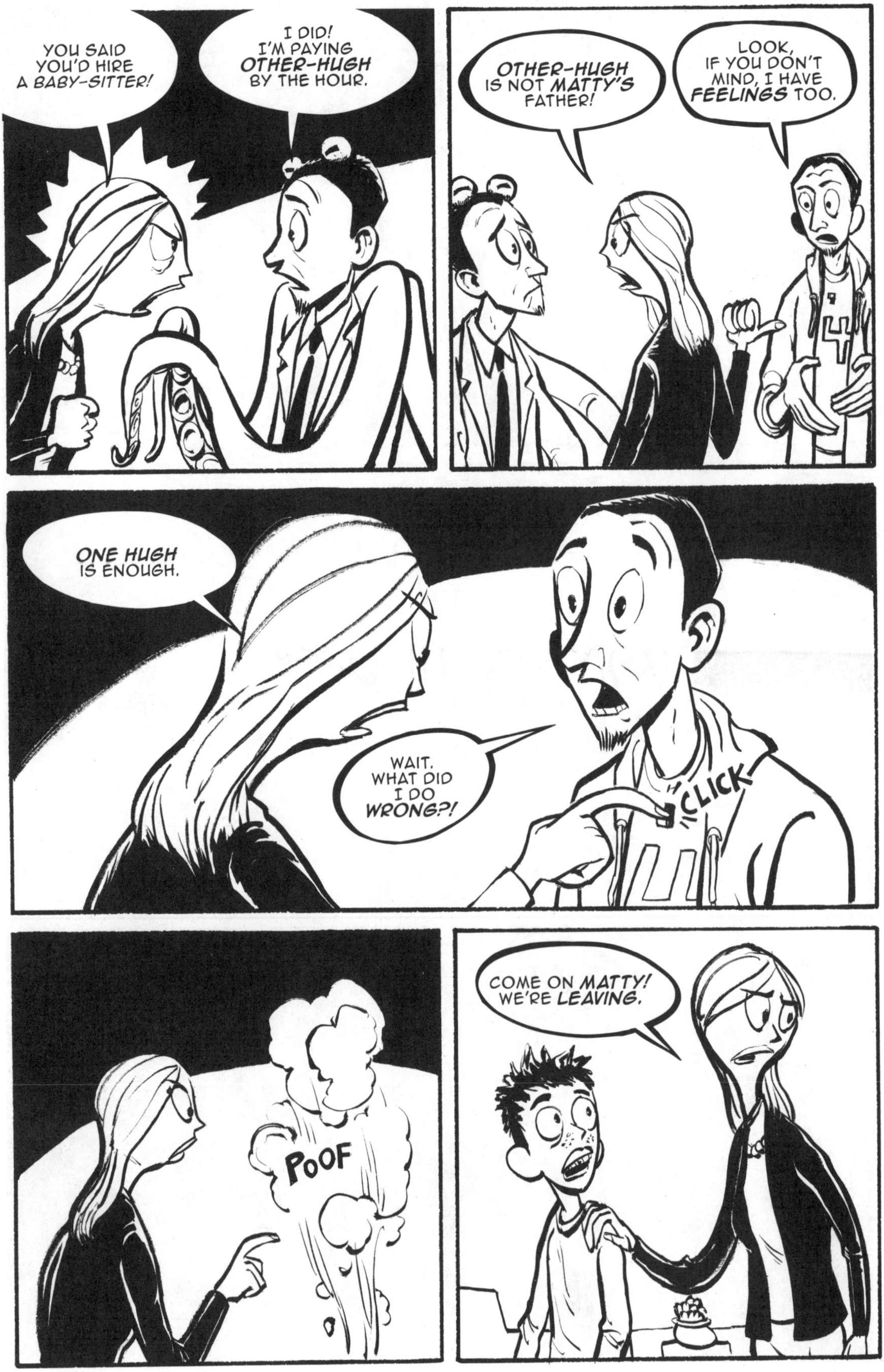
YOU SAID YOU'D HIRE A BABY-SITTER!
I DID! I'M PAYING OTHER-HUGH BY THE HOUR.
OTHER-HUGH IS NOT MATTY'S FATHER!
LOOK, IF YOU DON'T MIND, I HAVE FEELINGS TOO.
ONE HUGH IS ENOUGH.
WAIT. WHAT DID I DO WRONG?!
CLICK
POOF
COME ON MATTY! WE'RE LEAVING.

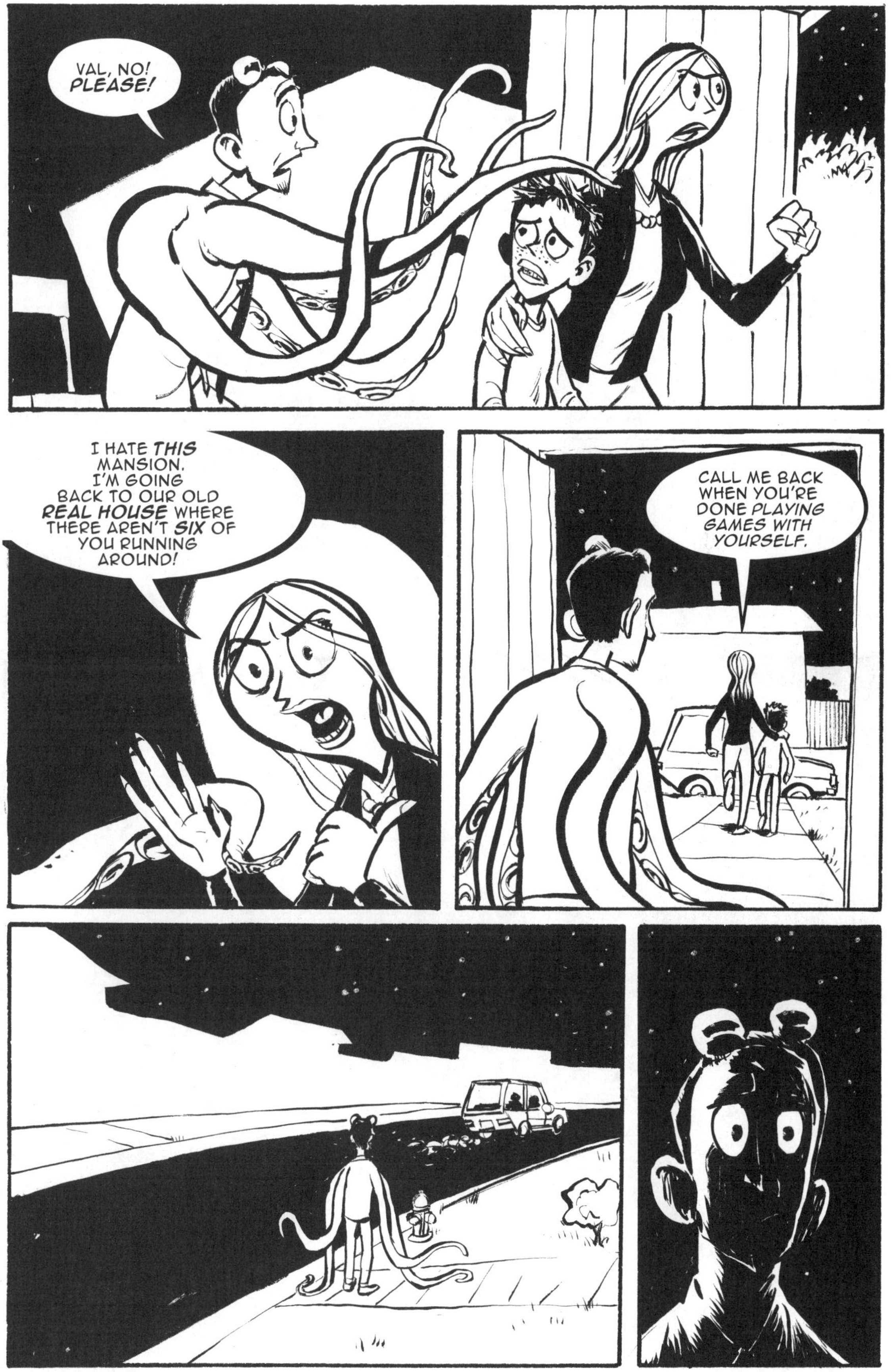
VAL, NO! PLEASE!
I HATE THIS MANSION. I'M GOING BACK TO OUR OLD REAL HOUSE WHERE THERE AREN'T SIX OF YOU RUNNING AROUND!
CALL ME BACK WHEN YOU'RE DONE PLAYING GAMES WITH YOURSELF.

ALL WHO CHALLENGE LORD DOOMUS MUST PERISH!

FLIP

BLOOP

RRRAAH!

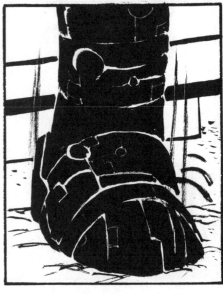

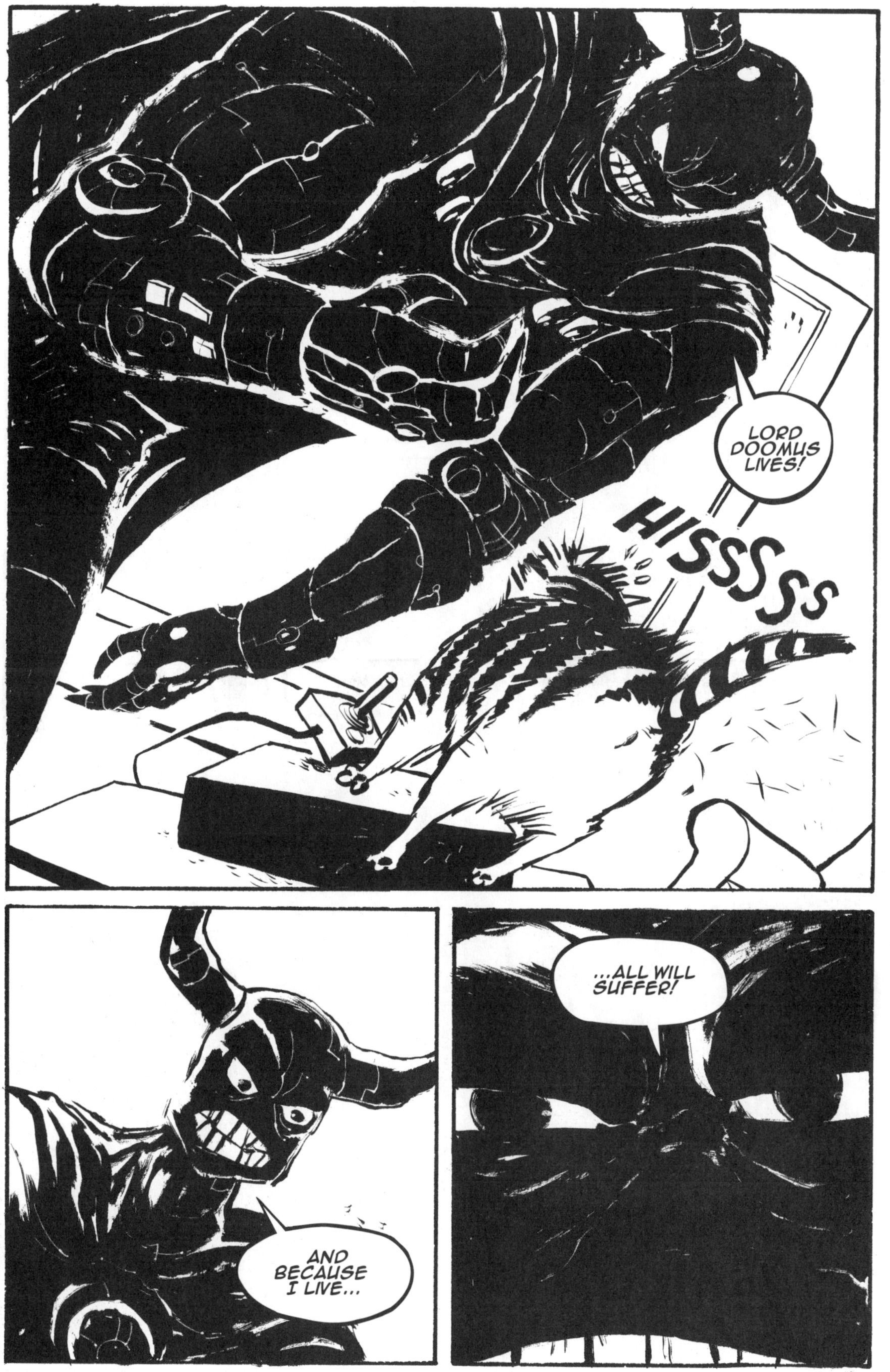
LORD DOOMUS LIVES!
HISSSSS
AND BECAUSE I LIVE...
...ALL WILL SUFFER!

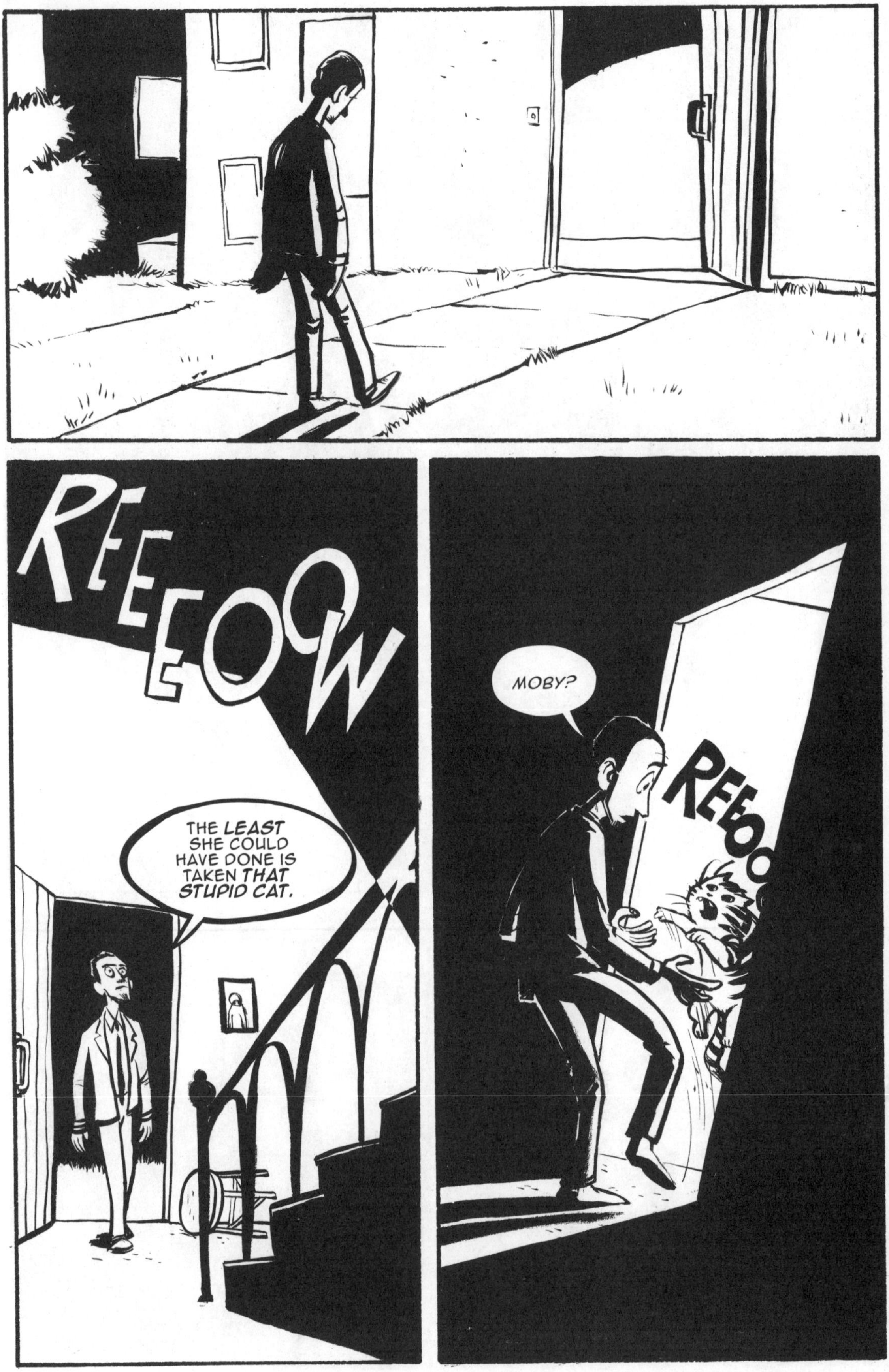
REEEOOW
THE LEAST SHE COULD HAVE DONE IS TAKEN THAT STUPID CAT.
MOBY?
REEOO

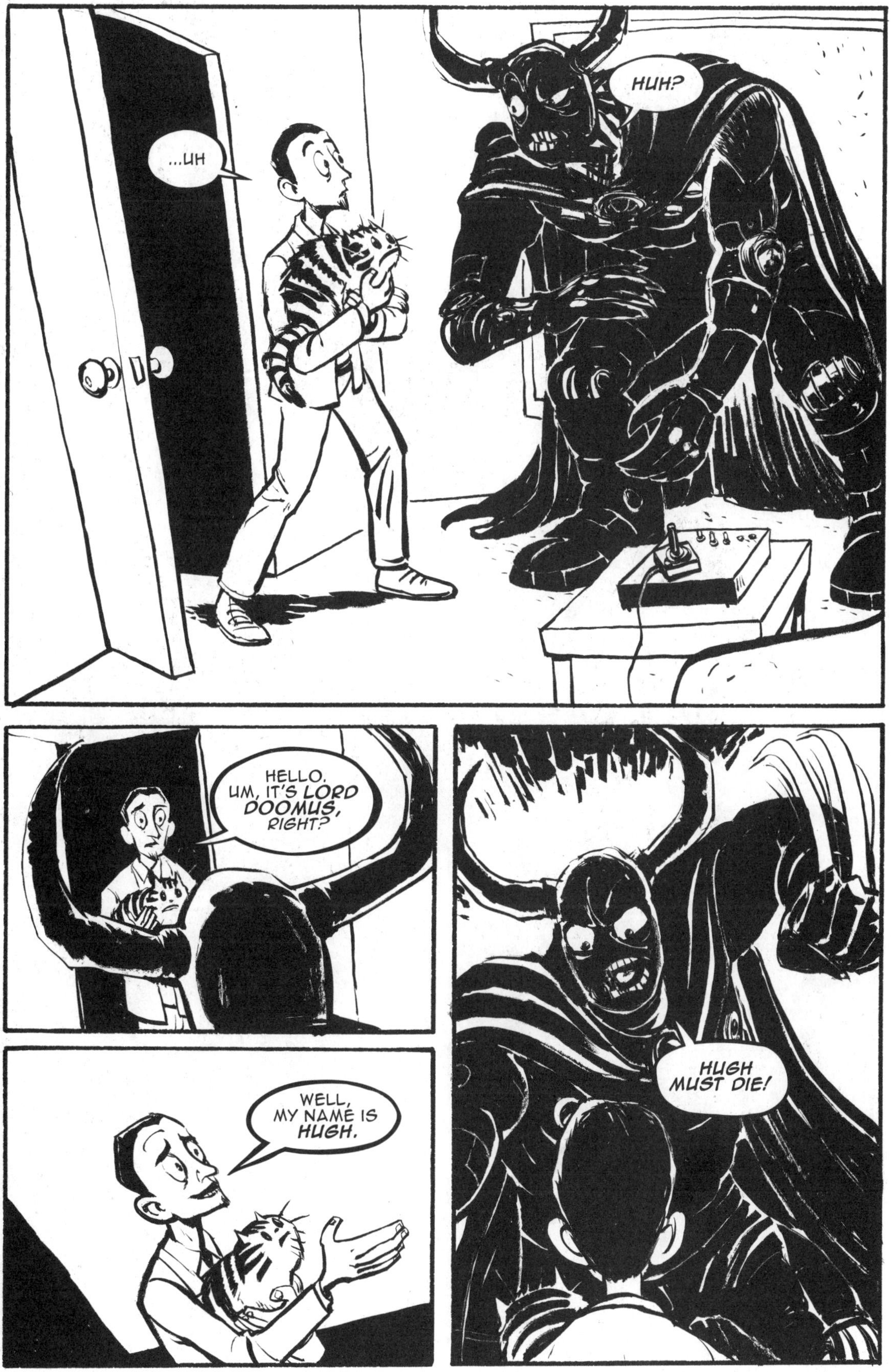
...UH
HUH?
HELLO. UM, IT'S LORD DOOMUS, RIGHT?
WELL, MY NAME IS HUGH.
HUGH MUST DIE!

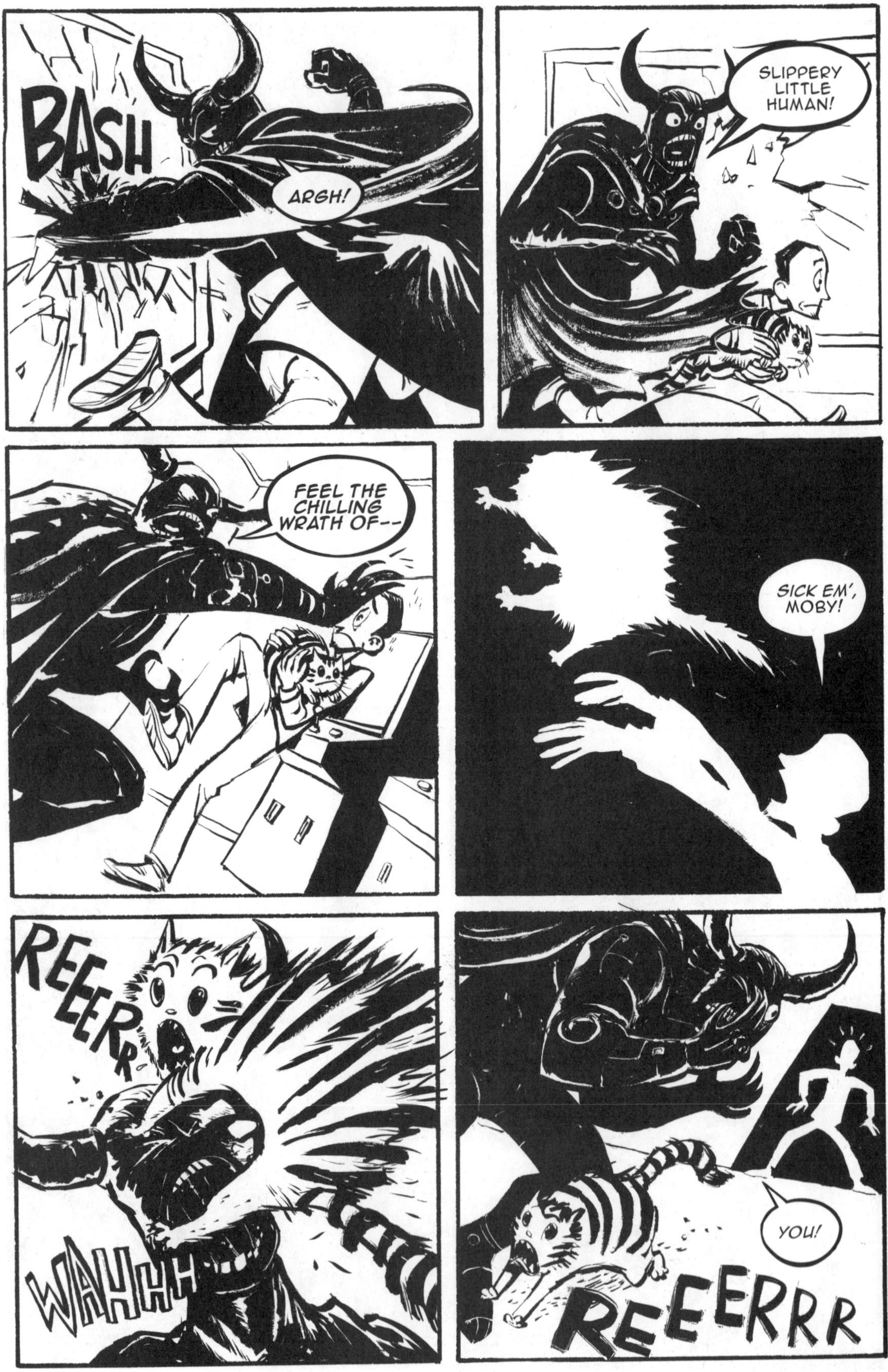
BASH
ARGH!
SLIPPERY LITTLE HUMAN!
FEEL THE CHILLING WRATH OF--
SICK EM', MOBY!
REEERRR
WAHHH
YOU!
REEERRRR

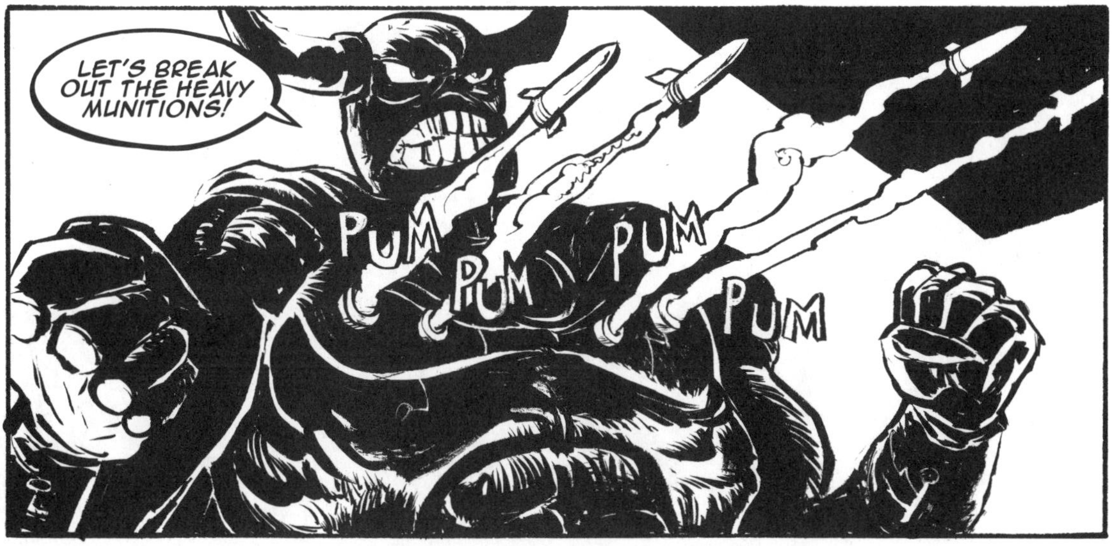
LET'S BREAK OUT THE HEAVY MUNITIONS!
PUM
PUM
PUM
PUM

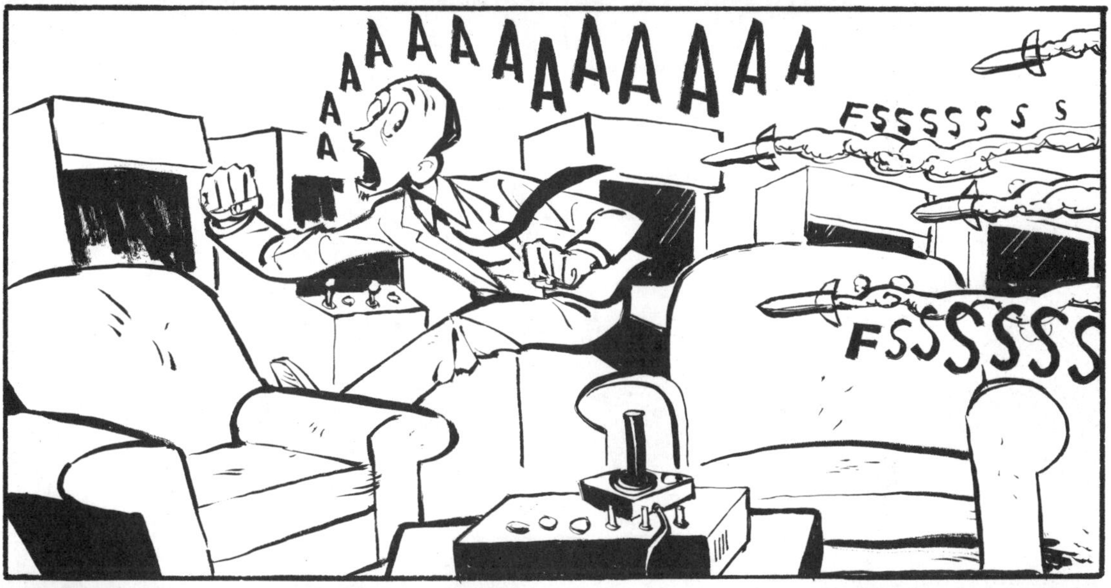
AAAAAAAAAAAAAA
FSSSSSSS
FSSSSSS

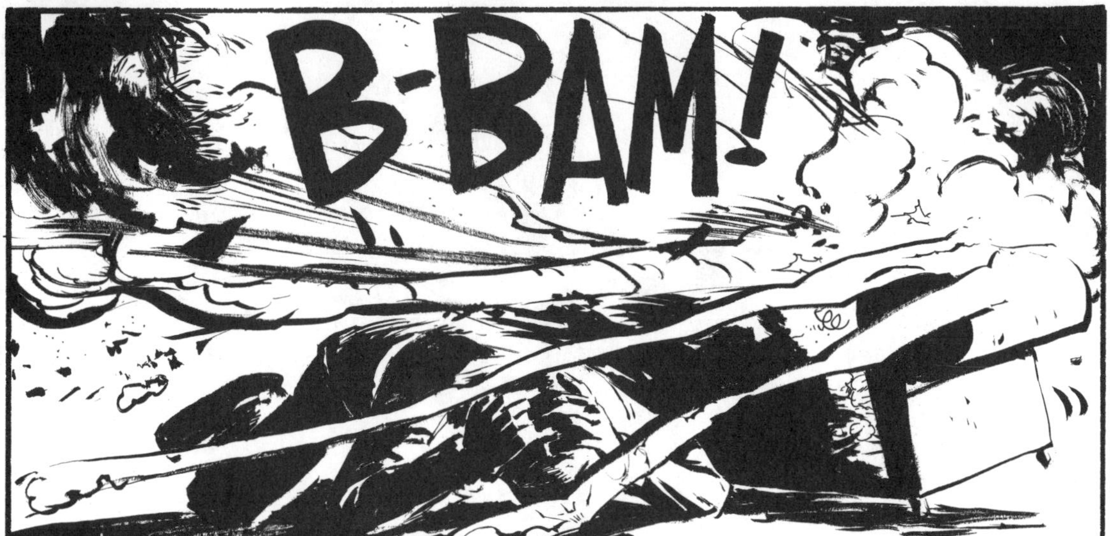
B-BAM!

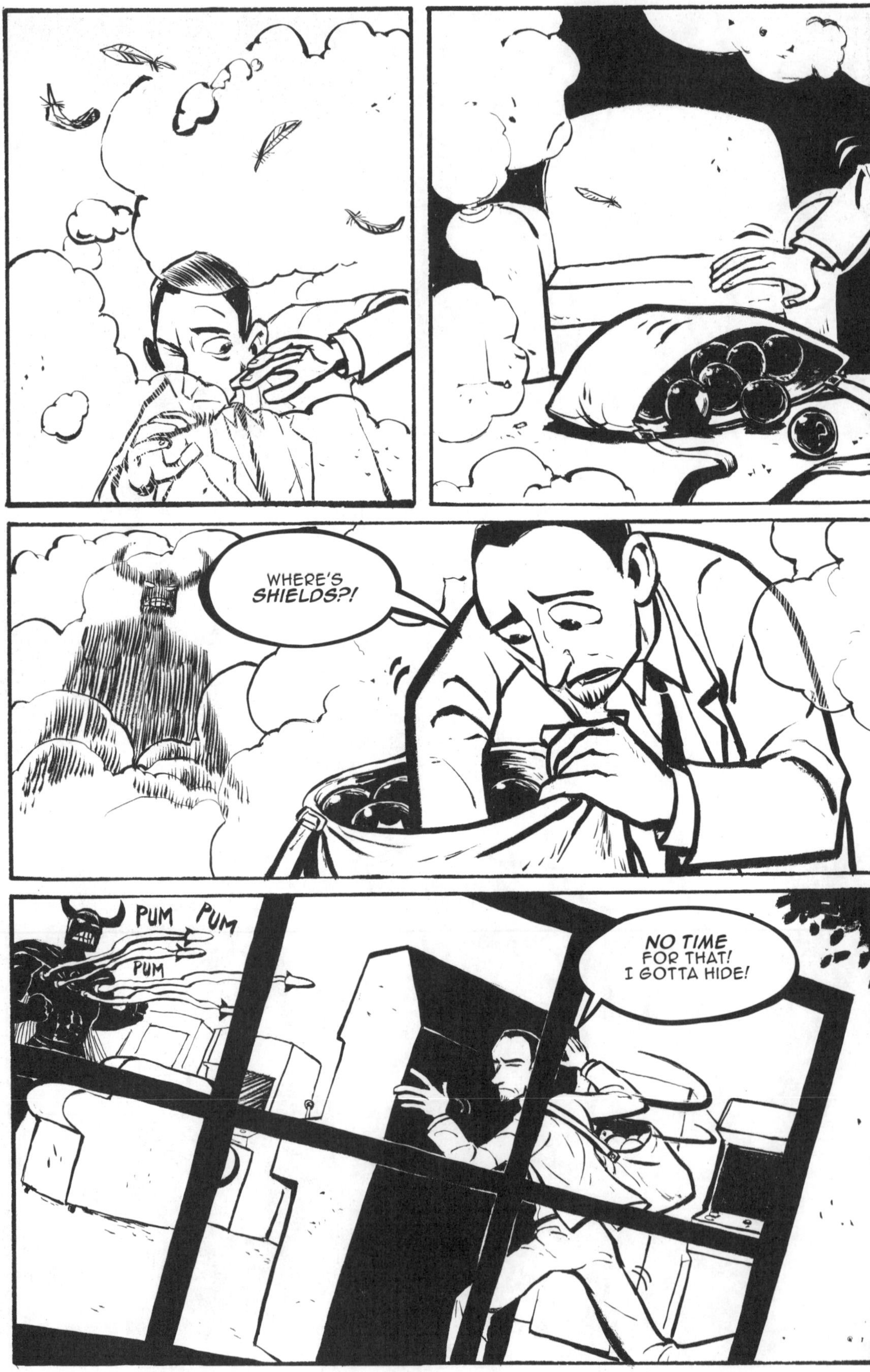
WHERE'S SHIELDS?!
PUM PUM
PUM
NO TIME FOR THAT! I GOTTA HIDE!

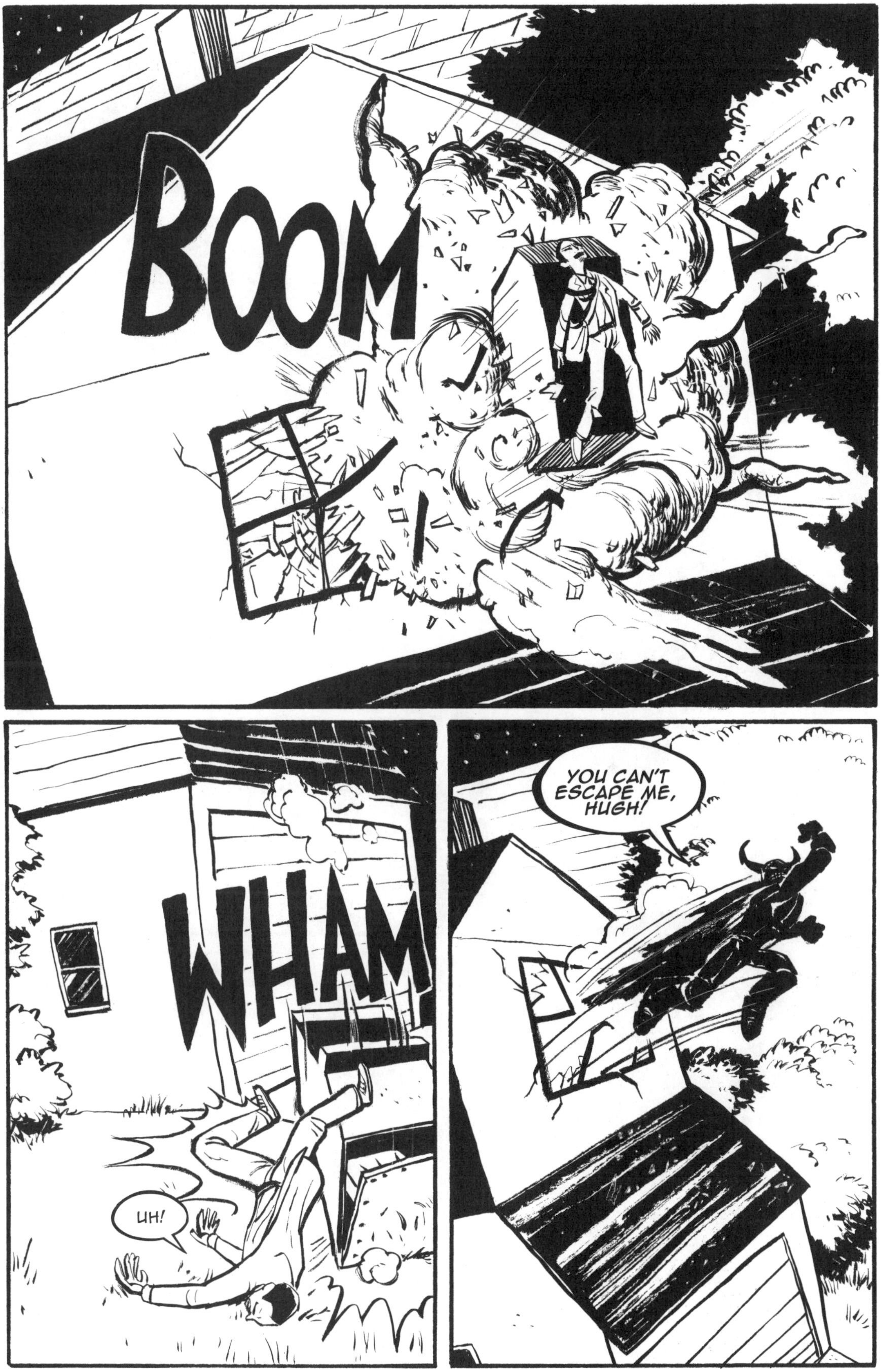
BOOM
WHAM
UH!
YOU CAN'T ESCAPE ME, HUGH!

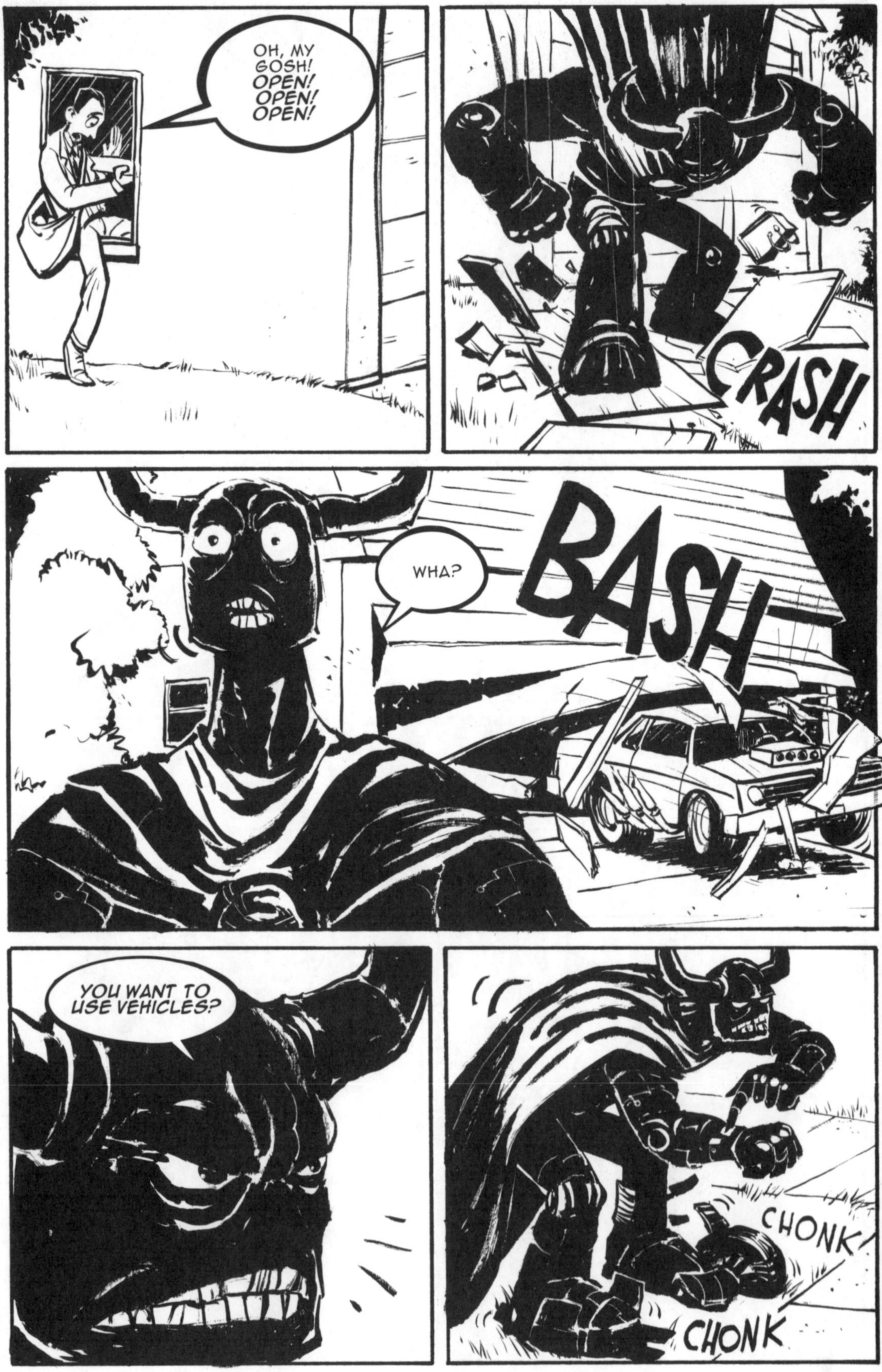

OH, MY GOSH! OPEN! OPEN! OPEN!
CRASH
WHA?
BASH
YOU WANT TO USE VEHICLES?
CHONK
CHONK

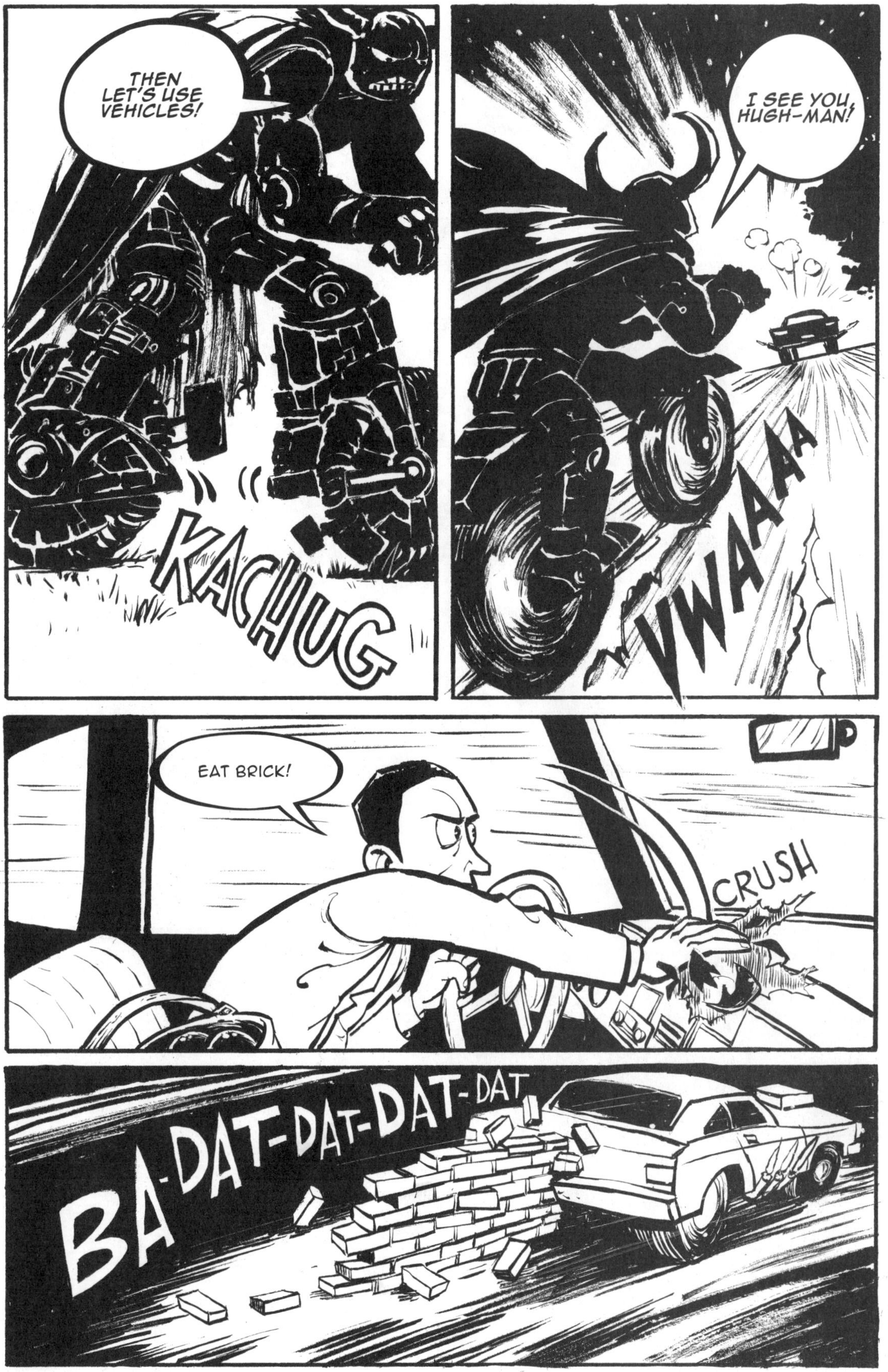

THEN LET'S USE VEHICLES!
KACHUG
I SEE YOU, HUGH-MAN!
VWAAAA
EAT BRICK!
CRUSH
BA-DAT-DAT-DAT-DAT

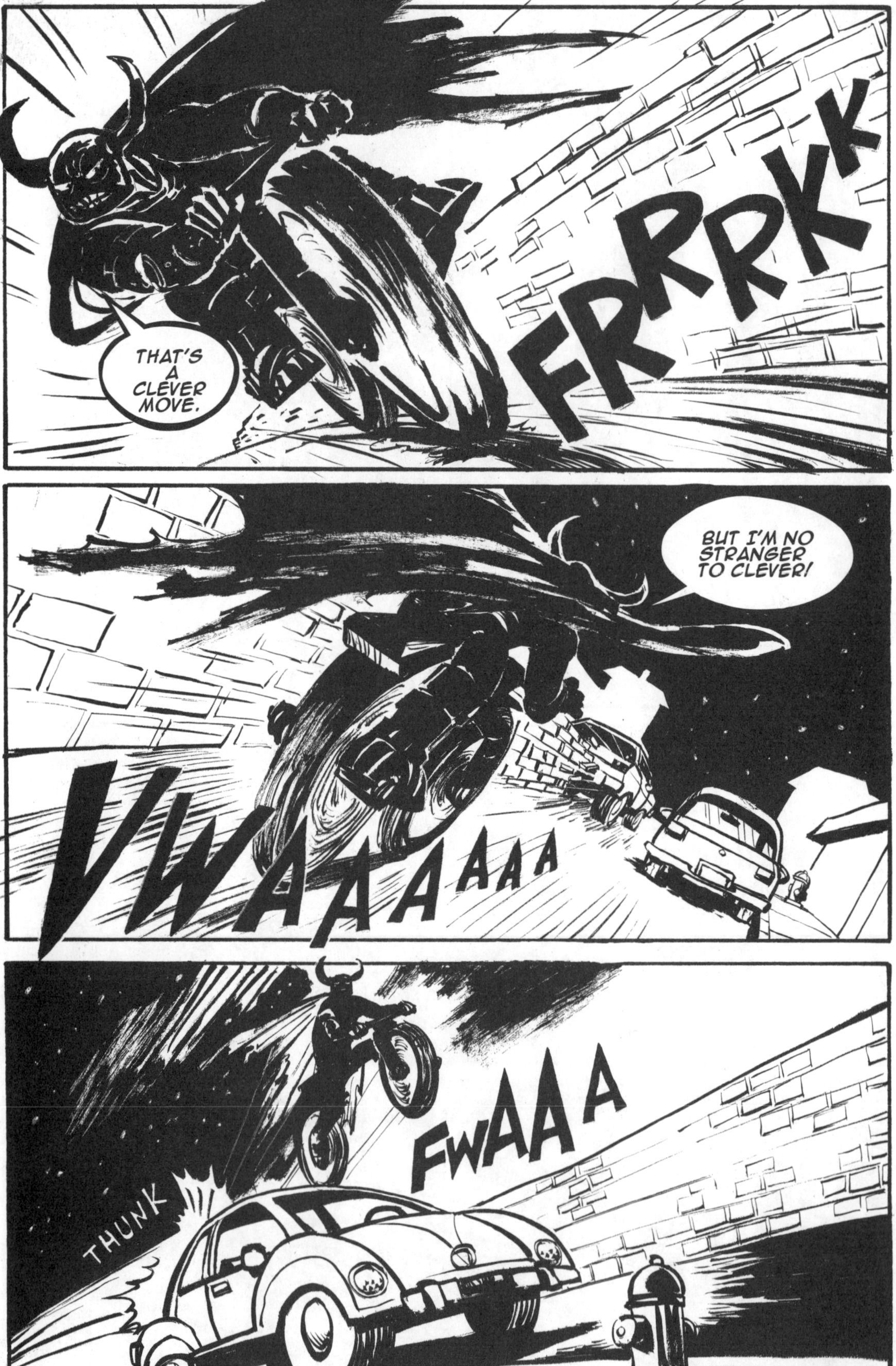
THAT'S A CLEVER MOVE.
FRRRKK
BUT I'M NO STRANGER TO CLEVER!
VWAAAAAAA
FWAAAA
THUNK

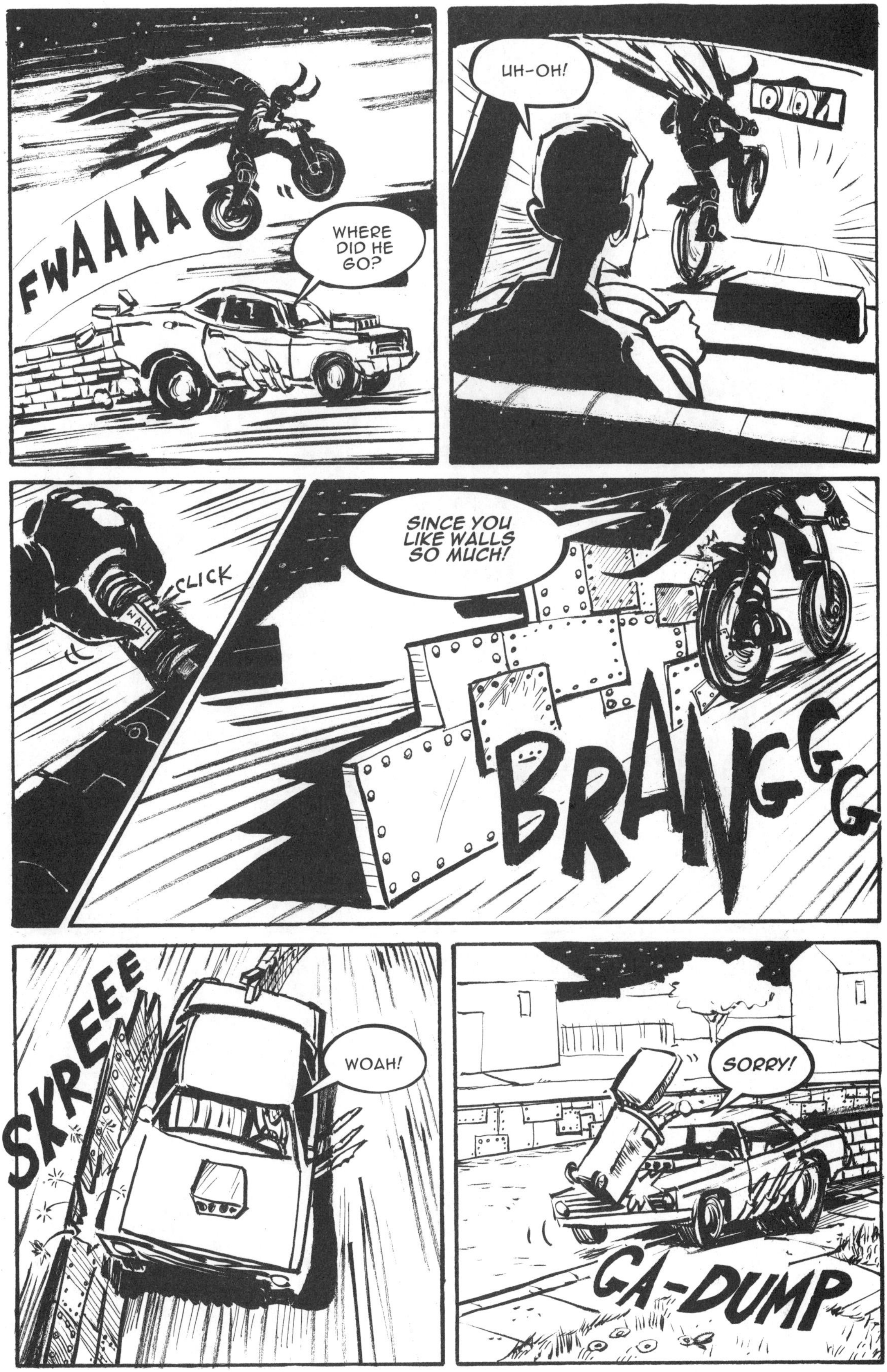
FWAAAA
WHERE DID HE GO?
UH-OH!
SINCE YOU LIKE WALLS SO MUCH!
CLICK
WALL
BRANGGG
SKREEEE
WOAH!
SORRY!
GA-DUMP

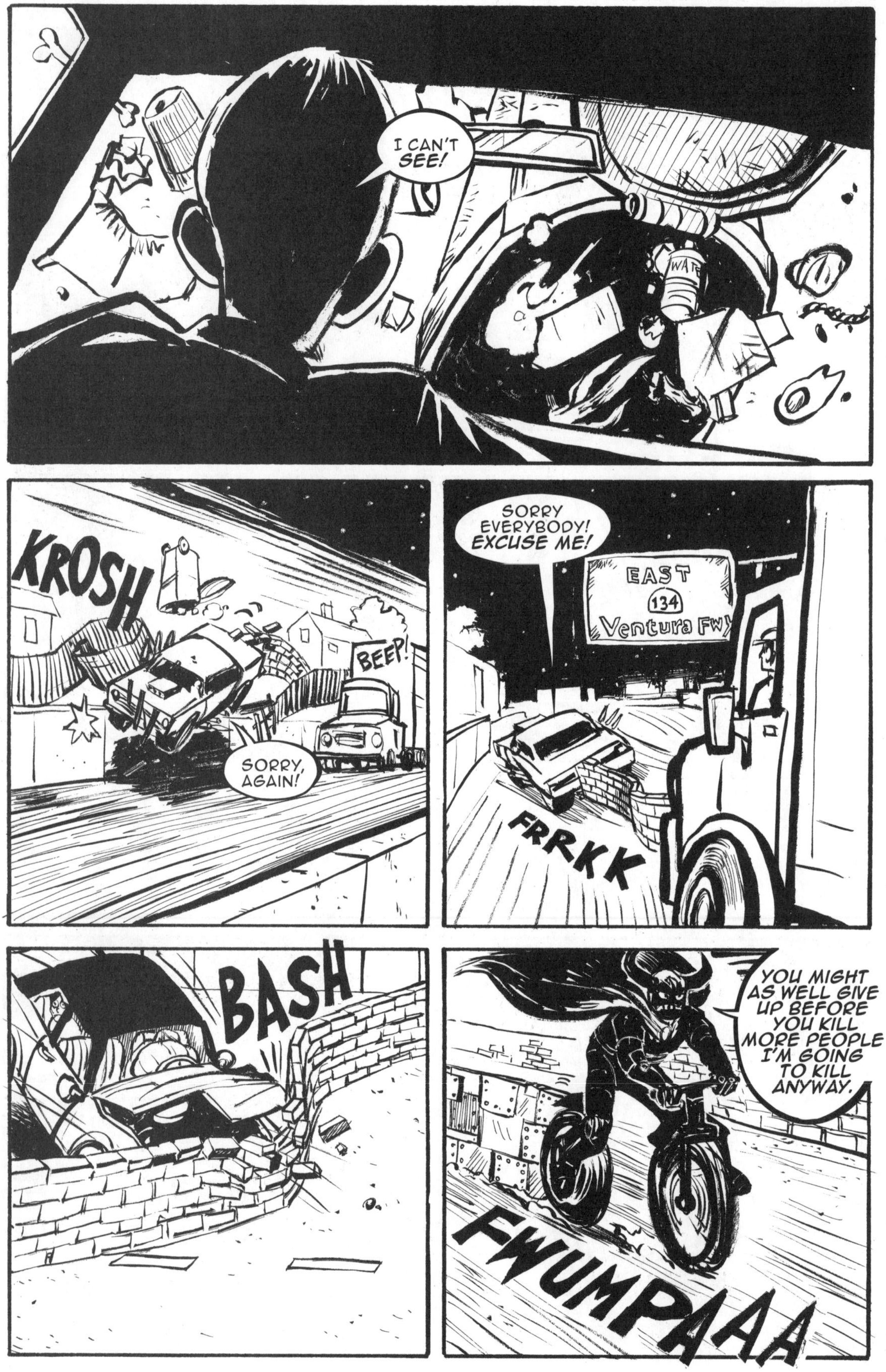
I CAN'T SEE!
KROSH
BEEP!
SORRY, AGAIN!
SORRY EVERYBODY! EXCUSE ME!
EAST
134
Ventura Fwy
FRRKK
BASH
YOU MIGHT AS WELL GIVE UP BEFORE YOU KILL MORE PEOPLE I'M GOING TO KILL ANYWAY.
FWUMPAAA

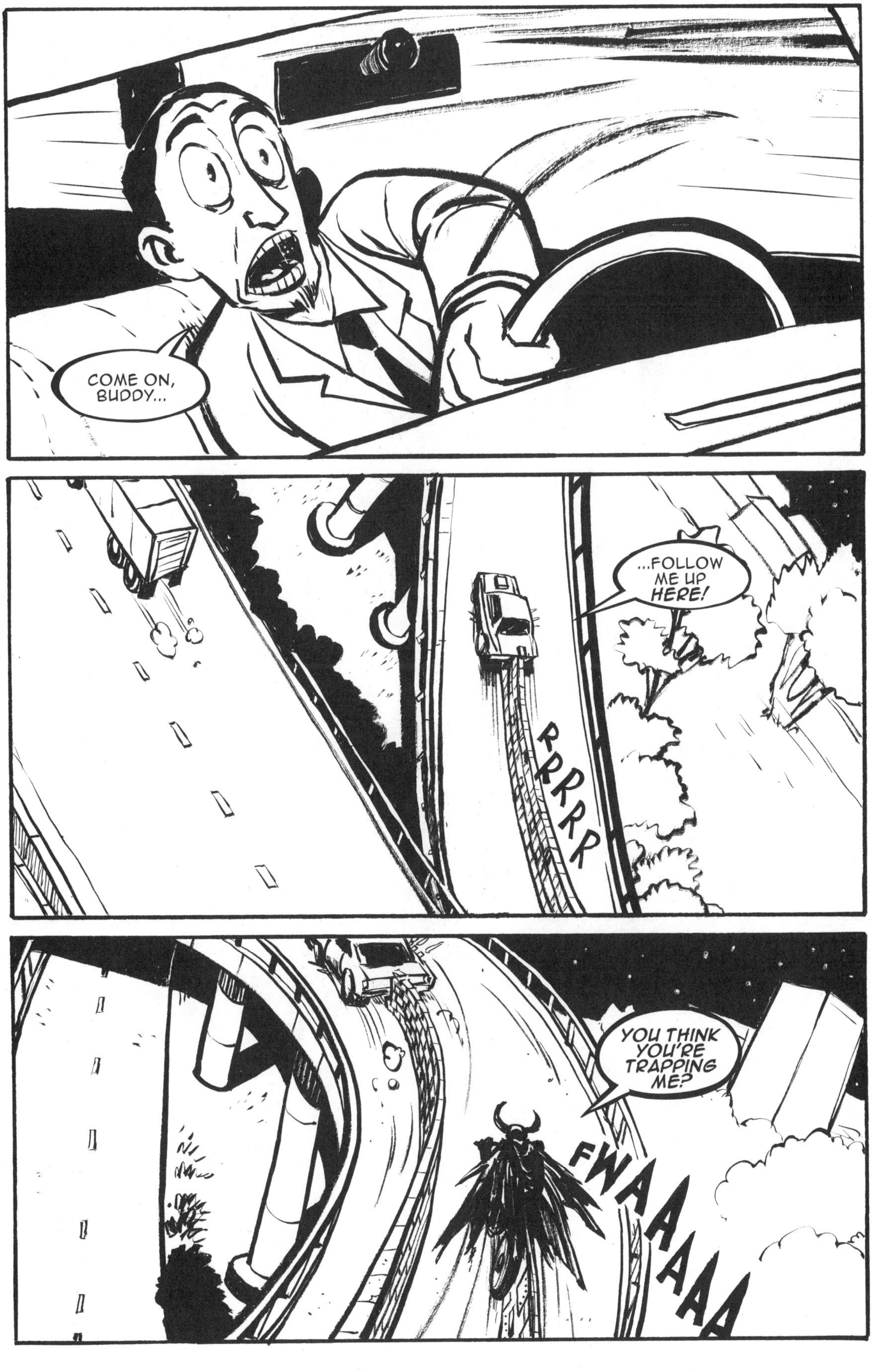

COME ON, BUDDY...
...FOLLOW ME UP HERE!
RRRRR
YOU THINK YOU'RE TRAPPING ME?
FWAAAAAA

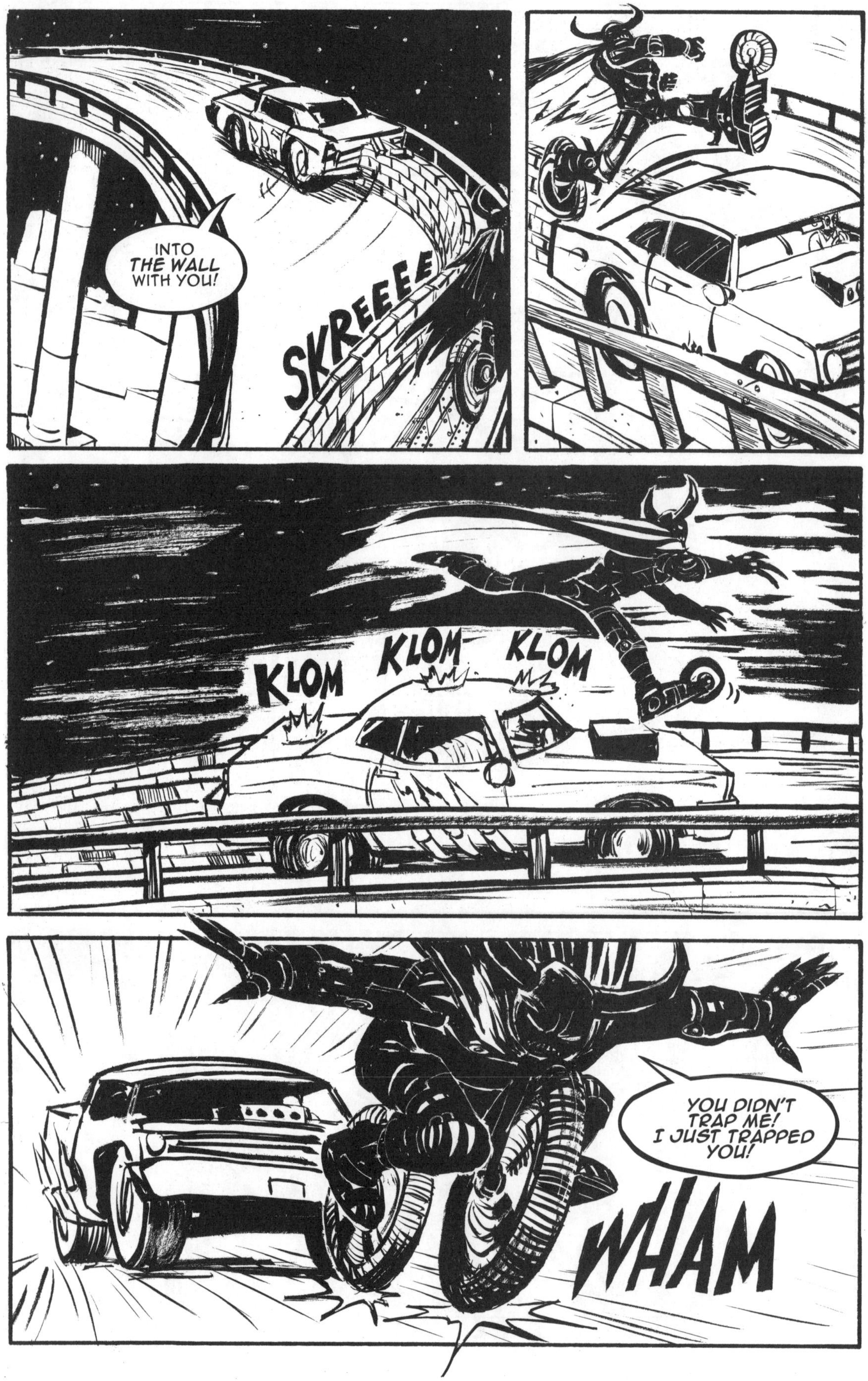
INTO *THE WALL* WITH YOU!
SKREEEEE
KLOM
KLOM
KLOM
YOU DIDN'T TRAP ME! I JUST TRAPPED YOU!
WHAM

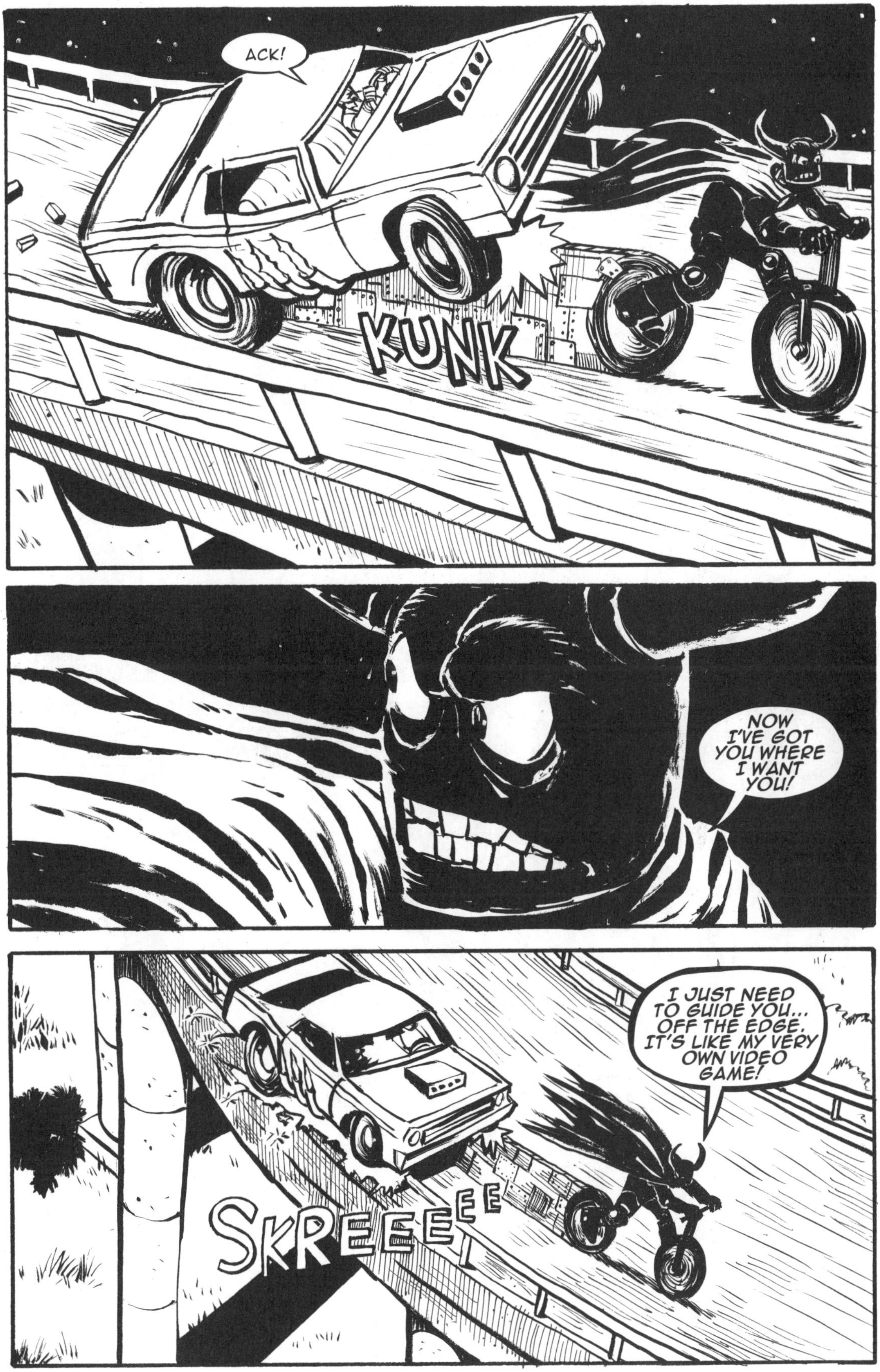
ACK!
KUNK
NOW I'VE GOT YOU WHERE I WANT YOU!
I JUST NEED TO GUIDE YOU... OFF THE EDGE. IT'S LIKE MY VERY OWN VIDEO GAME!
SKREEEEE

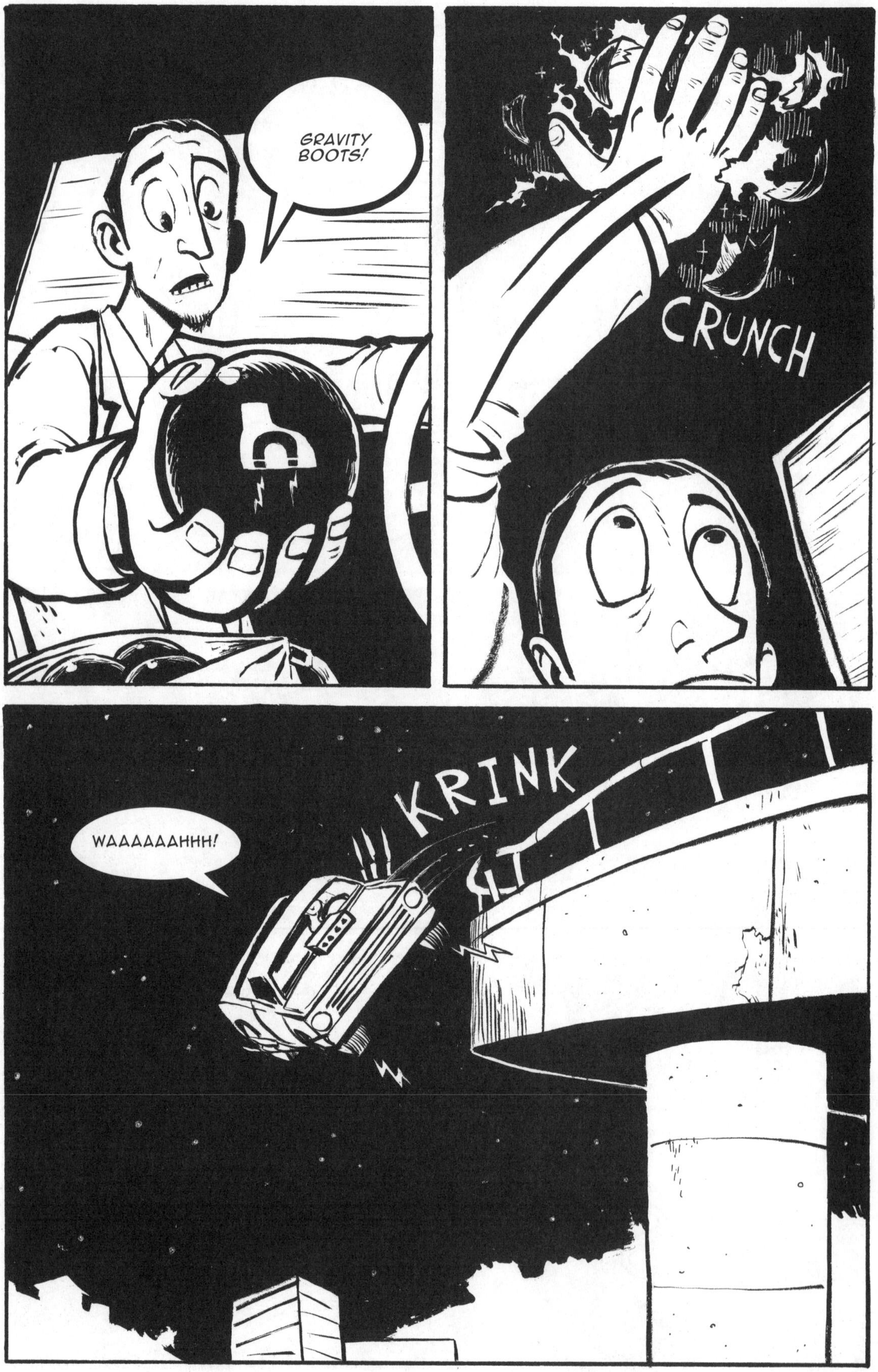
GRAVITY BOOTS!
CRUNCH
KRINK
WAAAAAAHHH!

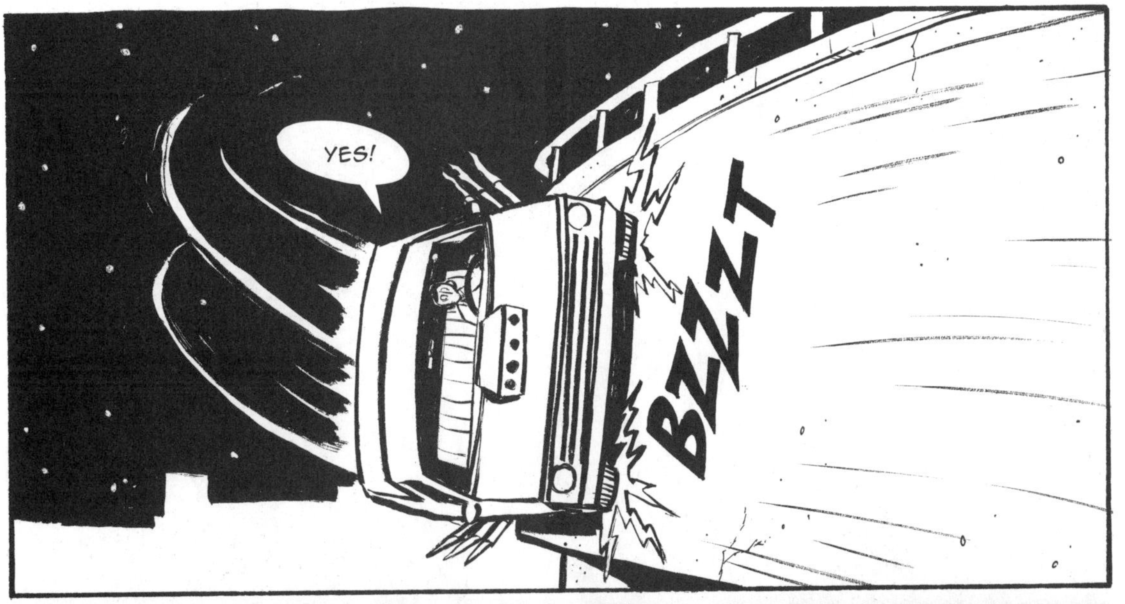
YES!
BZZZT

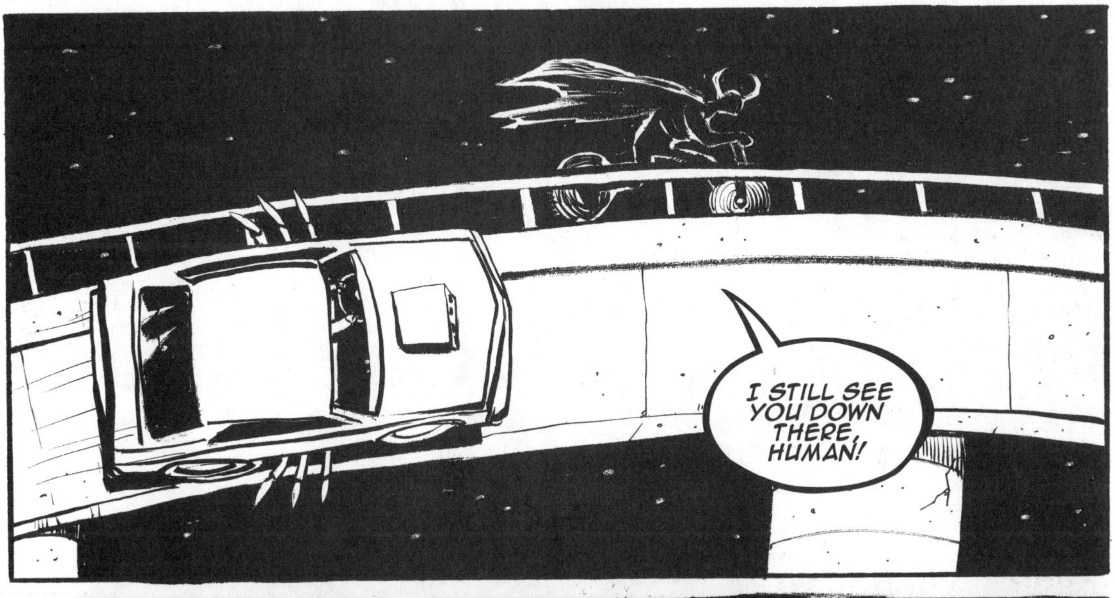
I STILL SEE YOU DOWN THERE, HUMAN!

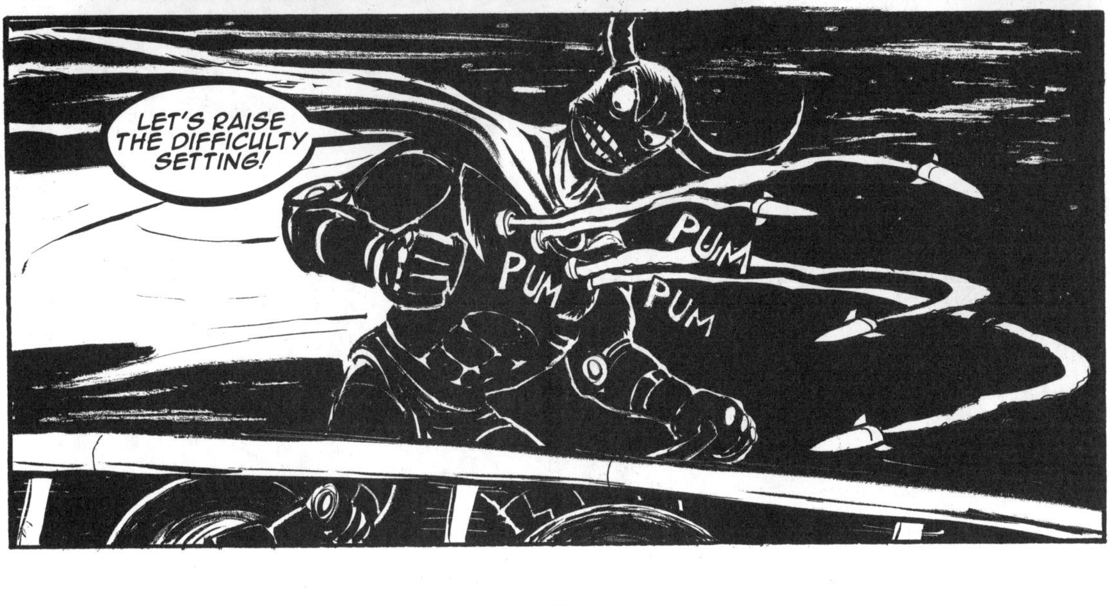
LET'S RAISE THE DIFFICULTY SETTING!
PUM
PUM
PUM
PUM

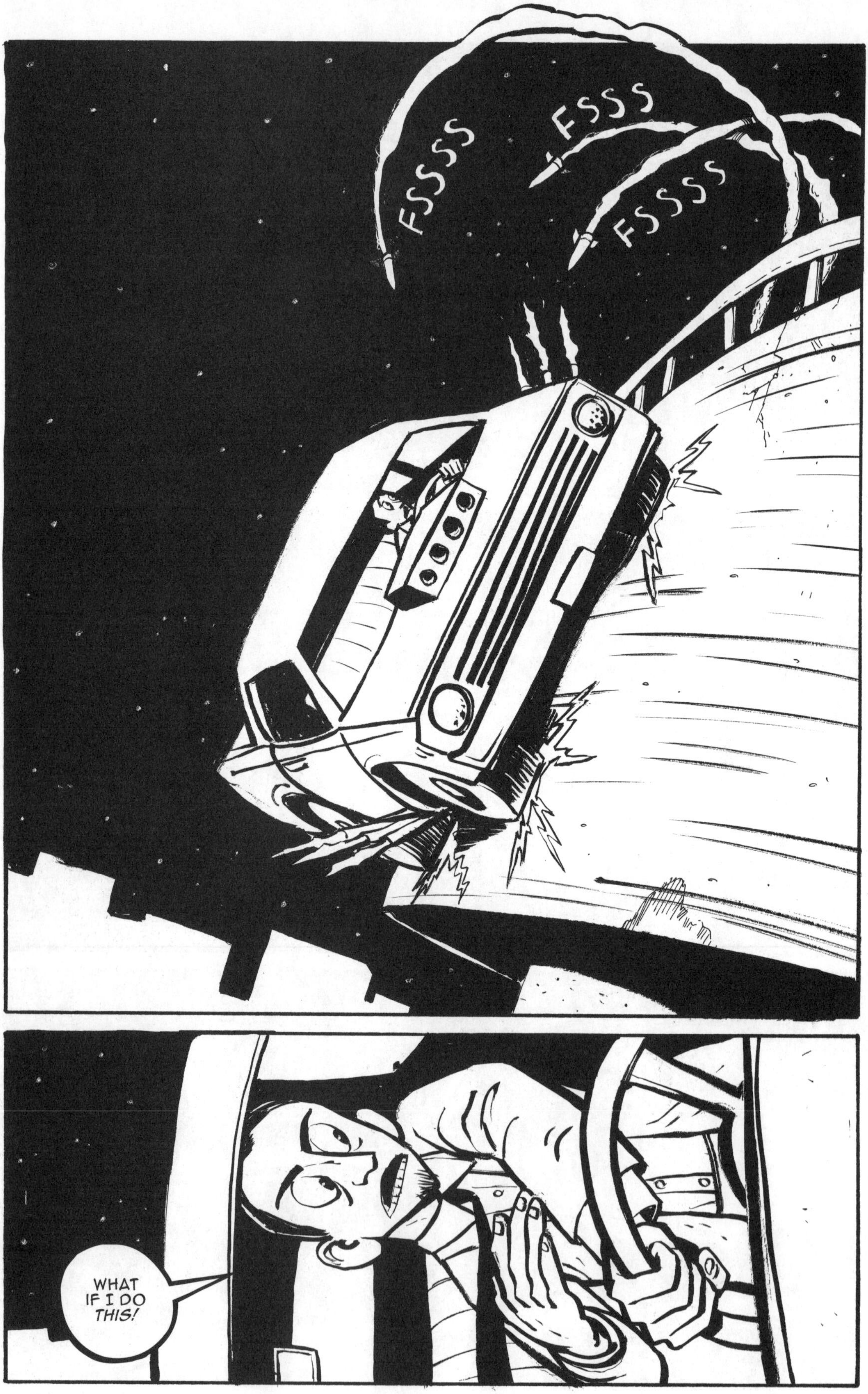
FSSSS
FSSS
FSSSS
WHAT IF I DO THIS!

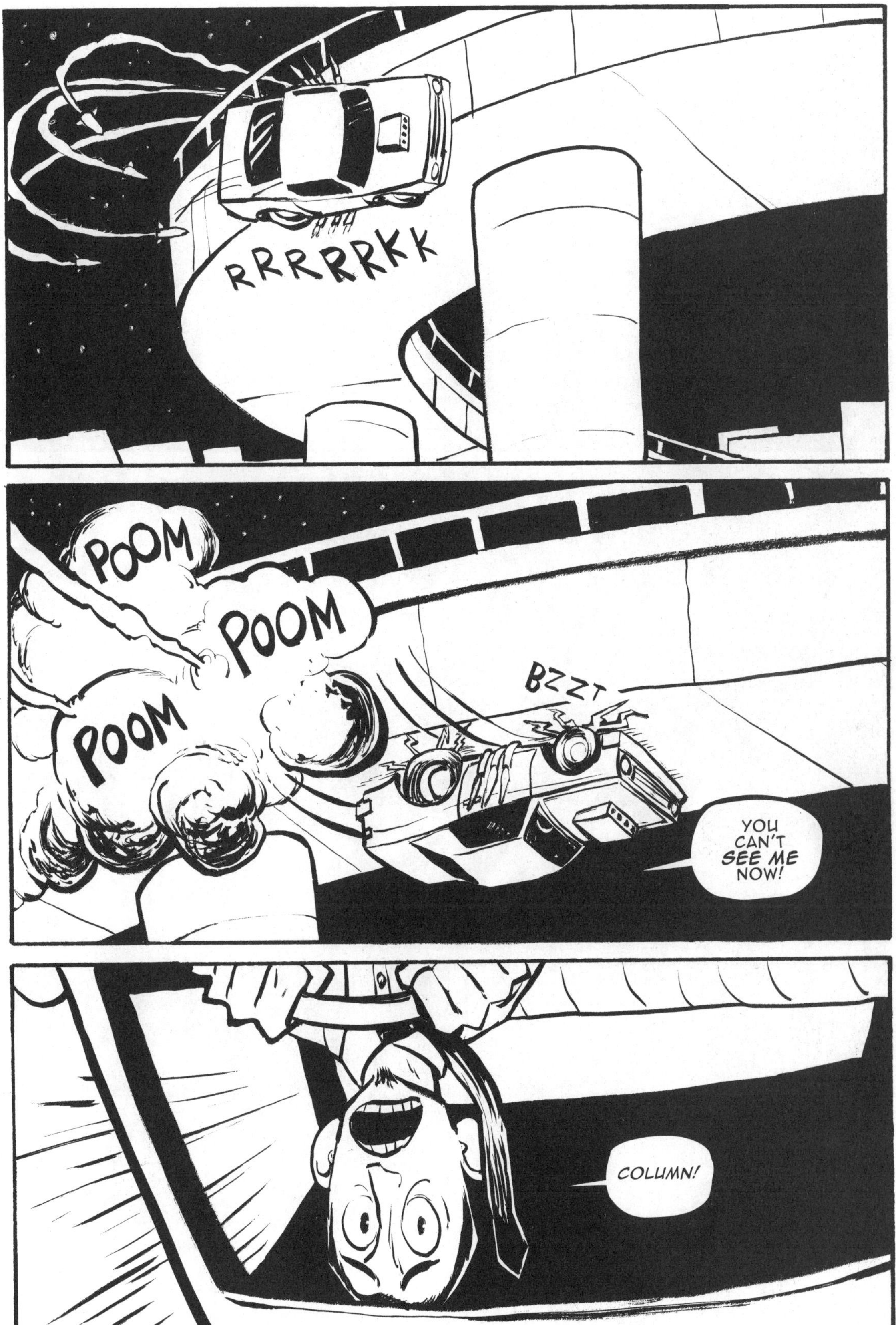
RRRRRKK
POOM
POOM
POOM
BZZT
YOU CAN'T SEE ME NOW!
COLUMN!

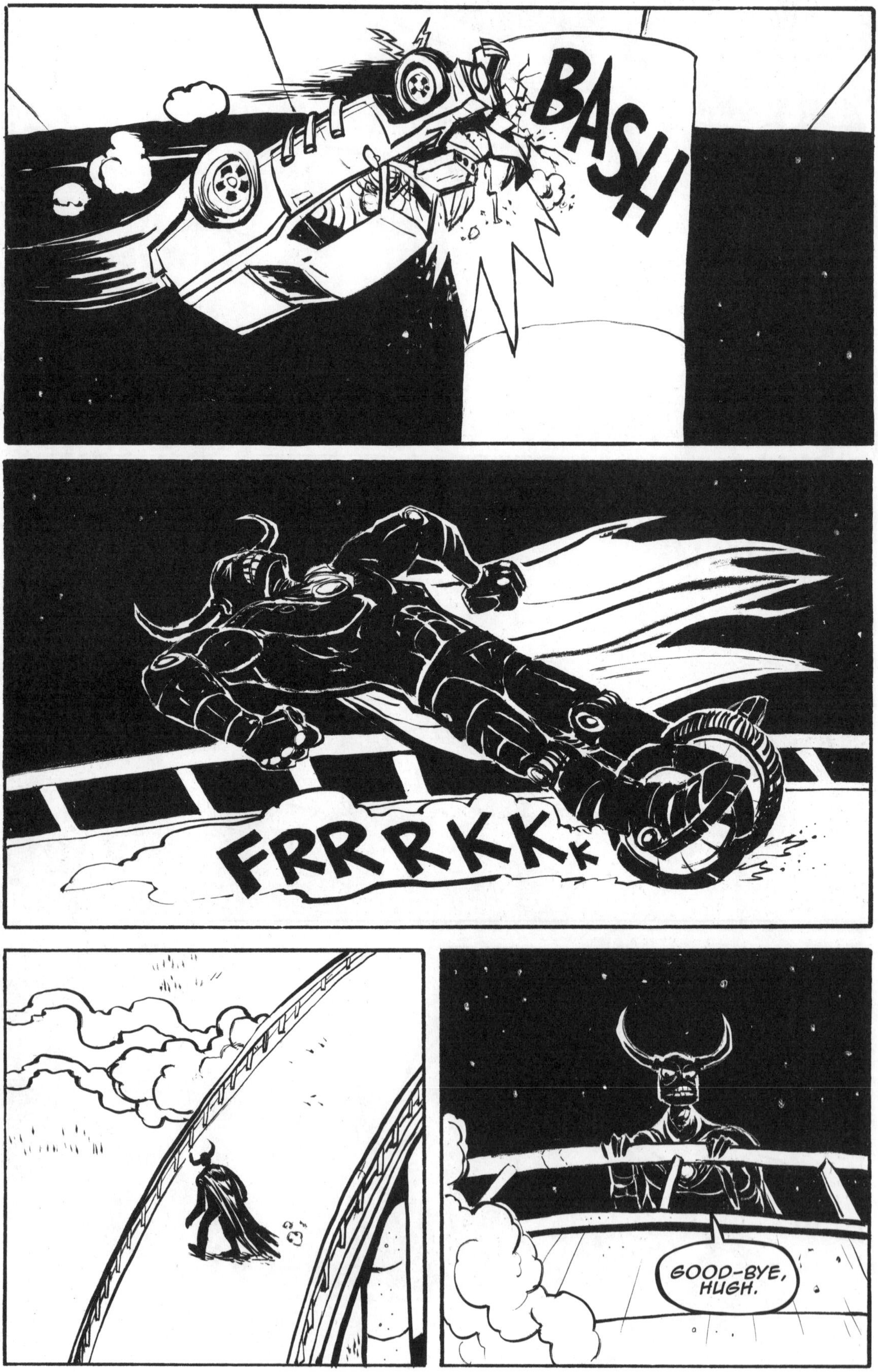
BASH
FRRRKKK
GOOD-BYE, HUGH.

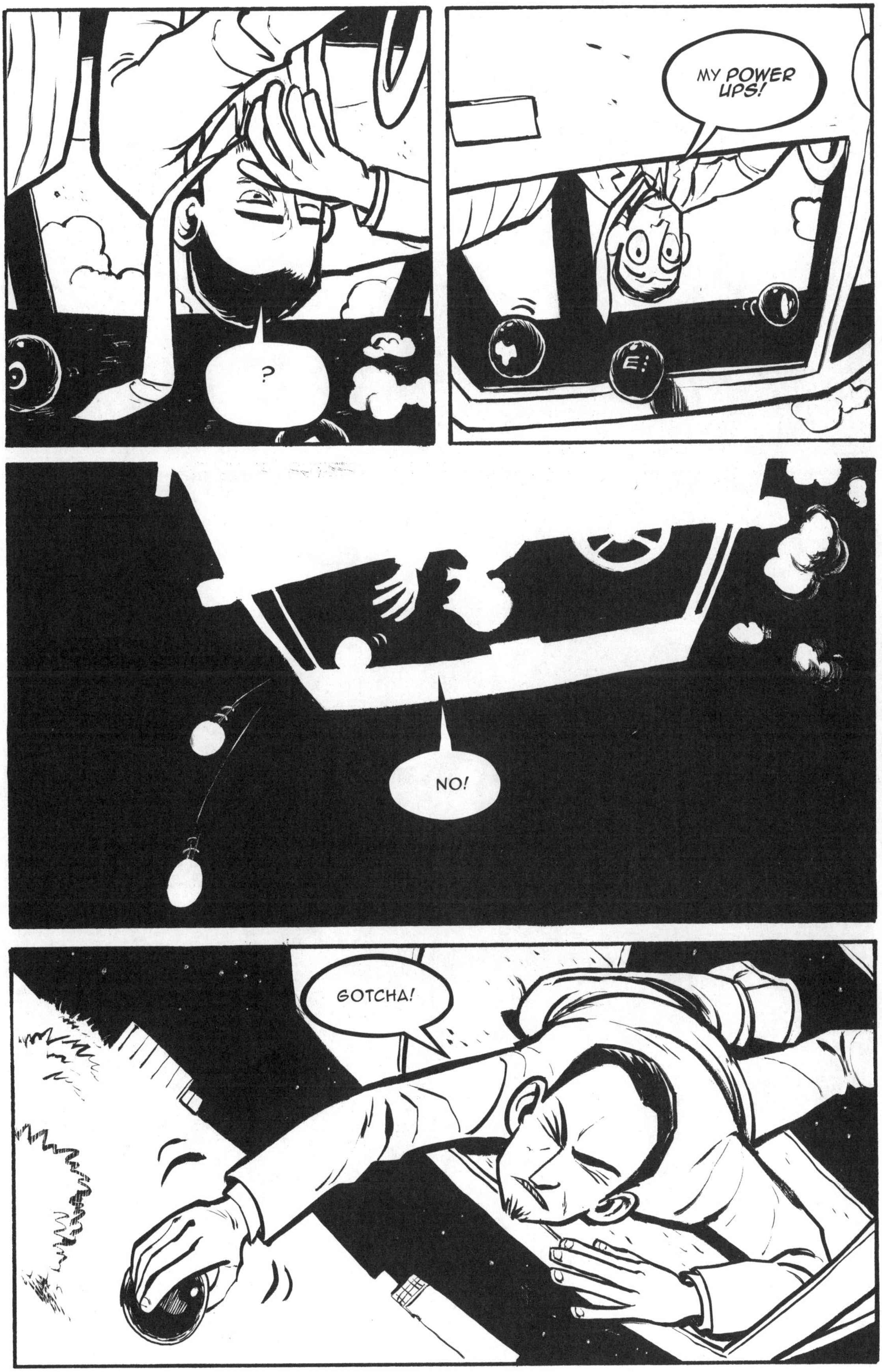
?
MY POWER UPS!
NO!
GOTCHA!

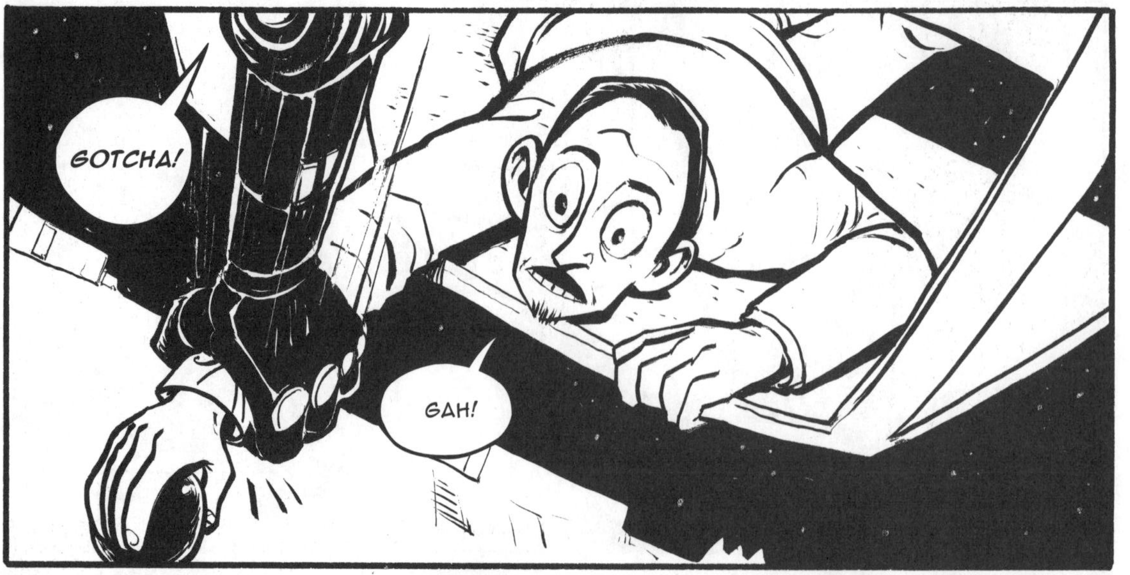
GOTCHA!
GAH!

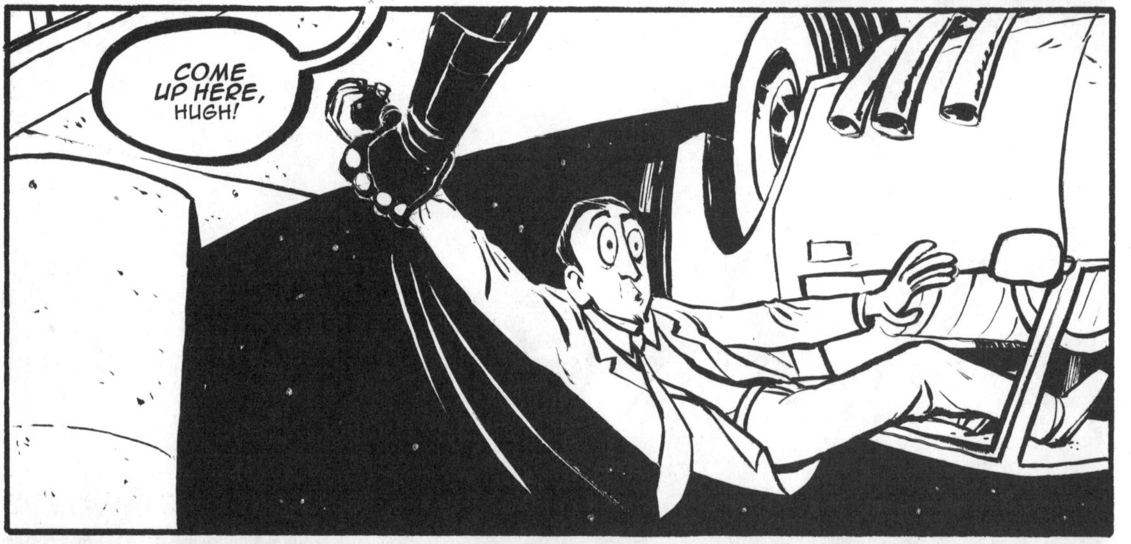
COME UP HERE, HUGH!

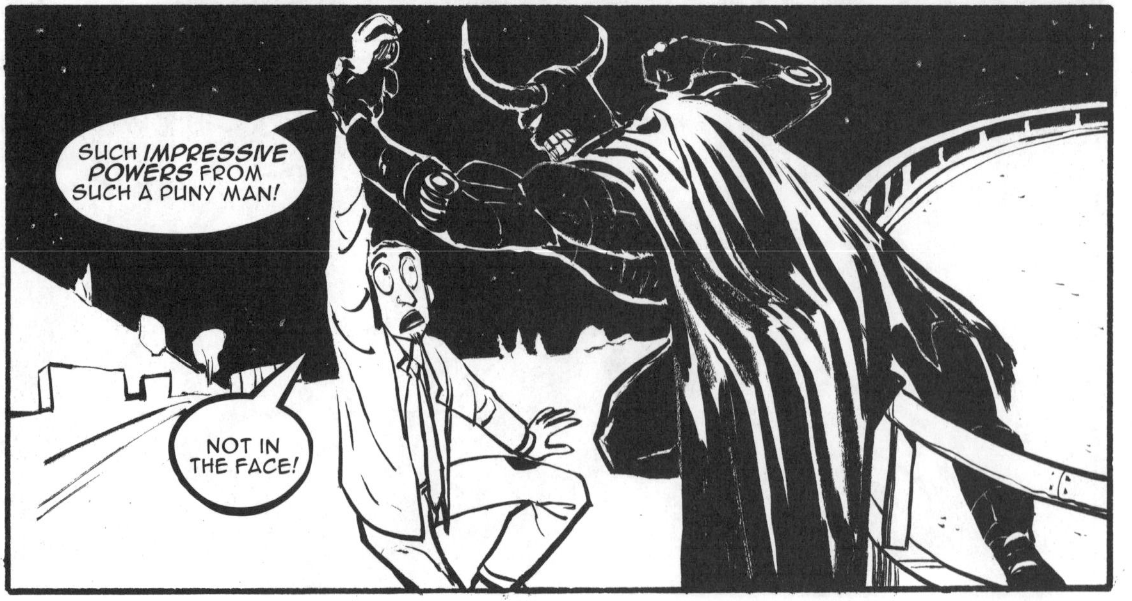
SUCH IMPRESSIVE POWERS FROM SUCH A PUNY MAN!
NOT IN THE FACE!

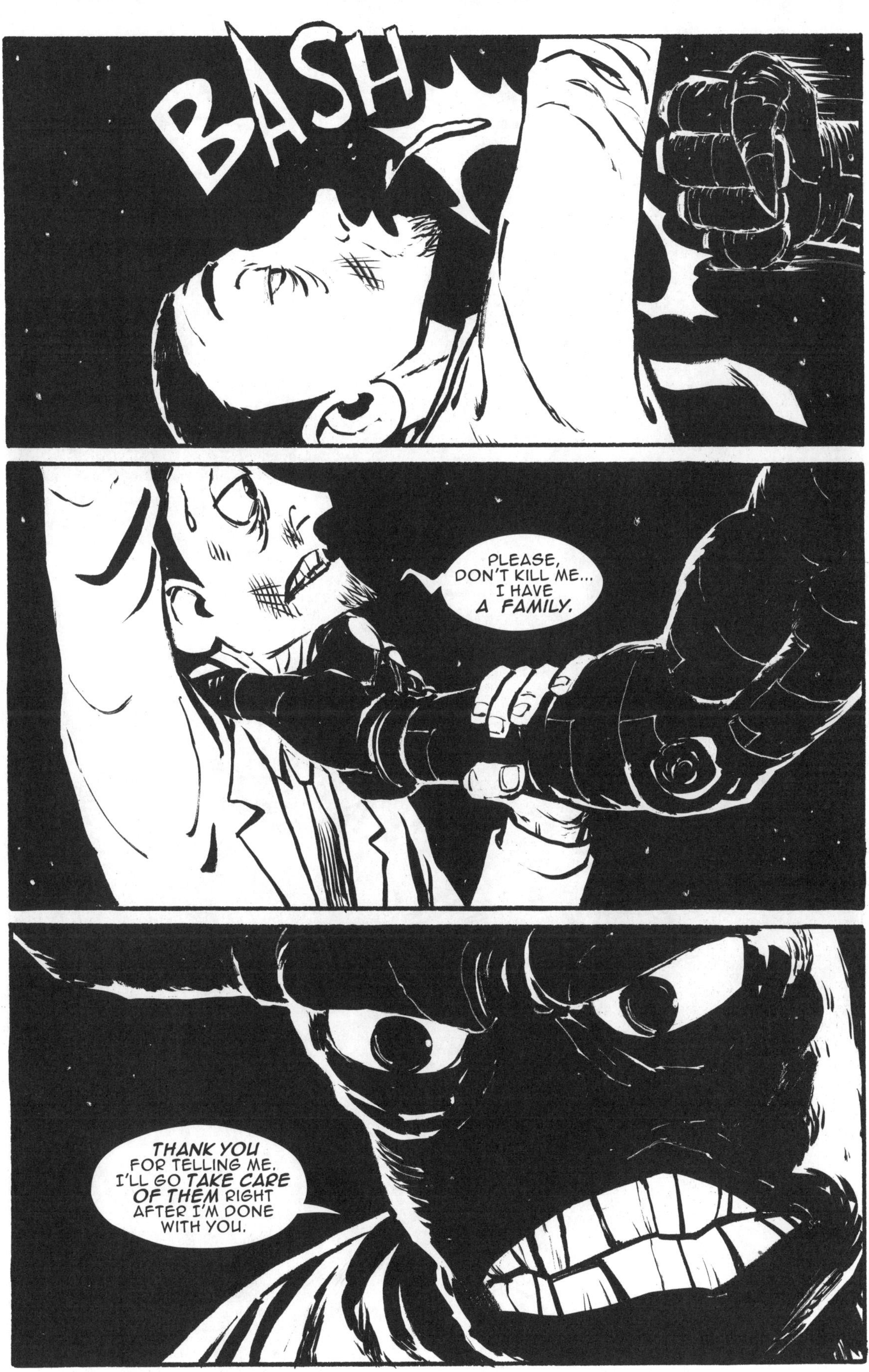
BASH
PLEASE, DON'T KILL ME... I HAVE A FAMILY.
THANK YOU FOR TELLING ME. I'LL GO TAKE CARE OF THEM RIGHT AFTER I'M DONE WITH YOU.

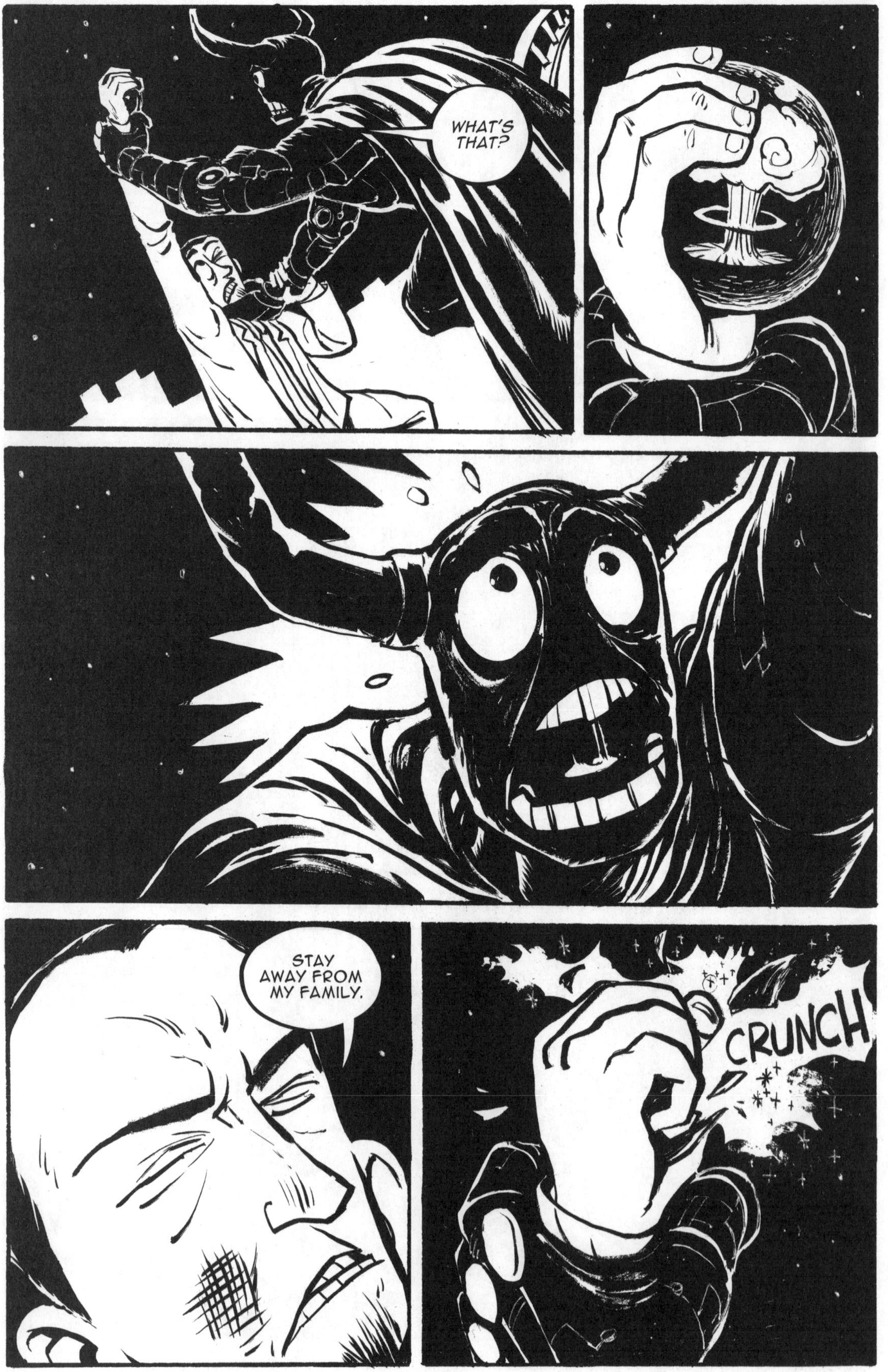
WHAT'S THAT?
STAY AWAY FROM MY FAMILY.
CRUNCH

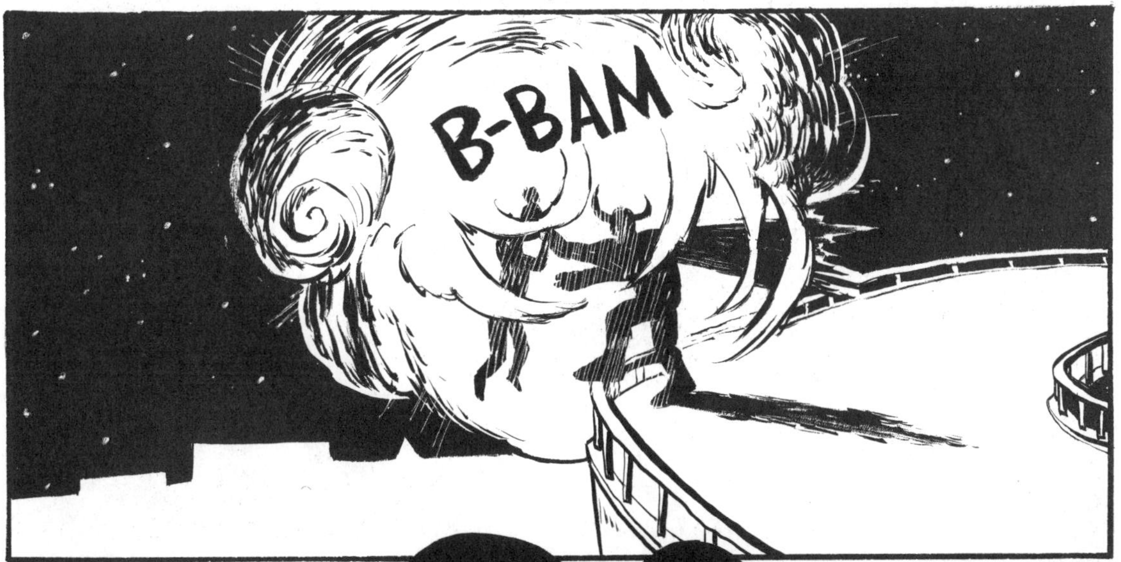
B-BAM

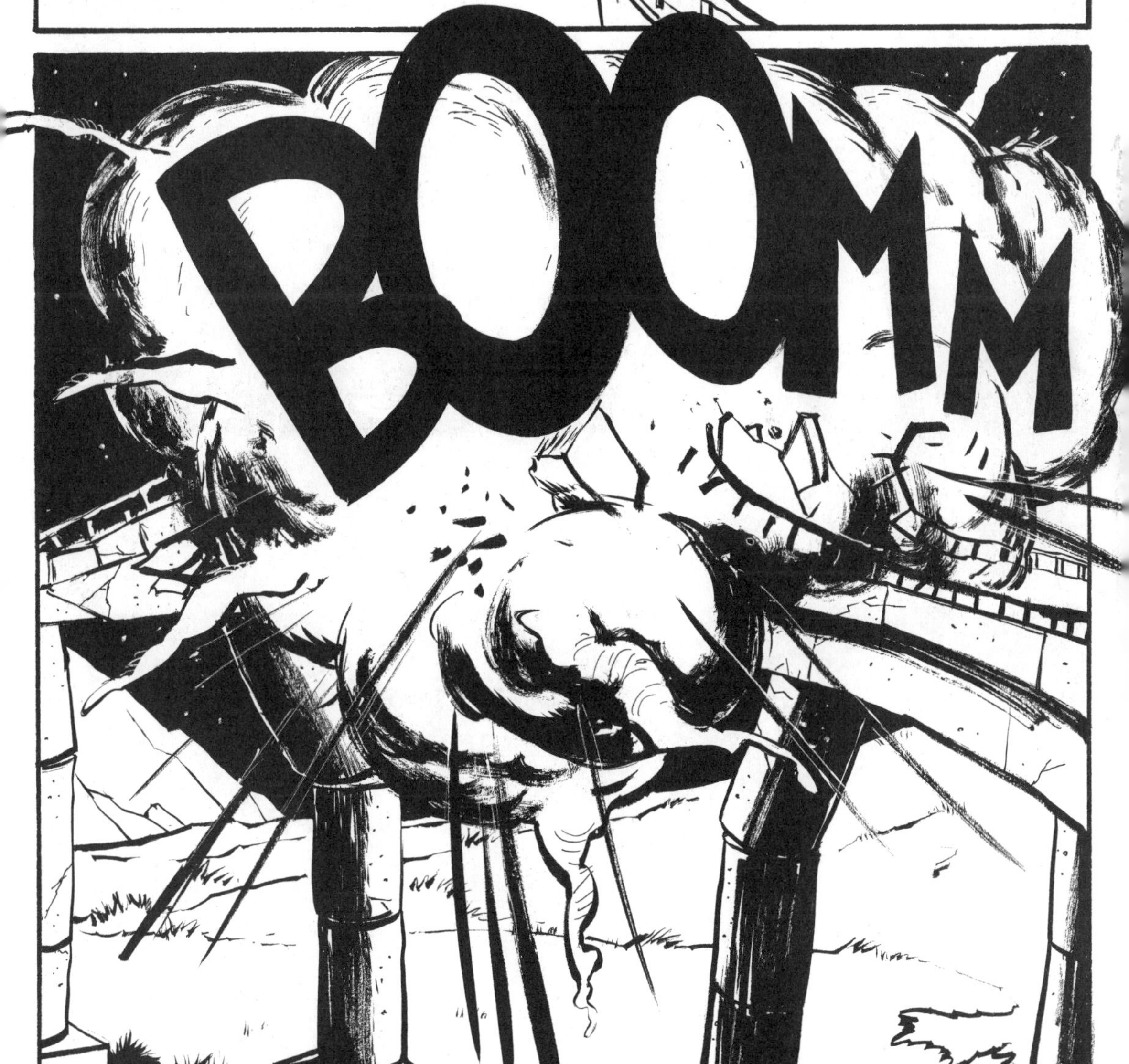
BOOMM

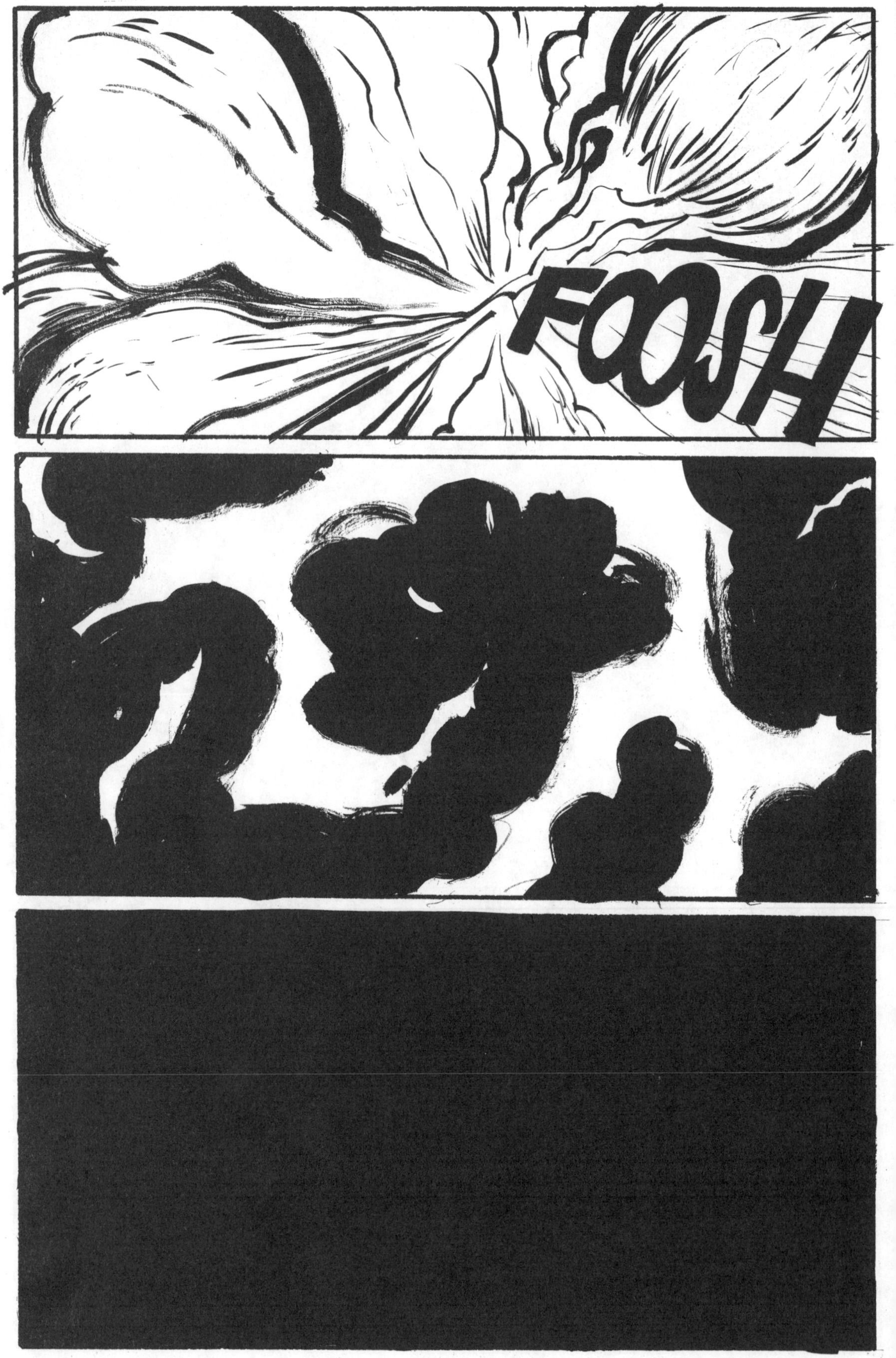
FOOSH

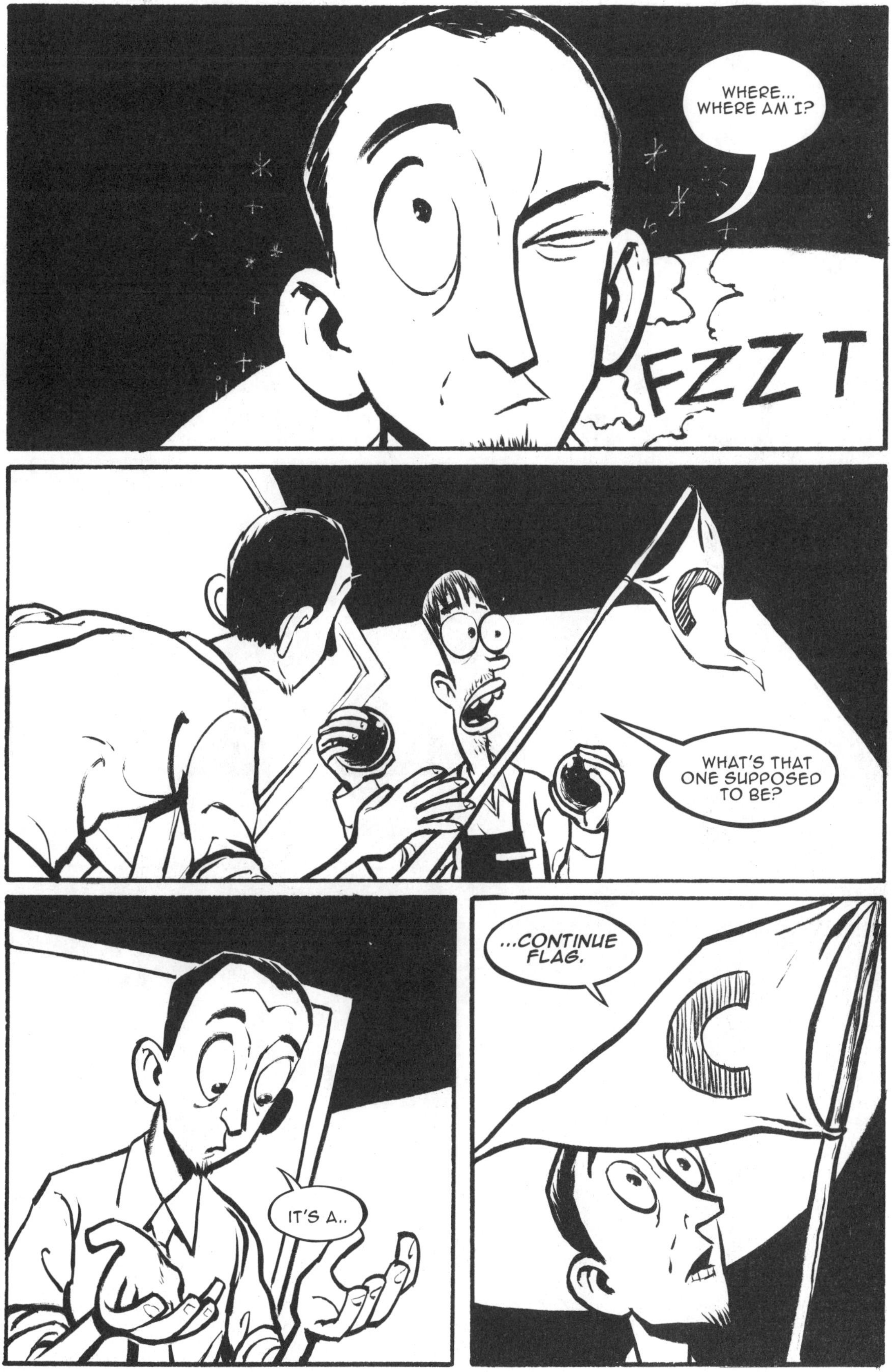
WHERE...
WHERE AM I?
FZZT
WHAT'S THAT ONE SUPPOSED TO BE?
IT'S A..
...CONTINUE FLAG.

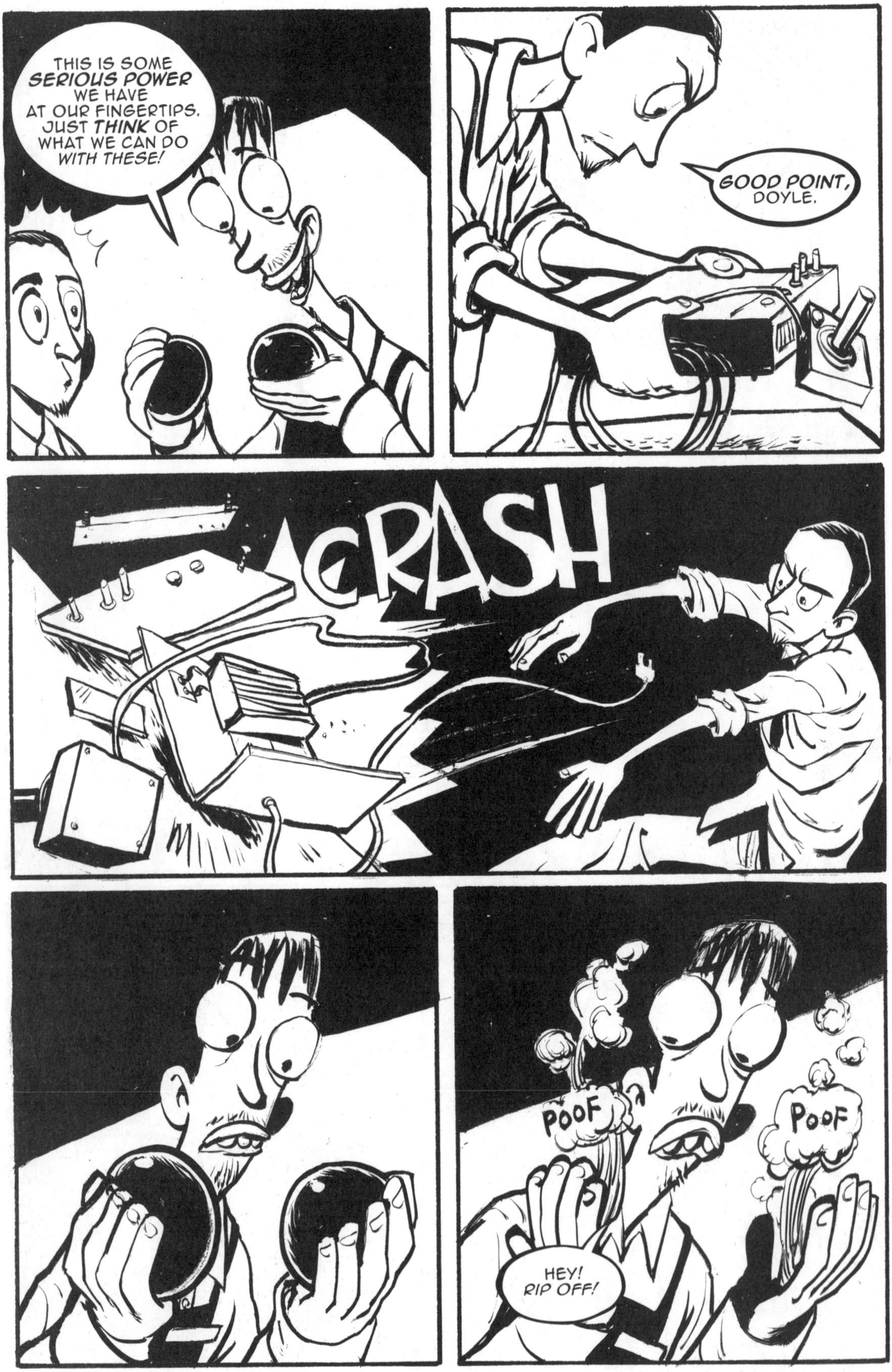
THIS IS SOME *SERIOUS POWER* WE HAVE AT OUR FINGERTIPS. JUST *THINK* OF WHAT WE CAN DO WITH THESE!
GOOD POINT, DOYLE.
CRASH
POOF
POOF
HEY! RIP OFF!

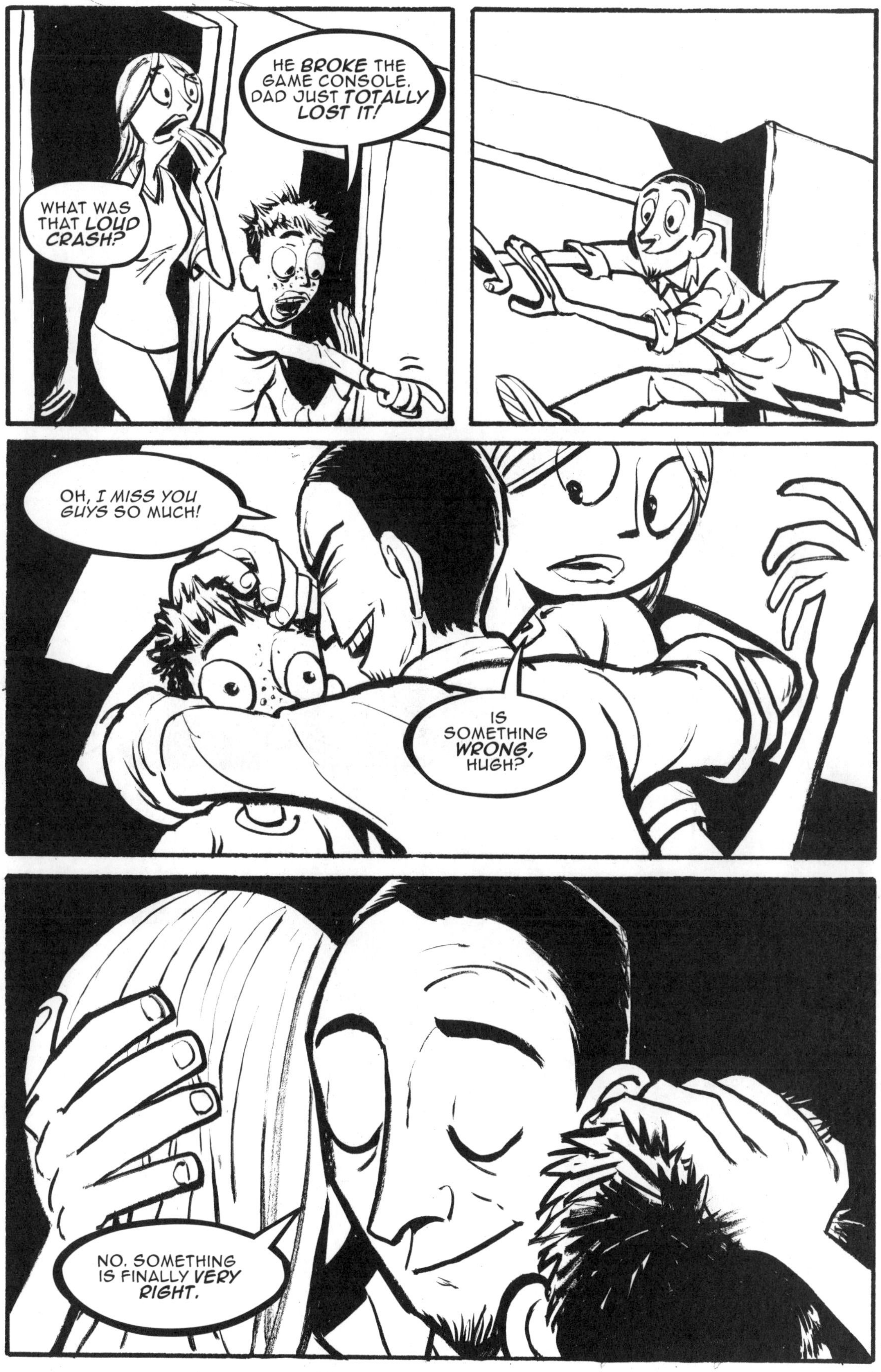
WHAT WAS THAT LOUD CRASH?
HE BROKE THE GAME CONSOLE. DAD JUST TOTALLY LOST IT!
OH, I MISS YOU GUYS SO MUCH!
IS SOMETHING WRONG, HUGH?
NO. SOMETHING IS FINALLY VERY RIGHT.

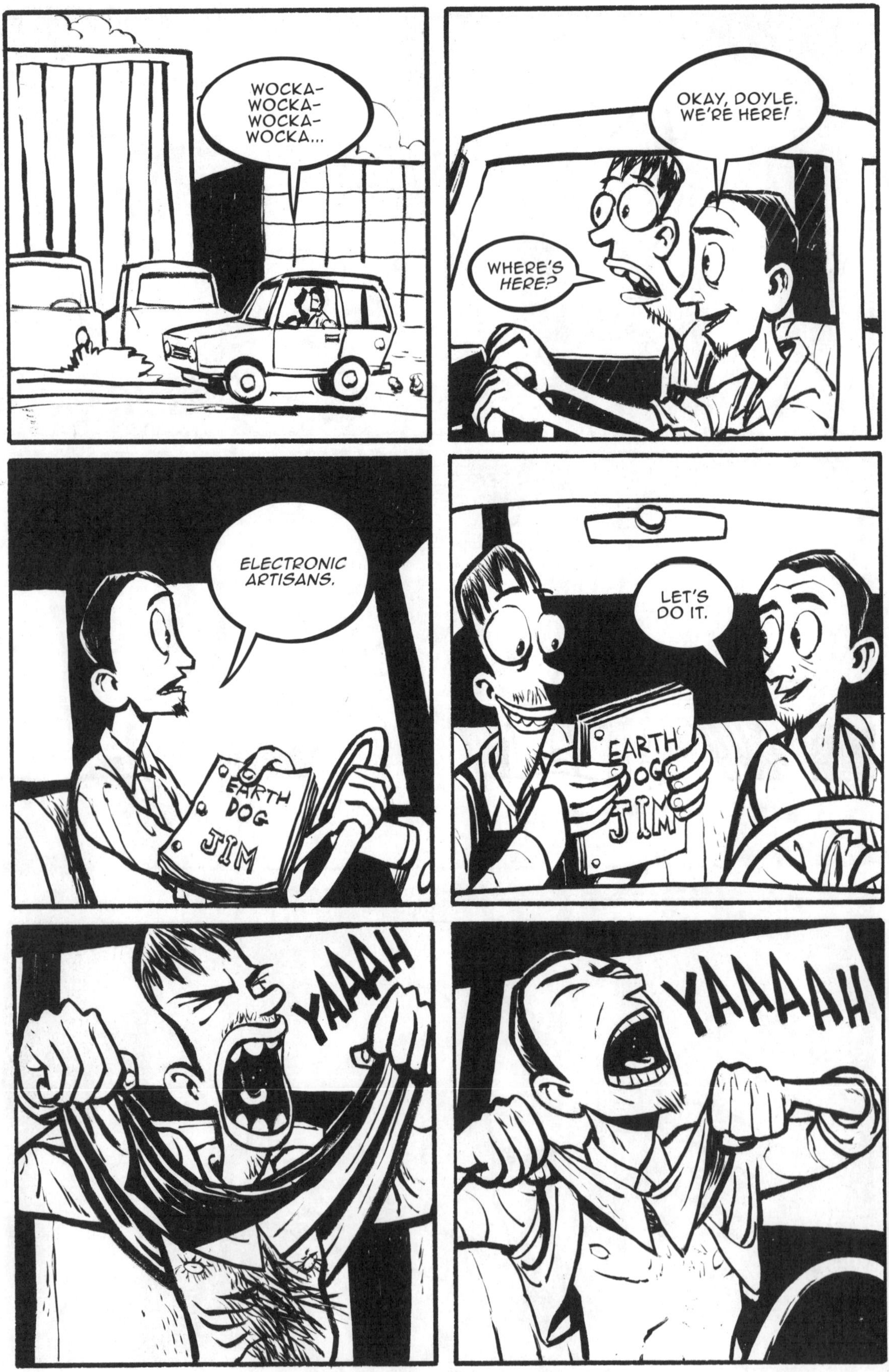
WOCKA-
WOCKA-
WOCKA-
WOCKA...
OKAY, DOYLE.
WE'RE HERE!
WHERE'S
HERE?
ELECTRONIC
ARTISANS.
EARTH
DOG
JIM
LET'S
DO IT.
EARTH
DOG
JIM
YAAAH
YAAAAH

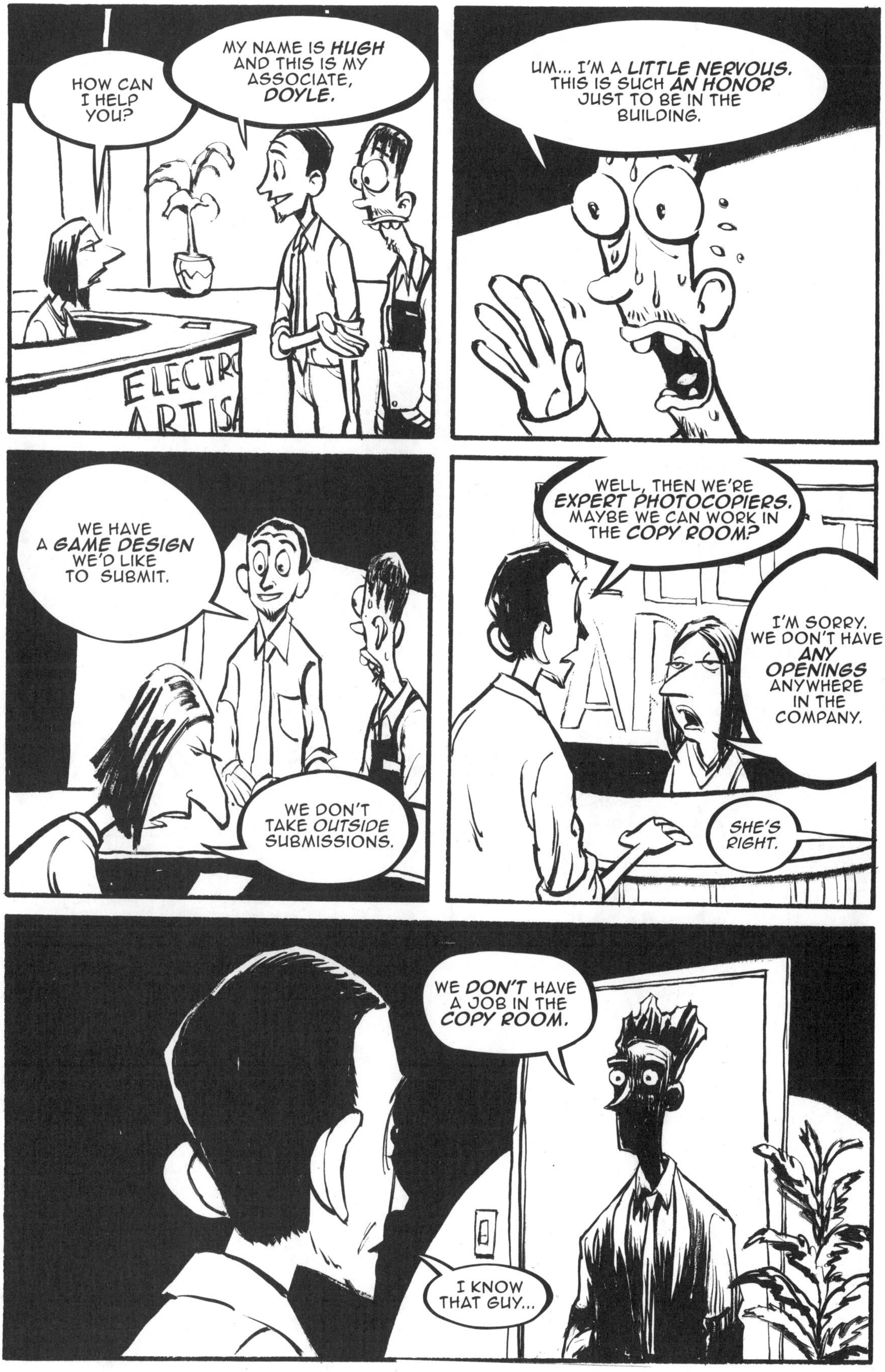
HOW CAN I HELP YOU?
MY NAME IS HUGH AND THIS IS MY ASSOCIATE, DOYLE.
ELECTRO ARTISA
UM... I'M A LITTLE NERVOUS. THIS IS SUCH AN HONOR JUST TO BE IN THE BUILDING.
WE HAVE A GAME DESIGN WE'D LIKE TO SUBMIT.
WE DON'T TAKE OUTSIDE SUBMISSIONS.
WELL, THEN WE'RE EXPERT PHOTOCOPIERS. MAYBE WE CAN WORK IN THE COPY ROOM?
I'M SORRY. WE DON'T HAVE ANY OPENINGS ANYWHERE IN THE COMPANY.
SHE'S RIGHT.
WE DON'T HAVE A JOB IN THE COPY ROOM.
I KNOW THAT GUY...

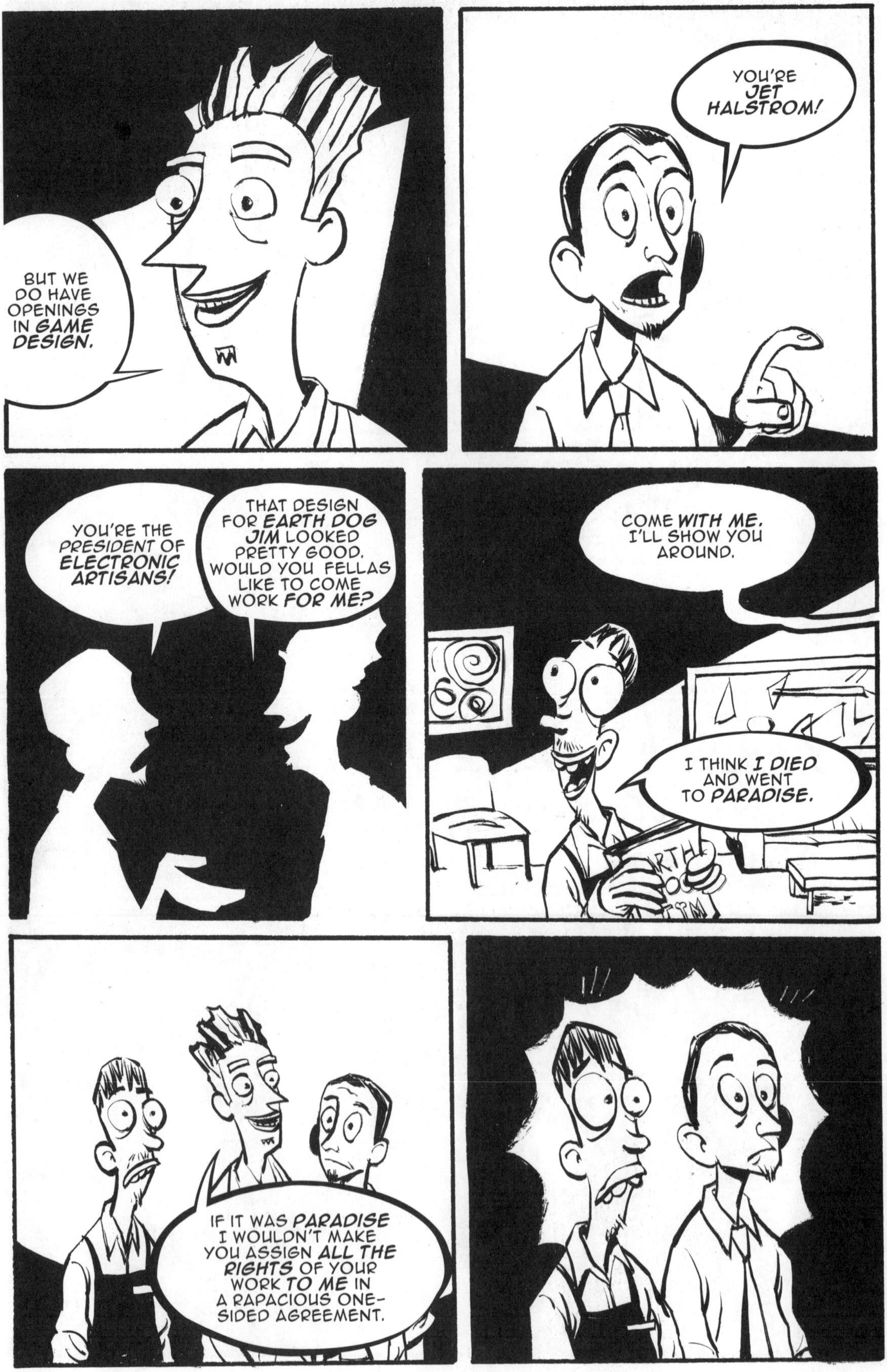
BUT WE DO HAVE OPENINGS IN GAME DESIGN.
YOU'RE JET HALSTROM!
YOU'RE THE PRESIDENT OF ELECTRONIC ARTISANS!
THAT DESIGN FOR EARTH DOG JIM LOOKED PRETTY GOOD. WOULD YOU FELLAS LIKE TO COME WORK FOR ME?
COME WITH ME. I'LL SHOW YOU AROUND.
I THINK I DIED AND WENT TO PARADISE.
IF IT WAS PARADISE I WOULDN'T MAKE YOU ASSIGN ALL THE RIGHTS OF YOUR WORK TO ME IN A RAPACIOUS ONE-SIDED AGREEMENT.

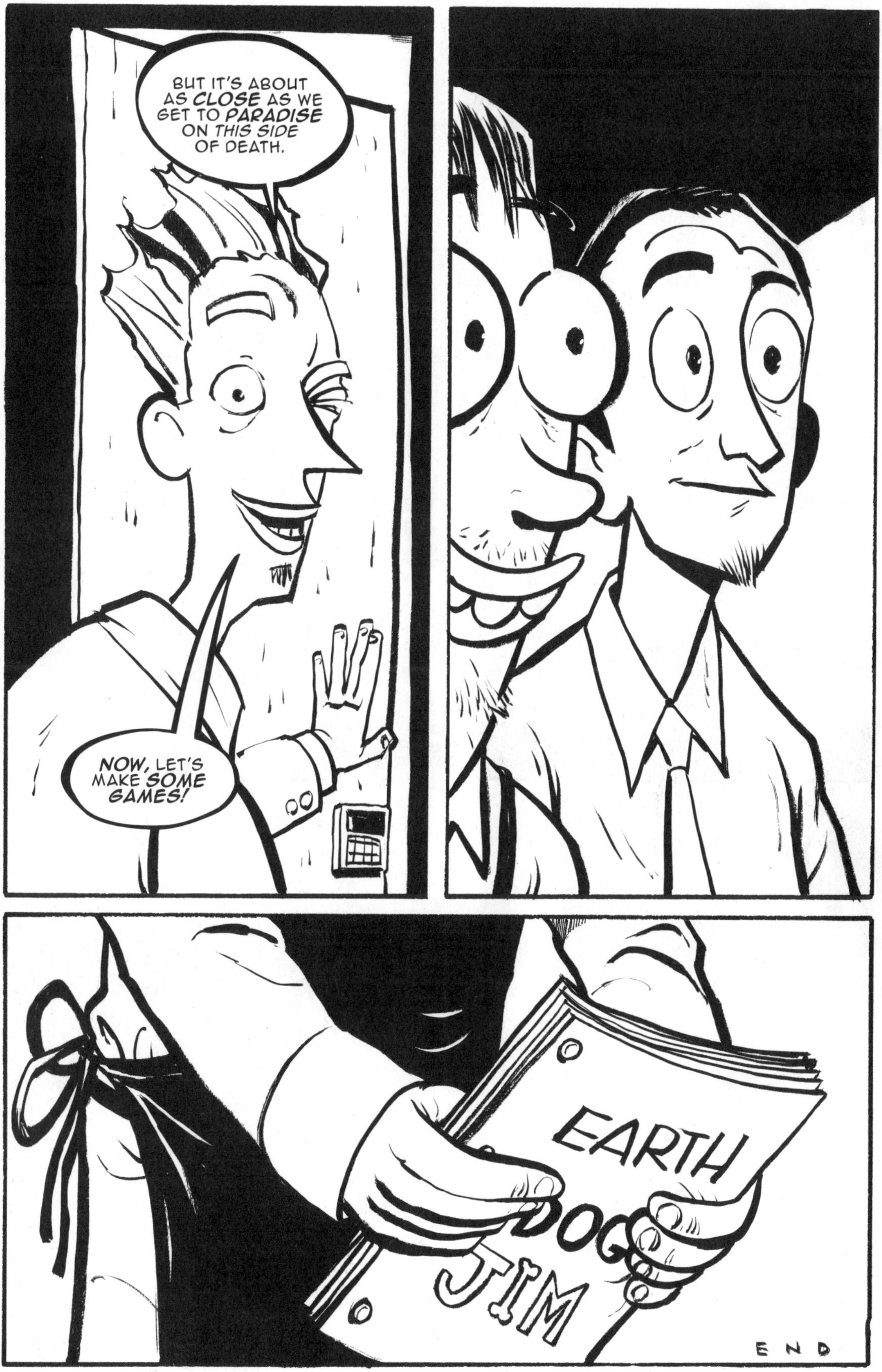
BUT IT'S ABOUT AS CLOSE AS WE GET TO PARADISE ON THIS SIDE OF DEATH.
NOW, LET'S MAKE SOME GAMES!
EARTH DOG JIM
END